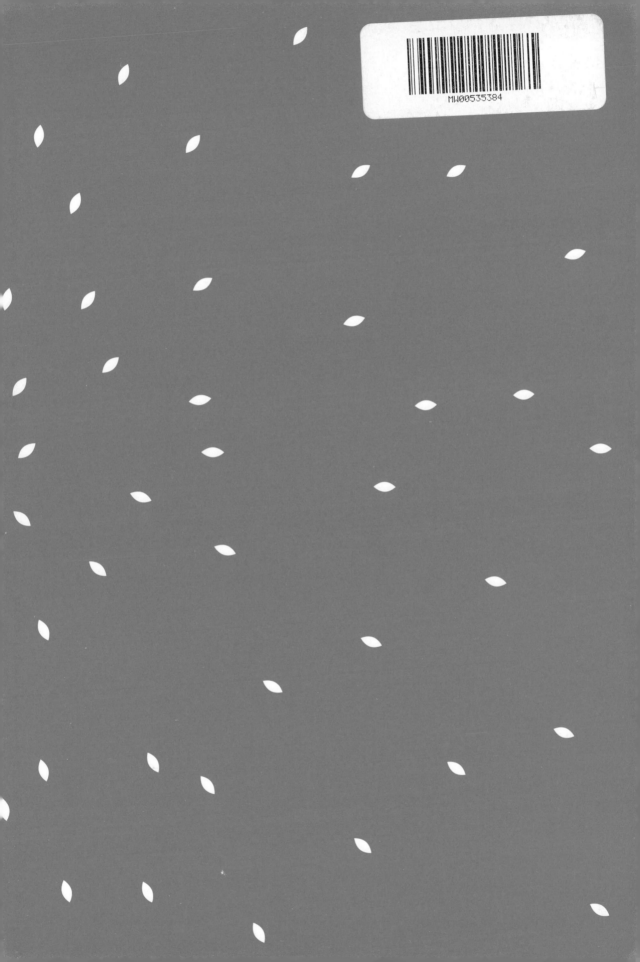

Photography
Caroline Faccioli, assisted by Margaux Besnier

**Photo Styling
and Joint Art Direction of Photography**
Marion Chatelain

Editor
Ryma Bouzid

ENGLISH EDITION

Editorial Director
Kate Mascaro

Editor
Helen Adedotun

Translation from the French
Ansley Evans

Copyediting
Wendy Sweetser

Typesetting
Claude-Olivier Four

Proofreading
Nicole Foster

Indexing
JMS Books/Chris Bell

Production
Christelle Lemonnier

Color Separation
IGS, L'Isle-d'Espagnac

Printed in Bosnia and Herzegovina
by GPS Group

Originally published in French as
Faites Votre Pâtisserie comme Lenôtre
© Flammarion, S.A., Paris, 1975–2020

English-language edition
© Flammarion, S.A., Paris, 2021

87, quai Panhard et Levassor
75647 Paris Cedex 13

editions.flammarion.com

21 22 23   3 2 1

ISBN: 978-2-08-020693-0

Legal Deposit: 09/2021

FRENCH PASTRIES
and Desserts by
LENÔTRE

More than 200 Classic Recipes

Flammarion

CONTENTS

RECIPE SKILL LEVEL
★ Basic ★★ Intermediate ★★★ Advanced

GENERAL ADVICE

Apricot glaze (abricotage)

Adds an attractive sheen when brushed over pastries, tarts, and sweet breads and prevents fruit toppings from drying out. It can be purchased ready to use or made at home. Heat apricot jam until it melts, adding a little water or lemon juice to thin it, if necessary. Strain the jam through a fine-mesh sieve and, while still warm, brush it over in a thin, even layer.

Blind-baking

To blind-bake a tart shell, line it with parchment paper and fill with pie weights. Bake until the pastry is lightly golden around the edges. Remove the parchment paper and weights, then brush the pastry with egg yolk to seal it. Return it to the oven for an additional 3–5 minutes, until the pastry is evenly golden.

Butter

Unless otherwise specified, unsalted butter is used in the recipes in this book, preferably with a fat content of at least 82%. Look for European-style or cultured butters but, if these are unavailable, use a butter with a fat content of around 80%. It is especially important to use butter with a higher fat content when making laminated doughs such as puff pastry or croissant dough.

Remove butter from the refrigerator 30 minutes before use to come to room temperature.

· Clarified butter: Used in recipes to impart a rich flavor. To clarify butter, melt it in a saucepan over very low heat without stirring until a white foam forms over the surface. Skim off the foam, letting the milk solids settle at the bottom. Carefully pour the clear, golden, clarified butter through a strainer into a separate container, leaving the milk solids behind. Butter can be clarified in large quantities and stored in a covered container for up to 1 month at room temperature and up to 2 months in the refrigerator.

· Browned butter (beurre noisette): Adds a caramelized and nutty flavor to cakes and desserts such as financiers and crêpes. Heat butter in a skillet, stirring until it melts, then continue cooking until the butter turns golden brown and develops a nutty aroma. Take care not to let it burn. Strain through a fine-mesh sieve before using.

· Softened butter (beurre pommade): To soften butter, cut room-temperature butter into dice, place in the bowl of a stand mixer fitted with the paddle beater, and work until it is smooth, creamy, and spreadable. Alternatively, place the diced butter briefly in the microwave, then work by hand using a spatula. Place back in the microwave for a few seconds and whisk until smooth.

Cream

If whipping, use cream that contains at least 35% fat (whipping or heavy cream in the US, whipping or double cream in the UK). Only remove cream from the refrigerator when ready to use it: the colder it is, the easier it will be to whip. Chilling the bowl will also allow the cream to be whipped more quickly. Begin by whipping on medium speed until the cream just begins to thicken, then reduce the speed to low, or finish whipping by hand, to avoid over-whipping which can give the cream an unattractive, grainy texture.

Eggs

Use eggs at room temperature, removing them from the refrigerator 30 minutes before use.

· Sizes: Unless otherwise indicated, the recipes in this book are made using eggs weighing approximately 2 oz. (55–60 g) in their shell ("large" eggs in the US and Canada, or "medium" in the UK), with an average composition of: **whole egg without shell:** 3½ tbsp (1¾ oz./50 g); **white:** 2 tbsp (1 oz./30 g); **yolk:** 1½ tbsp (¾ oz./20 g). Sizes can vary, however, so weighing eggs is recommended for optimal results.

· Raw eggs: Some of the recipes in this book contain raw or lightly cooked eggs. Ensure they are as fresh as possible. Pasteurized eggs can also be substituted, or egg products such as refrigerated liquid eggs or dried eggs. Powdered egg white can be used for making meringues, but must first be diluted in water to reconstitute the egg whites (about 2 tsp powdered egg white to 2 tbsp/30 ml water).

Gelatin

Used for setting custards, jellies, and creams. Gelatin is available in powder form (to be dissolved in 5 times its volume of water) or as transparent sheets. Although interchangeable, gelatin sheets are used in the recipes in this book. Sheets are graded by Bloom—the setting strength of the gelatin—with four main grades: bronze, silver, gold, and platinum. Gold sheets, weighing 0.1 oz. (2 g) each, with a Bloom strength of around 200, are mostly used in this book.

To use gelatin sheets, soak them in a bowl of cold water for 5–10 minutes until softened. Squeeze out the sheets to remove excess water and, if adding to a hot liquid (maximum temperature 158°F/70°C), stir in the sheets until dissolved. If adding to a cold liquid or meringue, place the squeezed-out sheets in the center of a bowl and microwave on high for 5–10 seconds, or until melted. Alternatively, place the bowl over a saucepan of barely simmering water (bain-marie). Stir the melted gelatin into the cold mixture.

Lining baking rings and pans with pastry dough

Roll the dough to the required thickness and gently ease it into the greased ring or pan. Take care not to stretch it or it will shrink back during baking. Press the pastry over the base to exclude any pockets of air, which will cause the pastry to rise in the oven, and ease it up the sides. Pinch around the top to make a border. Chill the pastry for at least 30 minutes to relax it before baking.

Measuring ingredients

Both imperial and metric measures are given in the recipes in this book. It is important to use one or the other, and not mix the two. Spoon and US cup measures are also included. However, weighing ingredients is more precise and accurate, especially important in pastry-making, and the use of digital scales (and, preferably, metric weights) is recommended to ensure consistent results. All spoon and cup measures are level, unless otherwise indicated.

Paper piping cones

Used for piping intricate decorations in chocolate or icing on cakes and desserts. Cut a large square or rectangle of parchment paper in half diagonally to make two right-angled triangles. Form a cone from one triangle by holding the center of the longest side with one hand and wrapping the points around with the other to give a tightly closed tip. Fold the excess parchment down into the cone and secure by creasing it tightly or with a staple. Stand upright in a tall glass or mug to fill. Spoon melted chocolate or icing into the cone, filling it about one-third full. Fold over the top to seal the cone and snip off the tip with scissors. The smaller the hole is, the thinner the piping will be.

Pastry rulers

These make it easier to roll pastry dough or marzipan into an even layer (and thus help to ensure even baking). This is particularly important when it needs to be very thin. Pastry rulers can be purchased, or handmade by cutting several strips of heavy cardboard measuring 10 in. (25 cm) in length. Place one, or stack several strips (depending on the desired thickness), on either side of the dough or marzipan and roll until it is flush with the tops of the rulers.

Pectin NH

Used to make many of the glazes in this book. This type of pectin can be melted, reset, and re-melted, as required, allowing glazes to be prepared ahead of time and reheated when needed.

Sugar

Unless otherwise indicated, granulated white sugar or superfine sugar (also known as baker's or caster sugar) is used in these recipes. In many of the recipes, the two are interchangeable but the latter is recommended for making meringues and creams, as it dissolves more easily. Decorative white sugars—such as coarse, sanding, or pearl—have larger crystals that do not dissolve when baked. They are used for decoration and for adding crunch to the tops of yeast breads, cakes, and choux puffs. In recipes calling for brown sugar, light or dark can be used.

· **Vanilla sugar:** Available to buy in 1½ tsp (7.5–8 g) packets, or make your own. Split a vanilla bean lengthwise and place it in a storage jar of sugar, completely immersing the bean. Seal the jar and leave for 24 hours, or longer, for the vanilla to impart its flavor to the sugar. Vanilla sugar can also be made by grinding a bean to a fine powder in a spice grinder and mixing it with sugar.

Thermometers

Use an instant-read thermometer to measure the temperature of a mixture quickly and accurately. If your thermometer cannot read the high temperatures required for sugar boiling, a candy thermometer will also be needed.

Yeast

Fresh yeast (also known as compressed, cake, or baker's yeast) is recommended for making many traditional French pastries, especially viennoiseries such as croissants and brioches. However, it is not always easy for home cooks to source, particularly in the US. Active dry and instant yeasts can both be substituted.

· **Using fresh yeast:** Fresh yeast does not need proofing and can be added directly to doughs. However, it is best to dilute it first in a little lukewarm water (no hotter than 122°F/50°C, or the yeast will be killed) before mixing it with the other ingredients, as this will help distribute the yeast more evenly throughout the dough. Fresh yeast must never come into direct contact with salt and sugar, as this can prevent it working properly and may even kill it.

· **Using active dry yeast:** If a recipe uses fresh yeast, divide the weight by 1.5 when substituting active dry yeast. This yeast must first be proofed to activate it. Dissolve it in either lukewarm water or another liquid used in the recipe and let sit for about 10 minutes until foamy. It can then be added to the other ingredients.

· **Using instant yeast:** When substituting instant yeast for fresh, use half of the weight of fresh. Instant yeast does not need proofing and can be stirred directly into the flour. However, it is important that the yeast is thoroughly incorporated into the flour before any liquid is added.

A SCHUSS*
OF MEMORIES

I loved preparing for the show. The PA system had announced that "at 3 p.m. French chef Gaston Lenôtre will reveal the secrets of Italian meringue." It was 1977 and the first edition of *Lenôtre's Desserts and Pastries* was prominently displayed on the immense countertop in Bloomingdale's, New York's great department store. The book had recently been published, and Gaston Lenôtre, my father, was about to revitalize the art of French patisserie and become famous around the world.

After unpacking all the boxes of ingredients and equipment, there was just enough time for my father to don his white chef's jacket and chef's hat—tucking in a few unruly strands of hair—and steal a brief glance at the audience before the grand event began. Acting as interpreter, I gripped the microphone while keeping one eye on the sugar syrup that was beginning to boil in the saucepan. The scraping of the whisk against the copper bowl was unmistakable, as the still-liquid egg whites swirled up in a kind of dance, following the rhythm of my father's wrist. With each beat, more air bubbles became trapped in the egg whites, and so the metamorphosis began.

The excitement felt by this audience of amateur pâtissiers was palpable, and every spectator leaned forward a little, mesmerized by the transformation taking place. They were all wondering just how high the whites would rise, well aware that they could collapse, break up, or separate. The sugar syrup had now boiled to the hard ball stage and, very carefully, I poured it into the foamy cloud of egg white. It was already silky but, as the whisk worked its magic, it soon became pearly-white and glossy, with a sweet fragrance. Finally, my father stopped whisking and turned the bowl upside down, as everyone in the audience held their breath. The stiff peaks of meringue held firm, and my father faced the camera with a big smile on his face. Very gently, so as not to crush the fragile white cloud, he scooped the meringue into a pastry bag, then piped it over small choux puffs. For my father, this was just another demonstration, performed for the sheer pleasure of it.

The memories we shared were literally edible ones. These tangible impressions have often triggered a powerful and mysterious current in me that goes straight to my heart and makes my mouth water. It is a reflex I have experienced all my life.

My mother, like all mothers, carried her children for nine months, but when she was at her patisserie store, she was always attentive to her customers and the team of girls who served them. As soon as she brought us home from the hospital, warmly wrapped up with our tiny faces peeking out from bonnets she had hand-knit, my mother returned to work, nursing us on the job. It is to Colette, my mother, that I dedicate this new edition of the book. She is the part of the cake that has most nourished the Lenôtre family.

Just as my father devoted himself to his passion, totally immersing himself in his work and tackling challenges head on, my mother, a *Parisienne* at heart, steered their lives with panache. It was she who saved Le Pré Catelan, the historic Parisian restaurant in the Bois de Boulogne, from closure in 1976. Seeking advice from artisans who had worked at the Palace of Versailles, she was able to restore the Napoléon-III pavilion to its original splendor. Work was certainly the driving force in both their lives. They thrived on challenges, whether it was hiring chefs and sales assistants, training apprentices, or seeking to enhance their products.

Another memory I would like to share takes us into the archives of the French National Audiovisual Institute and a television program recorded in 1977. The first edition of *Lenôtre's Desserts and Pastries* had just been published, and Gaston was asked to prepare a recipe from the book on the program. I encouraged him to make a gâteau that had been created for the opening of our store in Deauville. My mother had loved the cake and named it *Clairefontaine*, after the local racecourse. For the book, I had modified the recipe slightly and changed its name: *Rosace à l'Orange* (Orange Upside-Down Cake, see p. 212). My father agreed with my suggestion to make it on the program.

To be honest, we were not always in agreement. I'll never forget the weekly show we presented in 1982 for the radio station Europe 1. All week long, I would test the recipes in our atelier at Plaisir, near Paris, and continue testing at home under the inquisitive eyes of my three sons. Every Thursday evening, I'd type up the results, before heading to Le Pré Catelan early on Friday morning to collect my father. In the twenty minutes it took for his chauffeur to drive us to the radio station, he would read through what I'd written and scribble down notes. He would never allow himself to be contradicted and his entire being declared, "*Le patron, c'est moi,*" (I am the boss.) I'd be so tense by the time we reached the studio that it took all the kindness and charm of the presenter, Dénise Fabre, to put me at ease. My father, on the other hand, would be in his element throughout the entire show. Our loyal listeners and Lenôtre fans were divided—some couldn't stand it when I corrected my father, whereas others took my side. The show was a real verbal duel. We would finish with our hearts racing, before rushing back to Plaisir. The program was broadcast over six months, and it gave me the motivation I needed to finish writing our next cookbook, published in 1983.

But, let us return to *Rosace à l'Orange* and the recording studio in 1977. Knowing his recipes by heart was always a priority for my father. On the program, which was broadcast with only a very brief time delay, he had to juggle all the ingredients for a recipe using half-finished or completed components, having previously prepared two of each in case they were needed. In just twenty-five minutes, we covered every step of the recipe—oranges sliced and candied; genoise sponge layers prepared, baked, and cut; orange pastry cream made; pans readied; and, finally, the finished cake unmolded. On top of that, we'd provide the quantities to serve eight, as well as professional tips for home bakers. All using studio equipment from the 1970s.

Only an expert with my father's dexterity could beat the genoise batter to the ribbon stage live on air, without forgetting the specific temperatures required and the precise way each mixture needed to be assembled. He described everything in detail and was even playful, quipping, "If all goes well . . ." just before turning out the dessert, sending a little shiver of apprehension through us all. Unlike other methods of cooking, the end results in patisserie are never guaranteed and that was what my father so enjoyed— the element of risk.

He once confessed to me that, in 1936—as a sixteen-year-old looking for work, freshly crowned "Premier Apprenti de Normandie" (Best Apprentice in Normandie)—he had occasionally bet on horses at the Vincennes racecourse. I understood what he meant when he compared the sound of the whisk against the mixing bowl with the thud of horses' hooves: as he whipped the cream, evoking the gallop of champions, he must subconsciously have been reminded of his youth. For Gaston, it was all about playing to win, being first across the finish line, and making lucrative deals, sometimes by taking a gamble.

Sylvie Gille-Naves Lenôtre

* Schuss is an iconic Lenôtre gâteau (see p. 216 for the recipe). Created in 1968, the year of the Winter Olympic Games in Grenoble, this all-white cake evokes the snow-covered slopes frequented by schussing skiers.

Gaston and Colette Lenôtre.

FOREWORD BY ALAIN LENÔTRE

Origins. My family's culinary tradition began with my grandparents, Éléonore and Gaston, who were both professional chefs. My grandmother worked for the Rothschild family and was one of the first female chefs in France, while my grandfather was chef saucier at the historic Grand Hotel in Paris. I'm so proud of them.

After working for several years in Paris, my grandfather's health deteriorated, and my grandparents were forced to leave the capital. They returned to their native Normandy, where they bought a modest farmhouse in Bernay. My father, Gaston, was born there in 1920, followed by his brother Marcel a year later.

My grandparents were unable to afford the cost of sending the brothers to continue their studies beyond the age of fourteen, so my grandfather encouraged them to "choose a vocation that will guarantee that you never go hungry." Gaston chose an apprenticeship in pastry, while Marcel opted for bread making.

After earning their professional certification, the brothers headed to Paris in search of fortune. On the eve of World War II, jobs were scarce in the capital and, initially, they were only able to find work as porters at Les Halles, Paris's central market. Unloading market goods from trucks at night was grueling work, but they eventually found steady employment: Gaston with a chocolatier and Marcel with a baker.

When the war broke out, the brothers rushed back to Bernay, where the mayor tasked them with reopening the town's two bakeries in order to provide bread to the many refugees who were fleeing German persecution. One of the refugees, Colette Courallet, would later become my mother. Gaston and Colette married, and after the war they opened the first Lenôtre patisserie in nearby Pont-Audemer, where I was born along with my sisters, Sylvie and Annie.

Ideally located halfway between Paris and the elegant seaside resort of Deauville, many Parisians would stop in to enjoy Gaston and Colette's pastries. Over the next decade, encouraged by the growing demand and enthusiastic patronage of their Parisian customers, my parents decided to try their luck in Paris.

In 1957, they opened a new Lenôtre patisserie at 44 Rue d'Auteuil in the sixteenth arrondissement. My parents, two sisters, brother-in-law, and I all worked together over twenty-five years to build what would become known as the Maison Lenôtre.

My father and I. I apprenticed for my father at 44 Rue d'Auteuil for two years, rather than the habitual three. At the end of my apprenticeship, I had to take a trade exam, so I memorized our famous brioche recipe in preparation. But my father forbade me from divulging the Lenôtre recipe to the judges—he didn't want our competitors to steal it—and asked me to improvise an alternative recipe instead. Further complicating my situation, I learned the night before the exam that I would probably be asked to prepare choux pastry for the judges—a recipe that I didn't know, so I spent the night frantically learning how to make it. At the exam, I became acutely aware that my fellow apprentices had not been properly trained. The realization planted a seed in me that grew into a desire to reform the culinary education system.

Letting go of the baker's peel. We baked everything in our tiny atelier on Rue d'Auteuil, but Gaston was master of the oven. Made of multiple shelves, the oven was extremely hot at the back and cooler at the front, but my father knew how to load and unload it, how to safely slide the metal baking trays in and out, and how long different doughs needed to rise. My father was guardian of the fire, wielding his fourteen-foot-long wooden peel, and he always had the final word on everything that left his atelier, until the day he deemed me worthy of taking his place at the oven.

Years later, he confided that it was only after he had handed over the reins to me that he began to make money; he was able to focus on the business side of things, dedicating more time to our burgeoning catering business and to the opening of new patisseries.

He who opens a school door, closes a prison
(Victor Hugo). Gaston Lenôtre, a pioneer in modern
patisserie, was humble enough to believe that he still
had much to learn, particularly in the intricate art of
chocolate making. At the time, there were no schools
of continuing education in France devoted to the craft
of chocolate making, so he selected Coba, a world-
renowned Swiss pastry school. He figured that he could
take the overnight train from Paris to Basel, remain at
the school from Monday through Friday, and return
to Paris for the weekend to attend to the business at
Rue d'Auteuil. He enrolled under a different name, but
his real identity was soon discovered. The chefs at the
school, who were mostly from Alsace, passed on their
knowledge to my father in French.

Delighted by his experience, my father enrolled
me in the school, telling me it would do me a world of
good. I gladly accepted this study vacation, and I hit it
off with the owner by speaking with him in German.
On one occasion, when we were talking together, he
confided to me that he would soon be retiring and
closing the school. He had just informed his chefs,
who included Paul Rey and the director Gilbert Ponée.
Very excited, I called my father to suggest that we open
our own professional school and invite these two chefs
to join us.

This was in 1968, and we had just moved the
Lenôtre headquarters to Plaisir, a suburb of Paris;
it was here that my father visualized a space where the
school could be built. I then spoke to the chefs and
we set a date to meet six months later. It wasn't long
before we were welcoming our first students to teach
them the art of patisserie. Officially opened in 1971,
the École Lenôtre also trained the chefs working at our
franchise in KaDeWe, the iconic Berlin department
store. Our school has only grown since then, and
today it continues to offer top-level training to both
professionals and amateurs from around the world.

Across the Atlantic, my father's legacy lives on in
Houston, Texas—the fourth largest US city. It is where
my wife Marie and I settled with our five children and,
for many years, we've been passing on the knowledge
and expertise I acquired at my father's side.
We established the CULINARY INSTITUTE
LENÔTRE® in Houston in 1988. For the past three
years, it has been selected out of 170 schools by
Niche.com as the #1 Best College for Culinary Arts
in America. At the institute, twelve chefs—most of
them French—train three hundred students a year.

In memory of my father, Marie and I have created the
Gaston Lenôtre Scholarship Foundation: a perpetual
endowment fund to help deserving students fulfill their
dreams and build a career.

This comprehensive volume of pastry and dessert
recipes *à la française* that you are holding in your hands
will no doubt be an indispensable tool in bringing
a taste of French tradition to kitchens worldwide,
including your own.

All our thanks go to Flammarion and the Lenôtre
company for making this new edition possible.

Alain Lenôtre

On the terrace of Le Pré Catelan restaurant in 1980.
From left to right: Annie, Alain, Colette, Gaston, Sylvie, and Alain Gille-Naves.

DOUGHS, SPONGES, AND MERINGUES

BISCUITS À LA CUILLER

LADYFINGER SPONGE ★

Makes
40 individual ladyfingers or
10 × 4¾-in. (12-cm) round
sponge layers

Active time: 25 minutes

Cooking time: 18 minutes
per batch

Storage: Up to 2 weeks
in an airtight container
or up to 1 month
in the freezer

INGREDIENTS
5 egg yolks
    (scant ½ cup/110 g)
¾ cup (5 oz./150 g) sugar,
    divided
⅔ cup (2½ oz./75 g)
    AP flour, sifted
½ cup (2½ oz./75 g)
    cornstarch, sifted
5 egg whites (⅔ cup/
    150 g)
Confectioners' sugar,
    for dusting

EQUIPMENT
Stand mixer fitted
    with the whisk
Pastry bag fitted with
    a ¾-in. (2-cm) plain tip
2 cookie sheets lined
    with parchment paper

---

1. **Preheat the oven** to 340°F (170°C/Gas Mark 3).
2. **Whisk together the egg yolks** and ⅔ cup
(4½ oz./125 g) of the sugar on medium speed for
5 minutes, until pale and falling in thick ribbons
from the beaters when lifted. Using a flexible spatula,
gently fold in the flour and cornstarch, taking care not
to deflate the mixture.
3. **Whisk the egg whites** on high speed for 5 minutes,
adding the remaining sugar halfway through, until they
hold firm peaks.
4. **Briskly stir one-third of the whites** into the yolk
mixture, before gently folding in the remainder until
evenly incorporated.
5. **Transfer the batter to the pastry bag** and stick
the parchment paper to the cookie sheets with a dot
of batter in each corner. Pipe out 20 ladyfingers
measuring 3½ in. (9 cm) in length on each sheet
(see Chef's Notes).
6. **Lightly dust with confectioners' sugar** and leave
to soak in. Sift over another layer of confectioners'
sugar: this second dusting will form attractive little
bubbles when baked.
7. **Bake one sheet at a time** for 18 minutes; if necessary,
rotate the sheets after 12 minutes for even coloring.
To check the ladyfingers are cooked, carefully lift one
corner of the parchment; if golden underneath, they
are ready. Slide the ladyfingers, still on the parchment,
onto a rack and let cool completely before removing.

Chef's Notes
• Ladyfinger batter must be piped and baked immediately.
• The batter can be flavored with 5 tsp (20 g)
vanilla sugar; 1 tbsp (15 ml) orange flower water; or,
if serving the ladyfingers on their own, the finely grated
zest of ½ lemon.
• To make round sponge layers, draw a circle
of the required diameter on a sheet of parchment paper.
Place the parchment on a rimmed baking sheet with
the pencil line underneath and, starting in the center,
pipe the batter in a tight spiral to the circle edge.
Bake as above.
• When making a charlotte (see pp. 338–43), pipe
the ladyfingers side by side so they are almost touching.
As they bake, they will spread slightly and stick
together, forming a band.
• After freezing, let thaw at room temperature for
24 hours.

BISCUIT JOCONDE

JOCONDE SPONGE ★

Makes
3 sponge layers

Active time: 25 minutes

Cooking time:
7–8 minutes per layer

Storage: Up to 2 days
in the refrigerator or
2 weeks in the freezer

INGREDIENTS
1⅓ cups (6 oz./180 g)
    confectioners' sugar
⅓ cup (2½ oz./45 g)
    AP flour
1¾ cups + 2 tbsp (6 oz./
    180 g) almond powder
5 eggs (1 cup/250 g)
5 egg whites
    (¾ cup/165 g)
2 tbsp (25 g) granulated
    or superfine sugar

EQUIPMENT
10½- × 14½-in.
    (27- × 37-cm) Joconde
    sponge frame, ¼ in.
    (5 mm) deep
Cookie sheet
Stand mixer with
    the paddle beater
    and whisk

1. **Preheat the oven** to 450°F (240°C/Gas Mark 8). Set the frame on the cookie sheet and cut a sheet of parchment paper to line the frame.
2. **Sift the confectioners' sugar** and flour together into a large bowl and stir in the almond powder.
3. **Put 1 egg in the stand mixer bowl,** add the dry ingredients, and, using the paddle beater, beat on medium speed for 2 minutes. Scrape down the sides and bottom of the bowl and the beater.
4. **Add another egg** and beat on medium speed for 5 minutes, until the mixture is pale and has the consistency of a light mousse. Scrape down the bowl and beater again.
5. **Repeat until all the eggs** have been incorporated. Transfer the mixture to a large mixing bowl. Fit the stand mixer with the whisk and wash and dry the bowl.

6. **Whisk the egg whites** until they hold soft peaks, add the sugar, and whisk until the peaks are firm. Gently fold into the mousse mixture a third at a time, until evenly combined.
7. **Pour one-third of the batter** into the frame and spread it out with a palette knife to fill the frame, using as few movements as possible. The batter must be evenly spread as any thin areas could dry out in the oven. Bake for 7–8 minutes, until golden and springy to the touch.
8. **As soon as the sponge** comes out of the oven, remove the frame and slide the sponge onto the work surface. Wait 1–2 minutes for the sponge to cool a little. Lay a fresh sheet of parchment paper on top and flip the sponge upside down. Let cool between the two sheets of parchment paper, so the sponge remains moist and does not dry out.
9. **Repeat with the remaining batter** to make 3 sponge layers in total.

BISCUIT ROULÉ

ROULADE SPONGE ★

Makes	INGREDIENTS	EQUIPMENT
4 sponge layers	3 egg yolks (scant ¼ cup/60 g)	Stand mixer fitted with the whisk
Active time: 15 minutes	1 tsp (5 g) honey	16- × 12-in. (40- × 30-cm) rimmed baking sheet lined with parchment paper
	1¼ cups (8½ oz./240 g) sugar, divided	
Cooking time: 7–8 minutes per layer	½ cup (2 oz./60 g) AP flour, sifted	
	⅓ cup (2 oz./60 g) cornstarch, sifted	
Storage: Up to 4 days in the refrigerator or 2 months in the freezer	5 egg whites (¾ cup/ 160 g)	

1. **Preheat the oven** to 350°F (180°C/Gas Mark 4).
2. **Whisk together the egg yolks**, honey, and half the sugar on medium speed for 5 minutes, until pale and falling in thick ribbons from the whisk when lifted.
3. **Transfer to a large mixing bowl** and gently fold in the flour and cornstarch, taking care not to deflate the mixture. Wash and dry the whisk and mixer bowl.
4. **Whisk the egg whites** with the remaining sugar until they hold firm peaks. Gently fold the yolk mixture into the egg whites until just combined.
5. **Spread one-quarter of the batter** (about 5 oz./145 g) over the baking sheet in a ¼-in. (5-mm) layer. Bake for about 8 minutes, until golden and springy to the touch. Avoid overbaking or the sponge will dry out and crack when it is rolled. Lay a clean sheet of parchment paper on the work surface.
6. **As soon as the sponge** comes out of the oven, slide it onto the work surface. Wait 1–2 minutes for the sponge to cool a little. Lay a fresh sheet of parchment paper on top and flip the sponge upside down. Let cool between the two sheets of parchment paper, so the sponge remains moist and does not dry out.
7. **Repeat with the remaining batter** to make 4 sponge layers in total.
8. **Once cooled**, carefully peel away the lining parchment. The sponge is now ready to be filled and rolled, or rolled and stored in the freezer (see Chef's Notes).

Chef's Notes
• To fill the sponge, trim the edges neatly using a bread knife, spread with your chosen filling, and roll.
• If storing the sponge without filling it, let cool completely between the two sheets of parchment paper, then remove the lining paper and roll up the sponge, with the fresh sheet of parchment paper inside. Wrap it airtight and refrigerate or freeze.
• After freezing, let thaw overnight, ready to be filled and re-rolled the following day.

FEUILLETAGE CLASSIQUE

CLASSIC PUFF PASTRY ★★

Makes
1¼ lb. (600 g)

Active time: 30 minutes

Chilling and resting time:
5 hours

Storage: Up to 4 days
in the refrigerator
(see Chef's Notes) or
1 month in the freezer

INGREDIENTS
Water dough
½ cup (125 ml) water
1½ tsp (7 g) salt
2 cups (9 oz./250 g)
   AP flour
3 tbsp (1½ oz./40 g)
   butter, softened

For laminating
2 sticks (9 oz./250 g)
   butter, well chilled

EQUIPMENT
Stand mixer fitted with
   the dough hook
2 silicone baking mats
   (or parchment paper)
Cardboard pastry rulers
   (see Chef's Notes)

1. **To prepare the water dough,** place the water and salt in a bowl and mix until the salt dissolves.
2. **Beat the flour and butter** together in the mixer on low speed for 30 seconds. Add the salted water and mix for an additional 30 seconds to make a smooth dough. If necessary, finish kneading the dough by hand using a bowl scraper.
3. **Shape the dough** into a ball and slash the top in a criss-cross pattern using a bread knife. Transfer to a clean bowl, cover, and refrigerate for 2 hours to relax the dough.
4. **To laminate the dough,** place the butter between the silicone mats or sheets of parchment paper and beat it with a rolling pin until it is as malleable as the dough, but still cold and firm. Shape the butter into a square.
5. **Roll the water dough** into a square roughly twice the size of the butter. Place the butter in the center and fold over the corners of the dough to enclose the butter completely.
6. **Dust the work surface** lightly with flour and roll the dough into a rectangle three times as long as it is wide. Fold in three and give the dough a quarter turn. This is known as a single turn.
7. **Roll and fold the dough** again in the same way to make a second turn, making sure you always give the folded dough a quarter turn in the same direction. If necessary, dust the work surface with a little more flour to prevent the dough from sticking. If, between turns, the dough becomes too soft to roll and fold without the butter breaking through, wrap and return to the refrigerator to firm it up before continuing.
8. **Cover the dough** with plastic wrap and chill for 1 hour.
9. **Give the dough two more single turns**, making a total of four. Cover with plastic wrap and chill for an additional hour (see Chef's Notes).
10. **Give the dough two more turns** to make a total of six. Cover and return it to the refrigerator to rest for 1 hour before using. The dough can then be rolled out and used as required.

Chef's Notes
• Pastry rulers make it easier to roll dough evenly to a desired thickness, such as ¹⁄₁₆ or ⅛ in. (2 or 3 mm) for tartlets. Cut 10-in. (25-cm) strips from thick cardboard and stack as many as are needed to obtain the desired thickness on either side of the dough, before rolling it out.
• If refrigerating or freezing part or all of the dough, only give it four turns and then tightly wrap and store. Before using the dough, give it two more turns and let rest in the refrigerator for 1 hour.
• If left in the refrigerator for longer than 3–4 days, the dough will begin to discolor.
• Any dough trimmings can be used to make rings or other decorations.

FEUILLETAGE RAPIDE

QUICK PUFF PASTRY ★★

Makes
1¼ lb. (600 g)

Active time: 20 minutes

Chilling and resting time:
3 hours

Storage: Up to 1 month
in the freezer (see Chef's
Notes)

INGREDIENTS
Water dough
2½ cups (11 oz./320 g)
    AP flour
1 stick (4½ oz./130 g) cold
    butter, diced
½ cup (130 ml) water
2 tsp (10 g) salt

For laminating
1 stick (4½ oz./130 g)
    butter, well chilled

EQUIPMENT
Stand mixer fitted with
    the dough hook
2 silicone baking mats
    (or parchment paper)
Cardboard pastry rulers
    (see Chef's Notes)

---

1. **To prepare the water dough,** sift the flour
into the mixer bowl, add the butter, and mix on low
speed for 30 seconds. Add the water and salt and mix
again for 30 seconds to make a smooth dough. If
necessary, finish kneading the dough by hand using
a bowl scraper.
2. **Shape the dough** into a ball, place in a clean bowl,
cover, and refrigerate for 1 hour.
3. **To laminate the dough,** place the butter between
the silicone mats or sheets of parchment paper
and beat it with a rolling pin to make it more pliable.
On a lightly floured surface, roll out the dough into
a rectangle about ¼ in. (5 mm) thick. Cut the butter
into small pieces and place these evenly over the top
two-thirds of the dough.
4. **Fold the bottom third of the dough** up over
the butter and the top third down. Give the folded
dough a quarter turn and roll it into a rectangle again,
this time slightly less than ½ in. (1 cm) thick, lightly
dusting the work surface and the dough with more
flour, as necessary.

5. **Fold in the shorter ends of the dough** so they
touch in the center, then fold the dough in half
to give four layers. Give the dough a quarter turn,
in the same direction as before, and then roll and fold
again in the same way. The dough has now had
two double turns. Wrap tightly and refrigerate for
1 hour. If not using all of the dough, wrap airtight
and freeze the surplus straight away (see Chef's Notes).
6. **Before using the dough,** roll it out and give
it two additional double turns, as above. Wrap and let
rest in the refrigerator for 1 hour. The dough can then
be rolled out and used as required.

Chef's Notes
• Pastry rulers make it easier to roll dough evenly
to a desired thickness, such as 1⁄16 or ⅛ in. (2 or
3 mm) for tartlets. Cut 10-in. (25-cm) strips from
thick cardboard and stack as many as are needed
to obtain the desired thickness on either side
of the dough, before rolling it out.
• If not freezing, the pastry needs to be used on the day
it is made, as it does not keep for longer than a day
in the refrigerator.
• Any dough trimmings can be used to make rings or
other decorations.

GÉNOISE NATURE

GENOISE SPONGE ★

Makes
8-in. (20-cm) cake
to serve 8

Active time: 30 minutes

Cooking time: 30 minutes

Storage: Up to 1 week
in the refrigerator or
1 month in the freezer

INGREDIENTS
1 tbsp (15 g) softened
    butter and a little
    AP flour, for the pans
3 small eggs
    (scant ⅔ cup/140 g)
⅓ cup (2¾ oz./75 g) sugar
⅔ cup (2½ oz./75 g)
    AP flour, sifted
1 tsp (4 g) vanilla sugar
1½ tbsp (20 g) butter,
    clarified
    (see Chef's Notes),
    melted, and cooled

EQUIPMENT
8-in. (20-cm) round cake
    pan
Rimmed baking sheet
Electric hand beater
Instant-read thermometer

1. **Preheat the oven** to 350°F (180°C/Gas Mark 4).
2. **Grease the cake pan** with the softened butter
and dust with flour. Set on the baking sheet.
3. **Whisk together the eggs and sugar** in a large
heatproof bowl over a saucepan of barely simmering
water (bain-marie) for several minutes, until the mixture
thickens and reaches 104°F (40°C). Do not let it exceed
this temperature: if the batter gets too hot, the genoise
will be dry when baked. Remove the bowl from the heat
to the work surface.
4. **Continue whisking** on high speed for 8 minutes,
then reduce the speed to low and whisk for an
additional 15 minutes, until the mixture is light
and airy and the bowl is cool to the touch. The mixture
should fall from a spatula or the beaters in thick
ribbons.
5. **Gently fold in the flour** and vanilla sugar, followed
by the melted clarified butter, until just combined.
Do this quickly but lightly to avoid deflating the batter.
6. **Immediately pour the batter** into the prepared pan
and bake for 30 minutes, until the sponge turns a light
golden brown and begins to shrink from the sides
of the pan.
7. **Turn out onto a wire rack** while still warm and let
cool completely before filling or decorating as desired.

Chef's Notes
• It is preferable, but not essential, to use clarified
butter.
• After freezing, let thaw in the refrigerator for 24 hours
before using.

MERINGUE ITALIENNE

ITALIAN MERINGUE ★★

Makes
6½ oz. (190 g)

Active time: 15 minutes

Storage: Up to 2 days
in the refrigerator or
2 weeks in the freezer
(see Chef's Notes)

INGREDIENTS
3 small egg whites
   (⅓ cup/75 g)
⅔ cup (4½ oz./125 g)
   sugar
2 tbsp (30 ml) water
1 tsp (4 g) sugar

EQUIPMENT
Stand mixer fitted
   with the whisk
Instant-read thermometer

1. **Place the egg whites** in the mixer bowl.
2. **Stir the ⅔ cup (4½ oz./125 g) sugar** into the water in a saucepan. To ensure a successful meringue the following two steps must be done simultaneously.
3. **Dissolve the sugar** over low heat, then increase the heat and bring to a boil.
4. **As soon as the syrup** starts to boil, begin whisking the egg whites on high speed. When they hold soft peaks, add the 1 tsp (4 g) sugar and continue whisking until the peaks are firm (about 5 minutes in total).
5. **Check the temperature** of the sugar syrup and as soon as it reaches 250°F (121°C; see Chef's Notes), reduce the mixer speed to low and very carefully drizzle the syrup into the whites. Do not let the hot syrup touch the whisk, as it could spray up and burn you.
6. **Continue whisking on low speed** for about 5 minutes, until the meringue is firm and glossy, and it has cooled to room temperature.

Chef's Notes
• It is important for the temperature of the sugar syrup to reach 250°F (121°C), known as hard-ball stage. To test the temperature without using a thermometer, let a drop of the syrup fall into a bowl of very cold water. It should immediately form a ball that remains rigid when pressed.
• If freezing the meringue, cool it completely before storing it in a tightly sealed plastic bag or airtight container. Let thaw at room temperature for 30–60 minutes before using.
• To ensure successful results, this is the minimum quantity to be made.

MERINGUE SUISSE

SWISS MERINGUE ★

Makes
13 oz. (370 g)

Active time: 35 minutes

Cooking time:
45–50 minutes

Storage: Up to 2 weeks
in an airtight container
in a dry place

INGREDIENTS
4 egg whites (½ cup/
   120 g)
Scant 2 cups (8¾ oz./
   250 g) confectioners'
   sugar, or 1¼ cups
   (8¾ oz./250 g)
   superfine sugar
Unsweetened
   cocoa powder, for
   dusting (optional)

EQUIPMENT
Cookie sheet, lined
   with parchment paper
Instant-read thermometer
Electric hand beater
Pastry bag fitted with
   a ¼-in. (6-mm) plain tip

1. **Preheat the oven** to 250°F (130°C/Gas Mark ½).
2. **Whisk the egg whites and sugar** together in a bowl set over a saucepan of barely simmering water (bain-marie), until the mixture reaches 122°F (50°C).
3. **Remove from the saucepan** and continue whisking on high speed for 10 minutes, then on low for an additional 10 minutes, until the meringue is firm, glossy, and cool.
4. **Transfer to the pastry bag.** Pipe decorative shapes onto the parchment paper (see Chef's Notes). If wished, dust with a little sifted cocoa powder.

5. **Bake for 45–50 minutes**, propping the oven door ajar with the handle of a wooden spoon. The meringues should be dry on the outside and soft in the center. Cool on a wire rack.

Chef's Notes
• For chocolate meringue, whisk 1 cup (4¼ oz./120 g) cocoa powder into the whites in step 3, on high speed.
• Use Swiss meringue to make decorations, such as mushrooms for a Yule log (see pp. 168–69).

MERINGUE FRANÇAISE
FRENCH MERINGUE ★

Makes
about 1 lb. (465 g),
or 3 × 7-in. (18-cm) round bases, or 20 × 2¾- × 1½-in. (7- × 3.5-cm) individual meringues

Active time: 15 minutes

Cooking time: 1¼ hours

Storage: Up to 2 weeks in an airtight container in a dry place

INGREDIENTS
5 egg whites
  (scant ¾ cup/155 g)
Generous ¾ cup
  (5½ oz./155 g) superfine sugar, divided
Scant 1¼ cups (5½ oz./155 g) confectioners' sugar

EQUIPMENT
2 cookie sheets
Stand mixer fitted with the whisk
Pastry bag fitted with a ¾-in. (2-cm) plain tip

1. **Preheat the oven** to 200°F (100°C/Gas Mark ¼). If making round meringue bases, draw 3 × 7-in. (18-cm) circles on sheets of parchment paper with a pencil and place upside down on the cookie sheets. For individual meringues, simply line the cookie sheets with parchment paper.
2. **Set aside** 5 tsp (20 g) of the superfine sugar and combine the rest in a bowl with the confectioners' sugar.
3. **Whisk the egg whites** on high speed until they hold soft peaks. Add the reserved 5 tsp (20 g) superfine sugar and continue whisking for about 5 minutes or until a stiff, shiny meringue is obtained.
4. **Gently fold in** the combined superfine and confectioners' sugar, taking care not to deflate the mixture.
5. **The meringue must be used immediately.** Spoon it into the pastry bag and stick the parchment paper to the cookie sheets with a dab of meringue in each corner.

6. **To make round bases**, pipe the meringue in a tight spiral, starting at the center of each drawn circle and piping outward to the edge. To make individual meringues, pipe 20 oval-shaped mounds, each measuring approximately 2¾ × 1½ in. (7 × 3.5 cm). For oval meringues, start piping at the drawn circle and work inward to the center.
7. **Place the sheets of meringues** in the oven and bake for about 1¼ hours, watching them closely to ensure they do not color too much. The meringues should be a pale golden color and dry on the outside and underneath.
8. **Let cool completely on a wire rack** before storing in an airtight container.

FOND DE SUCCÈS

SUCCÈS MERINGUE BASES ★★

Makes
2 × 8-in. (20-cm) bases +
10 × 2½-in. (6-cm) bases,
or 40 × 2½-in. (6-cm)
bases

Active time: 15 minutes

Cooking time: 1 hour
20 minutes

Storage: Up to 2 weeks
in an airtight container
in a dry place

INGREDIENTS
5 egg whites
    (scant ¾ cup/155 g)
1 cup (6¾ oz./190 g)
    superfine sugar, divided
Scant ⅔ cup (3 oz./90 g)
    confectioners' sugar
Scant 1 cup (3 oz./90 g)
    almond powder
4 tbsp (50 ml) whole milk

EQUIPMENT
Stand mixer fitted
    with the whisk
Pastry bag fitted with
    a ¾-in. (2-cm) plain tip
    (for larger bases)
Pastry bag fitted with
    a ½-in. (1-cm) plain tip
    (for smaller bases)

1. **Preheat the oven** to 300°F (150°C/Gas Mark 2). Using a pencil, draw an 8-in. (20-cm) circle on two sheets of parchment paper and 5 × 1½-in. (4-cm) circles on each sheet around the larger circles. If you are only making smaller bases, draw 40 × 1½-in. (4-cm) circles on the parchment paper. Place upside down on two cookie sheets, so the pencil marks are underneath.
2. **Whisk the egg whites** on high speed until they form soft peaks. Whisk in 5 tsp (20 g) superfine sugar, a little at a time, until a stiff, shiny meringue is obtained.
3. **In a separate large bowl**, whisk together the remaining 1 scant cup (6 oz./170 g) superfine sugar, confectioners' sugar, almond powder, and milk. Stir a small amount of the first (meringue) mixture into the second until combined, then add this back to the rest of the first mixture, folding it in gently so as not to deflate the meringue.
4. **Stick the parchment paper** to the cookie sheets with a dab of meringue in each corner.

5. **For the larger bases**, spoon the meringue into the pastry bag fitted with the ¾-in. (2-cm) tip. Starting at the center and working outwards, pipe the meringue in a tight spiral to fill the circles.
6. **For the smaller bases**, spoon the meringue into the pastry bag fitted with the ½-in. (1-cm) tip. Pipe in a tight spiral to fill the circles, as above. The bases will expand slightly as they bake, resulting in 2½-in. (6-cm) rounds.
7. **Bake the larger bases** for about 1 hour 10 minutes and the smaller ones for 40–45 minutes, until the meringue is dry and crisp. Invert the positions of the cookie sheets halfway through the cooking time. Both the large and small meringue bases can color quickly, so watch them carefully and lower the oven temperature as necessary.
8. If cooking two sizes at once, remove the smaller bases from the oven when they are ready and transfer them to a wire rack to cool. Leave the larger bases in the oven until cooked, then remove and let cool on the rack.

BABAS

BABA CAKES ★★

Makes	INGREDIENTS	EQUIPMENT
2 babas, each serving 10 (see Chef's Notes)	¼ oz. (7 g) fresh yeast (see Chef's Notes)	Stand mixer fitted with the dough hook
	2 tbsp (30 ml) lukewarm water	2 × 8-in. (20-cm) baba molds (see Chef's Notes)
Active time: 15 minutes	2 cups (9 oz./250 g) AP flour, sifted	
Rising time: 55–60 minutes	Scant ½ cup (100 ml) milk, divided	
Cooking time: 15–20 minutes	2 tsp (6 g) fine salt	
	3 eggs (⅔ cup/150 g)	
	2 tsp (6 g) sugar	
Storage: up to 10 days in the refrigerator or 1 month in the freezer, baked (see Chef's Notes)	5 tbsp (2½ oz./75 g) butter, diced + more for the molds	

1. **Dissolve the yeast** in the lukewarm water in the bowl of the stand mixer.

2. **Add the flour,** 1 tbsp (15 ml) of the milk, and the salt (see Chef's Notes), and mix together on low speed.

3. **With the mixer running,** add the eggs one by one to make a fairly firm dough.

4. **Increase the speed** to medium and knead for 8 minutes, until the dough is smooth and elastic.

5. **Soften the dough** by gradually adding the remaining milk, followed by the sugar and butter. Continue to mix until the butter has been fully incorporated and the dough is smooth; it has been sufficiently kneaded when it can be easily stretched between your fingers without tearing.

6. **Shape the dough** into a ball, place in a clean bowl, cover, and leave in a warm place for about 15 minutes, until risen but not necessarily doubled in volume (this will take longer in a cold kitchen). The dough must not be left to rise for too long or the babas will be fragile.

7. **Deflate the dough** by picking it up with lightly floured hands and dropping it onto the work surface.

8. **Lightly butter the baba molds,** divide the dough between them, cover loosely, and let rise for 40–45 minutes at room temperature, or until the dough rises to the top of the molds.

9. **Preheat the oven** to 350°F (180°C/Gas Mark 4) and bake for 15–20 minutes. To check the babas are cooked, push the tip of a pointed knife into the center: if it comes out dry, they are ready.

10. **Turn out onto a wire rack** while still hot. If a baba sticks to the mold, overwrap in aluminum foil to create steam that will help to release the baba from its mold.

11. **Let the babas dry out** at room temperature for 1–2 days, as they will better absorb the imbibing syrup.

Chef's Notes

• This recipe makes 1 lb. 2 oz. (500 g) baba dough, which is the optimal quantity to make: the dough hook will be able to knead better and the result will be a smoother, more elastic dough.

• If you only have one baba mold, bake one large baba and use the other half of the dough to make 10 individual babas in savarin molds or muffin cups: bake for 15 minutes at 340°F (170°C/Gas Mark 3).

• The unbaked dough does not freeze well, so if only one baba is required, bake two and freeze the second one (unsoaked) for another occasion.

• If storing, wrap the baked baba tightly in plastic wrap while still slightly warm, and refrigerate or freeze. After freezing, let thaw in the refrigerator for 24 hours.

• Baba dough is traditionally made using fresh yeast, as it gives the best results. If fresh yeast is unavailable, you can substitute 1½ tsp (5 g) active dry yeast or 1¼ tsp (3.5 g) instant yeast. Instant yeast must be mixed directly into the flour before any liquid is added, rather than dissolved in the water, which can be omitted.

• Never allow fresh yeast to come into direct contact with salt and sugar, as this can prevent it working properly, or even kill it.

PÂTE À BRIOCHE

BRIOCHE DOUGH ★★

Makes
1¼ lb. (600 g)

Active time: 30 minutes

Rising time: 3½–4½ hours

Chilling time: overnight

Storage: Up to 1 month
in the freezer

INGREDIENTS
¼ oz. (7 g) fresh yeast
    (see Chef's Notes)
1½ tsp (7.5 ml) lukewarm
    water
3¾ tsp (15 g) sugar
1½ tsp (7 g) fine salt
1 tbsp (15 ml) whole milk,
    well chilled
2¾ cups (8¾ oz./250 g)
    high gluten or bread
    flour
3 eggs (⅔ cup/150 g)
1 stick + 2 tbsp
    (5¼ oz./150 g) butter

EQUIPMENT
Stand mixer fitted
    with the dough hook
2 silicone baking mats
    (or parchment paper)

---

1. **Dissolve the yeast** in the lukewarm water in a small bowl. In another small bowl, dissolve the sugar and salt in the milk.

2. **Pour the milk mixture** into the bowl of the stand mixer, add the flour, and finally the dissolved yeast, without letting the yeast come into direct contact with the sugar or salt (see Chef's Notes).

3. **Knead on low speed until combined.** Add 2 eggs and knead briefly to make a firm, smooth dough, before incorporating the remaining egg.

4. **Increase the speed to medium** and knead for about 15 minutes, until the dough is smooth and elastic and can be easily stretched between your fingers without tearing.

5. **While the dough is kneading,** place the butter between two silicone mats or sheets of parchment paper and beat with a rolling pin until the butter is as malleable as the dough.

6. **When the dough is ready,** reduce the mixer speed to low. Cut the butter into 3 or 4 pieces and add them, one at a time, kneading continuously until the butter is fully incorporated and the dough pulls away from the sides of the bowl.

7. **Transfer to a large clean bowl,** cover with a dish towel, and let rise at room temperature until doubled in volume (about 1½ hours).

8. **Deflate the dough** by lifting it out of the bowl with lightly floured hands and dropping it onto the work surface; do this twice. Shape the dough into a ball, return it to the bowl, and cover. Let rise for 2–3 hours in the refrigerator.

9. **Deflate the dough again,** reshape it into a ball, and return to the bowl. Cover tightly with plastic wrap and refrigerate overnight.

10. **Transfer the dough** to a floured work surface and knead it briefly with your hands until smooth. The brioche dough can then be shaped or placed in a mold, and baked.

Chef's Notes

• This recipe makes enough dough for about 20 individual brioches or 2 large brioches, each serving 5. This is the optimal quantity of dough to make: the dough hook will be able to knead better and the result will be a smoother, more elastic dough. Any leftover dough can be used to make buns or rolls, or can be frozen for another occasion.

• If freezing all or part of the dough, do not refrigerate overnight, but divide it into the desired portion sizes, wrap airtight, and freeze. Let thaw in the refrigerator for 24 hours before proceeding with step 10.

• Brioche dough is traditionally made using fresh yeast, as it gives the best results. If fresh yeast is unavailable, you can substitute 1½ tsp (5 g) active dry yeast or 1¼ tsp (3.5 g) instant yeast. Instant yeast must be mixed directly into the flour before any liquid is added, rather than dissolved in the water, which can be omitted.

• Never allow fresh yeast to come into direct contact with salt and sugar, as this can prevent it working properly, or even kill it.

PÂTE À CHOUX

CHOUX PASTRY ★

Makes
1¾ lb. (800 g)

Active time: 15 minutes

Cooking time: 30 minutes
per batch

Storage: Up to 1 week
in the refrigerator or
1 month in the freezer
(see Chef's Notes)

INGREDIENTS
½ cup (125 ml) water
½ cup (125 ml) whole milk
1 tsp (5 g) fine salt
1¼ tsp (5 g) sugar
7 tbsp (4 oz./110 g) butter,
    diced
1 cup + 1 tbsp (5 oz./140 g)
    AP flour, sifted
5 eggs (1 cup/250 g)
2½ tbsp (20 g)
    confectioners' sugar,
    for dusting

EQUIPMENT
Pastry bag fitted with
    a ½- or ¾-in.
    (1- or 1.5-cm) plain tip
2 cookie sheets lined
    with parchment paper

---

1. **Preheat the oven** to 425°F (220°C/Gas Mark 7).
2. **In a large saucepan**, place the water, milk, salt, sugar, and butter. Heat gently until the mixture just begins to boil. Meanwhile, warm a large mixing bowl.
3. **Remove the saucepan** from the heat and add the flour all at once. Begin by beating vigorously with a whisk, then a wooden spoon, until smooth. Return to low heat and cook for 1 minute, stirring continuously with the spoon so the mixture dries and comes away from the sides of the pan.
4. **Transfer to the warm mixing bowl**, cool slightly, and stir in 2 eggs. Stir in 2 more eggs until incorporated, followed by the final egg. Stop stirring as soon as the dough is smooth. The dough can now be used and should be piped and baked right away to prevent it drying out and cracking.
5. **To make choux puffs**, spoon the dough into the pastry bag and stick the parchment to the cookie sheets with a dab of dough in each corner.
6. **Pipe 1½-in. (4-cm) mounds** onto the sheets, well spaced apart; don't worry if the shapes are not identical as they will even out during baking. With practice, you can try piping shapes such as logs for éclairs (see pp. 272–78), ovals for Salambo Choux Puffs (see p. 290), or rings for Paris-Brest (see p. 210).

7. **Dust the puffs** with the confectioners' sugar, place in the oven, and prop the door ajar with the handle of a wooden spoon. Bake for 5 minutes, then reduce the oven temperature to 350°F (180°C/Gas Mark 4) and bake for another 25 minutes, until the puffs are golden and crisp but still soft inside. Watch them closely as, if they overbake, they will be too dry to work with. Puffs will cook more quickly than larger items such as a Paris-Brest, so follow the instructions in the recipe you are making.
8. **Transfer to a wire rack** to cool completely.

Chef's Notes
• This recipe makes enough dough for about 32 éclairs or choux puffs. To ensure successful results, this is the optimal quantity of dough to make.
• Once baked and cooled, choux pastry keeps well in the freezer, so it is worthwhile preparing the quantity of dough given in the recipe, baking it in your chosen shapes, and then freezing in airtight containers.
• After freezing, let thaw overnight in the refrigerator and re-crisp for 5 minutes in a 350°F (180°C/Gas Mark 4) oven.

PÂTE BRISÉE

SHORTCRUST PASTRY ★

Makes
1 lb. 2 oz. (500 g)

Active time: 15 minutes

Resting time: At least
2 hours, preferably
overnight

Cooking time:
15–25 minutes,
if blind-baking

Storage: Up to 1 week
in the refrigerator or
2 months in the freezer

INGREDIENTS
2½ tsp (10 g) sugar
1½ tsp (8 g) fine salt
1 stick + 5 tbsp
   (6¾ oz./190 g) butter,
   well chilled and diced
   (see Chef's Notes)
   + more for the pan
1 egg (3½ tbsp/50 g)
About 2 tbsp (30 ml)
   whole milk
3 cups (9½ oz./265 g)
   cake flour
1 egg yolk, lightly beaten,
   for glazing

EQUIPMENT
Stand mixer fitted with
   the paddle beater
Tart pan or ring
Cookie sheet, lined with
   parchment paper if
   using a ring
Pie weights or dried beans
   for blind-baking

---

1. **Prepare the dough** by beating the sugar, salt, and butter together in the stand mixer. Add the egg and 2 tbsp milk and beat for several seconds to incorporate.

2. **Add the flour** all at once and beat on low speed until the dough comes together, adding more milk, if necessary. The dough should not be elastic and it is fine if small clumps of butter remain. Take care not to overwork the dough, or the pastry will be tough.

3. **Gather the dough together** using your hand, shape it into a ball, and cover tightly with plastic wrap. Let rest in the refrigerator for at least 1 hour, or preferably overnight, as the dough will be even better and easier to roll out the following day.

4. **To line a tart pan or ring**, set the pan or ring on the cookie sheet. Butter the inside of the pan or edge of the ring to help stick the dough to it and prevent the edge from falling during baking. It will also make it easier to unmold the baked tart. Roll out the required amount of dough to the desired thickness on a lightly floured surface and carefully line it into the pan or ring. Gently press it right into the corners and against the sides, taking care not to stretch it.

5. **Either run a rolling pin** across the top to remove excess dough so it is flush with the rim, or leave a little overhanging and crimp by pressing the blunt edge of a knife blade into the dough at an angle at regular intervals. Line with plastic wrap and let rest in the refrigerator for at least 1 hour, or up to 24 hours, before baking.

6. **To blind-bake the crust**, preheat the oven to the required temperature and prick the base all over with a thin-tined fork. Do not prick the base if you are making a fruit tart as the juices will make the crust soggy. Line with parchment paper and fill with pie weights or dried beans to prevent the base from puffing up during baking.

7. **Bake until lightly golden**, remove the parchment paper and weights, and brush the pastry with lightly beaten egg yolk. Return to the oven for 5–10 minutes, until the crust is crisp and evenly golden.

8. **Let cool** before filling.

Chef's Notes

• This recipe makes enough dough for about 16 tartlets or 2 tarts, each serving 6. To ensure successful results, this is the optimal quantity of dough to make.

• If storing the dough, refrigerate or freeze at step 3. After freezing, let thaw for 24 hours in the refrigerator before using.

• Equal quantities of unsalted and salted butter can be used but reduce the quantity of salt by half.

• To prevent the dough from becoming elastic, before starting the recipe, place the flour and half the butter on a work surface. Combine with your fingertips and then, using the heel of your hand, smear the butter into the flour until it has the texture of coarse sand; the French term for this technique is *fraiser*. Continue with step 1, using the remaining butter, and then incorporate the butter and flour mixture at step 2.

PÂTE SABLÉE SUCRÉE

SWEET SHORTCRUST PASTRY ★

Makes	INGREDIENTS	EQUIPMENT
1 lb. 2 oz. (500 g)	1¼ sticks (5 oz./145 g) butter + more for the pan	2 silicone baking mats (or parchment paper)
Active time: 15 minutes	Generous ⅓ cup (1¾ oz./50 g) confectioners' sugar	Stand mixer fitted with the paddle beater
Resting time: At least 1 hour, preferably overnight	2 tsp (8 g) vanilla sugar	Tart pan or ring
	1 pinch fine salt	Cookie sheet, lined with parchment paper if using a ring
Cooking time: 15–25 minutes, if blind-baking	½ cup (1¾ oz./50 g) almond powder	Pie weights or dried beans for blind-baking
	2⅓ cups (7½ oz./210 g) cake flour	
Storage: Up to 1 week in the refrigerator or 2 months in the freezer	2 egg yolks (2½ tbsp/ 40 g) + 1 egg yolk, lightly beaten, for glazing	

1. **Place the butter** between the silicone mats or two sheets of parchment paper and beat it with a rolling pin until softened and pliable.
2. **Cut the butter into pieces** and place in the bowl of the stand mixer. Add the confectioners' sugar, vanilla sugar, salt, and almond powder and beat together.
3. **Scrape down the sides** of the bowl and then add the cake flour in 2 equal quantities, mixing until just combined. Scrape down the sides of the bowl again and continue mixing briefly, until the dough has the texture of coarse sand.
4. **Add the egg yolks** and mix just until the dough comes together; take care not to overwork the dough, or the pastry will be tough.
5. **Cover tightly with plastic wrap** (or divide into portions, as required, and then wrap tightly). Let rest in the refrigerator for at least 1 hour, or preferably overnight, as the dough will be easier to roll out the following day.
6. **To line a tart pan or ring**, set the pan or ring on the cookie sheet. Butter the inside of the pan or edge of the ring to help stick the dough to it and prevent the edge from falling during baking. It will also make it easier to unmold the baked tart. Roll out the required amount of dough to the desired thickness on a lightly floured surface and carefully line it into the pan or ring. Gently press it right into the corners and against the sides, taking care not to stretch it.

7. **Either run a rolling pin** across the top to remove excess dough so it is flush with the rim, or leave a little overhanging and crimp by pressing the blunt edge of a knife blade into the dough at an angle at regular intervals. Line with plastic wrap and let rest in the refrigerator for at least 1 hour, or up to 24 hours, before baking.
8. **To blind-bake the crust**, preheat the oven to the required temperature and prick the base all over with a thin-tined fork. Do not prick the base if you are making a fruit tart as the juices will make the crust soggy. Line with parchment paper and fill with pie weights or dried beans to prevent the base from puffing up during baking.
9. **Bake until lightly golden**, remove the parchment paper and weights, and brush the pastry with the lightly beaten egg yolk. Return to the oven for 5–10 minutes, until the crust is crisp and evenly golden.
10. **Let cool** before filling.

Chef's Notes
• This recipe makes enough dough for about 16 tartlets or 2 tarts, each serving 6. To ensure successful results, this is the optimal quantity of dough to make.
• If storing the dough, refrigerate or freeze at step 5. After freezing, let thaw for 24 hours in the refrigerator before using.

CREAMS, SAUCES, GLAZES, AND DECORATIONS

APPAREIL À BAVAROIS

BAVARIAN CREAM *

Makes
about 1 lb. 9 oz./700 g

Active time: 10 minutes

Storage: Up to 3 days
in the refrigerator, covered

INGREDIENTS
4–5 sheets
    gelatin (see Chef's
    Notes)
2 quantities vanilla custard
    sauce (1 lb. 9 oz./700 g;
    see p. 86), hot
2 tbsp (30 ml) kirsch
    (optional)

EQUIPMENT
Mold(s) of your choice

1. **Soak the gelatin** in a bowl of cold water until softened.
2. **Squeeze excess water** out of the gelatin and, using a flexible spatula or whisk, stir into the hot custard until dissolved.
3. **Let cool slightly**, then stir in the kirsch, if using.
4. **Pour the mixture** into one large mold or individual dessert cups and let cool completely. Chill until set.

Chef's Notes
• If adding kirsch, use 5 sheets of gelatin rather than 4.

APPAREIL À SOUFFLÉ
BASIC SWEET SOUFFLÉ ★★

Serves	INGREDIENTS	For the soufflé dish	EQUIPMENT
4	1 cup (250 ml) whole milk, divided	2 tbsp (25 g) butter, softened	Electric hand beater
Active time: 30 minutes	Generous ⅓ cup (2¾ oz./80 g) sugar, divided	Sugar	6-in. (16-cm) round soufflé dish, 2½ in. (6 cm) deep
Cooling time: 15 minutes	½ cup + 1 tbsp (2½ oz./45 g) AP flour		
Cooking time: 20 minutes	1 tbsp + 1 tsp (20 g) butter		
	4 egg yolks (scant ⅓ cup/ 80 g)		
	4 egg whites (½ cup/ 120 g)		
	Confectioners' sugar, for dusting		

1. **Preheat the oven** to 350°F (180°C/Gas Mark 4).
2. **Using a pastry brush**, thoroughly grease the bottom and sides of the soufflé dish with the butter, then sprinkle with sugar until evenly coated.
3. **Bring to a boil** ¾ cup (190 ml) of the milk in a large saucepan.
4. **Meanwhile, in a mixing bowl**, whisk together a scant ⅓ cup (2 oz./60 g) sugar, the flour, and the remaining milk.
5. **Whisk in a small amount** of the boiled milk, then return the entire mixture to the saucepan, whisking continuously. Let boil for 2 minutes, continuing to whisk nonstop. Remove from the heat.
6. **Stir the butter into the mixture** while it is still warm, until the butter has melted.
7. **Cover and let cool** for 15 minutes.
8. **Whisk in the egg yolks** to make a smooth custard. Stir in any alcohol or other flavorings, such as pistachios, almonds, or chocolate (see recipes pp. 320–27).
9. **Whisk the egg whites** in a large bowl until they hold soft peaks. Gradually whisk in the remaining 5 tsp (20 g) sugar, continuing to whisk until the peaks are medium-firm.
10. **Stir one-third of the whites** into the custard to loosen it, then gently fold in the remaining whites using a flexible spatula until evenly combined.
11. **Pour the batter** into the soufflé dish, filling it no more than three-quarters full (see Chef's Notes).

12. **Sift a light dusting** of confectioners' sugar over the top and bake for about 20 minutes, until well risen. To check if the soufflé is ready, insert the tip of a knife or skewer into the center: if it comes out clean, the soufflé is cooked. Serve immediately.

Chef's Notes
• Once you have filled the soufflé dish, you can wait up to 30 minutes to bake it. Cover the dish and keep it warm (86°F–104°F/30°C–40°C).
• You can make 4 individual soufflés with the mixture, baking them in ramekins as above. The quantities of ingredients can also be doubled or tripled to make 2 or 3 large soufflés, which can be baked together on the same baking sheet.

CARAMEL CUIT À SEC

DRY CARAMEL ★★

Makes
about 5 oz. (150 g)

Active time: 10 minutes

Cooking time: 5 minutes

Storage: Up to 1 month
in an airtight container
in a dry place

INGREDIENTS
1 cup (7 oz./200 g) sugar,
  divided
10 drops lemon juice

EQUIPMENT
Heavy-bottomed
  saucepan with
  a capacity of at least
  4 cups (1 L)

1. **Gently dissolve** ¼ cup (1¾ oz./50 g) of the sugar
in the saucepan over low heat, without stirring. If
using gas, make sure the flame does not extend beyond
the base of the pan or the sugar could burn on the sides.
2. **When the sugar has dissolved** into a clear syrup,
increase the heat so that it begins to boil. Do not stir.
Add the lemon juice, then gradually add the remaining
sugar, ¼ cup (1¾ oz./50 g) at a time, following
the same procedure as above. Melting the sugar in stages
helps to prevent lumps of crystals from forming.
3. **Boil until the syrup** begins to color, carefully swirling
the saucepan to encourage even browning.
4. **Remove from the heat** when the desired color has
been reached (about 5 minutes).
5. **Use immediately** if using as a base for crème caramel
or for decorations. Otherwise, let cool and store in an
airtight container.

Chef's Notes
• Caramel can range from light gold to mahogany
in color. As it starts to color, it must be closely watched:
if it becomes too dark, it will develop a bitter taste; if it
is too light, it will simply sweeten your dish instead
of adding a caramel flavor.
• Dry caramel is easier to prepare on an induction stove,
which gives more uniform results.

CARAMEL LIQUIDE

LIQUID CARAMEL ★★

Makes
about 10½ oz. (300 g),
to cover a dessert
serving 8

Active time: 15 minutes

Storage: Up to 1 month
in the refrigerator,
in an airtight container

INGREDIENTS
1 cup (7 oz./200 g) sugar
¼ cup (60 ml) water
10 drops lemon juice
¼ cup (60 ml) very hot
   water

EQUIPMENT
Heavy-bottomed
   saucepan with
   a capacity of at least
   2 cups (500 ml)

---

1. **Combine the sugar** and ¼ cup (60 ml) water
in the saucepan.
2. **Place over low heat** and stir with a spatula until
the sugar dissolves. Take care not to splash water
up the sides of the pan. If using a gas stove, make
sure the flame does not extend beyond the base
of the saucepan to avoid any sugar burning on the sides.
Brush down any sugar crystals that collect on the sides
of the pan to prevent them burning.
3. **Stir in the lemon juice,** increase the heat, and
continue cooking and stirring until the syrup comes
to a full boil. Once boiling, stop stirring immediately
to prevent the sugar from crystallizing.
4. **When the syrup begins to color,** carefully swirl
the saucepan to encourage even browning. Do not stir.
5. **When the caramel has reached the desired color,** put
on an oven mitt to protect your hand against boiling
splatters and very carefully add the hot water in 2 equal
quantities, stirring constantly. The caramel should be
quite runny at this point, or it will harden too much
as it cools.

CHANTILLY NATURE

CHANTILLY CREAM ★

Makes
about 2 cups (9 oz./250 g)

Active time: 10 minutes

Chilling time: 2 hours

Storage: Up to 24 hours
in the refrigerator,
in an airtight container

INGREDIENTS
Generous ¾ cup (200 ml)
    crème fraîche + ¼ cup
    (60 ml) whole milk
or
1 cup (250 ml) heavy
    cream (see Chef's
    Notes)
Generous 1 tbsp (15 g)
    sugar, preferably
    superfine or
    confectioners'
    (see Chef's Notes)

EQUIPMENT
Stand mixer fitted
    with the whisk
Pastry bag fitted
    with a plain or fluted tip
    (if piping)

---

1. Combine the ingredients in the bowl of the mixer
and place in the refrigerator to chill for at least 2 hours.
Chill the whisk at the same time (see Chef's Notes).
2. Whip on medium speed until the cream starts
to thicken. Increase the speed to high, and continue
whipping until the cream holds its shape (about
4 minutes in total). Take care not to overwhip the cream
or it will separate.
3. The cream is now ready to be used and can be piped
out, spread with a palette knife over tarts and cakes, or
spooned over desserts.
4. If storing the cream, stir a few times with a balloon
whisk before using.

Chef's Notes
• The cream must have a fat content of 30% or more,
or it will not thicken when whipped.
• It is best to use a fine sugar, such as superfine or
confectioners', as it will dissolve more easily
in the cream.
• For best results, the cream, bowl, and whisk must be
very cold, to avoid overwhipping.
• Plain whipped cream, which is often used to lighten
other creams, can be made in the same way, but
omitting the sugar.

COULIS DE FRUITS FRAIS

FRESH FRUIT COULIS *

Makes
about 11½ oz. (325 g)

Active time: 10 minutes

Storage: Up to 3 days
in the refrigerator or
2–3 months in the freezer,
in an airtight container
or ice-cube trays

INGREDIENTS
9 oz. (250 g) fresh fruit
(see Chef's Notes)
⅓ cup (2¾ oz./75 g) sugar
(see Chef's Notes)

EQUIPMENT
Food processor
Fine-mesh sieve, if needed

1. **Wash the fruit**, peel it, and remove any pits or cores. Cut larger fruits into bite-size pieces.
2. **Place the fruit** in the food processor, add the sugar, and process until smooth (about 2 minutes).
3. **Strain through a fine-mesh sieve**, if necessary, to remove any fibers or seeds.

Chef's Notes
• Coulis can be made with a single variety of fresh fruit or a combination of several different ones. For a single-fruit coulis, raspberries, strawberries, apricots, peaches, and mangos work very well. For combinations, try mixed berries, or a tropical blend of passion fruit, banana, and pineapple.
• As some fruits are sweeter than others, taste the coulis and adjust the sugar as necessary.
• If the coulis has been frozen, whisk or blend it while thawing until smooth and use straight away.

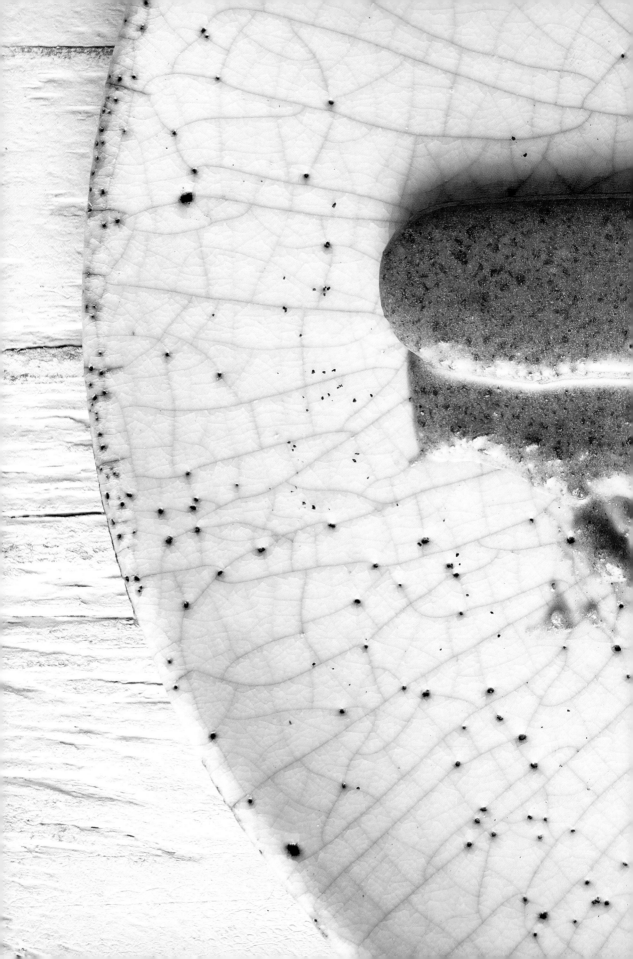

CRÈME AU BEURRE NATURE

PLAIN BUTTERCREAM ★

Makes
1½ lb. (700 g)

Active time: 30 minutes

Storage: Up to 3 days
in the refrigerator or
2–3 months in the freezer

INGREDIENTS
⅔ cup (165 ml) whole milk
Scant 1 cup (6 oz./170 g)
    sugar, divided
7 egg yolks (½ cup/140 g)
1½ sticks (6 oz./170 g)
    butter, diced
2¾ oz. (75 g) Italian
    meringue (see p. 32
    and Chef's Notes)

Optional flavorings
(see Chef's Notes)
Vanilla extract, almond
    extract, orange flower
    water, rose water, or
    other extracts
Cocoa powder or instant
    coffee dissolved in 1 tsp
    (5 ml) water
Very finely grated citrus
    zest and a little juice

EQUIPMENT
Instant-read thermometer
Fine-mesh sieve
Stand mixer with the whisk
    and paddle beater

1. **Pour the milk** into a saucepan and whisk in half the sugar. Bring to a boil, stirring until the sugar dissolves. Remove from the heat and let cool to 176°F (80°C).

2. **Whisk the egg yolks** and remaining sugar together on high speed until pale and thick. Pour one-quarter of the hot milk slowly into the egg yolks and sugar, whisking continuously until incorporated.

3. **Pour the mixture back into the saucepan** and stir over low heat to make a custard, using a spatula to make figure-eight movements. Do not let the mixture boil.

4. **When the temperature of the custard** reaches 181°F (83°C) and coats the back of a spoon, strain it through a fine-mesh sieve into a clean bowl. Whisk until cool.

5. **Clean and dry the mixer bowl.** Fit the mixer with the paddle beater and beat the butter on medium speed until softened and smooth.

6. **Beat in the cooled custard**, followed by the Italian meringue, until just smooth. If the ingredients are too cold to come together, gently warm the bowl in a bain-marie or by setting it over a saucepan of water at 140°F (60°C).

Chef's Notes
• If you are not using the buttercream immediately, press plastic wrap over the surface and refrigerate, or freeze in an airtight container, unflavored. Let frozen buttercream thaw in the refrigerator overnight. Before using, let it come to room temperature, stir until smooth, then incorporate any chosen flavorings.
• Italian meringue makes buttercream exceptionally silky and smooth. To ensure the best results, make a full quantity of the meringue recipe on p. 32 and weigh out the 2¾ oz. (75 g) needed. The meringue that is leftover can be used in another recipe, or frozen for later use.

CRÈME AU BEURRE CHOCOLAT

CHOCOLATE BUTTERCREAM ★

Makes
1 lb. 2 oz. (500 g)

Active time:
5 minutes + making
the plain buttercream

Storage: Up to 3 days
in the refrigerator or
2–3 months in the freezer

INGREDIENTS
4 oz. (115 g) dark
    chocolate, 70% cacao,
    roughly chopped
13½ oz. (385 g)
    plain buttercream
    (see p. 54)

EQUIPMENT
Instant-read thermometer

---

1. Melt the chocolate to 104°F (40°C)
in a heatproof bowl over a saucepan of barely simmering
water (bain-marie).
2. In a separate bowl, whisk the buttercream until
smooth.
3. Gradually whisk the melted chocolate
into the buttercream until well blended and smooth.

Chef's Notes
• If you are not using the buttercream immediately,
press plastic wrap over the surface and refrigerate, or
freeze in an airtight container. Let frozen buttercream
thaw in the refrigerator overnight. Before using, let
it come to room temperature and stir until smooth.

CRÈME AU BEURRE CAFÉ GUATEMALA

COFFEE BUTTERCREAM ★

Makes
1 lb. 2 oz. (500 g)

Active time: 1 hour

Infusing time: 24 hours

Cooking time: 15 minutes

Storage: Up to 3 days
in the refrigerator or
2–3 months in the freezer

INGREDIENTS
Coffee syrup
(make 1 day ahead)
¼ cup (1¾ oz./50 g) sugar
3½ tbsp (50 ml) very hot
    water (200°F/90°C)
¼ cup (25 g) ground
    coffee, preferably
    Guatemalan

Buttercream
3 small egg whites
    (⅓ cup/75 g)
⅔ cup (4½ oz./125 g)
    sugar
2 tbsp (30 ml) water
1½ tbsp (25 ml) coffee
    syrup (see left)
2 sticks (9 oz./250 g)
    butter, diced

EQUIPMENT
Fine-mesh sieve
Stand mixer with the whisk
    and paddle beater
Instant-read thermometer

1. **Prepare the coffee syrup** the day before needed. Make a dry caramel with the sugar (see p. 46). When the caramel is dark amber, put on an oven mitt to protect your hand against boiling splatters and very carefully pour in the hot water, stirring constantly with a wooden spoon.

2. **Whisk in the ground coffee**, cover with plastic wrap, and let infuse for 24 hours in the refrigerator.

3. **The following day**, strain through a fine-mesh sieve to obtain about 3½ tbsp (50 ml; see Chef's Notes).

4. **To prepare the buttercream**, first make an Italian meringue. Place the egg whites in the mixer bowl. Stir the sugar into the water in a saucepan. The following two steps must be done simultaneously to ensure success.

5. **Dissolve the sugar** over low heat, then increase the heat and bring to a boil. As soon as the syrup starts to boil, begin whisking the egg whites on high speed until they hold firm peaks.

6. **When the temperature of the syrup** reaches 250°F (121°C), reduce the mixer speed to low and very carefully drizzle in the syrup in a steady stream Do not let the hot syrup touch the whisk, as it could spray up and burn you. Continue whisking on low speed until the meringue cools to room temperature.

7. **Whisk in half the coffee syrup** and stop whisking straight away. Transfer to another bowl, wash and dry the mixer bowl, and fit with the paddle beater.

8. **Beat the butter** on medium speed until it is soft and smooth, then beat in the remaining coffee syrup, scraping down the sides of the bowl as needed.

9. **Slowly beat in the meringue** a third at a time, scraping down the sides of the bowl after each addition. Beat just until combined.

Chef's Notes

• If you are not using the buttercream immediately, press plastic wrap over the surface and refrigerate, or freeze in an airtight container. Let frozen buttercream thaw in the refrigerator overnight. Before using, let it come to room temperature and stir until smooth.

• As only half the quantity of coffee syrup is needed, the remainder can be stored for up to 2 weeks in the refrigerator in a sealed container and used for another recipe.

CRÈME AU BEURRE PRALINÉ

HAZELNUT PRALINE BUTTERCREAM *

Makes
1½ lb. (700 g)

Active time:
5 minutes + making
the plain buttercream

Storage: Up to 3 days
in the refrigerator or
2–3 months in the freezer

INGREDIENTS
1¼ lb. (560 g)
   plain buttercream
   (see p. 54)
2½ oz. (70 g) pure
   hazelnut paste
2½ oz. (70 g) hazelnut
   praline paste

1. **Whisk the buttercream** in a mixing bowl until smooth.
2. **Stir in the hazelnut paste** using a firm spatula, followed by the praline paste, until smooth and evenly blended.

Chef's Notes
• If you are not using the buttercream immediately, press plastic wrap over the surface and refrigerate, or freeze in an airtight container. Let frozen buttercream thaw in the refrigerator overnight. Before using, let it come to room temperature and stir until smooth.

CRÈME CHIBOUST

CHIBOUST CREAM ★★

Makes
1 lb. 3 oz. (550 g)

Active time: 30 minutes

INGREDIENTS

Pastry cream
2 sheets gelatin,
   180–200 Bloom
1 cup (250 ml) whole milk
½ vanilla bean, preferably
   Madagascar Bourbon
3 egg yolks
   (scant ¼ cup/60 g)
3 tbsp (1¼ oz./35 g) sugar
2 tbsp (20 g) AP flour
2 tbsp (20 g) cornstarch

Italian meringue
4 egg whites
   (scant ⅓ cup/130 g)
⅓ cup (2½ oz./70 g) sugar
1 tbsp (15 ml) water
1 tsp (4 g) sugar

EQUIPMENT
Stand mixer fitted
   with the whisk
Instant-read thermometer

1. **To prepare the pastry cream,** first soak the gelatin in a bowl of cold water until softened.

2. **While the gelatin softens,** make the pastry cream following the recipe on p. 66, flavoring it with the vanilla and using the reduced quantity of sugar given here (so it is less sweet).

3. **When the pastry cream is ready** and still hot, squeeze the gelatin to remove excess water and whisk the sheets into the cream until dissolved. Press plastic wrap over the surface to prevent a skin from forming and set the pastry cream aside (still in the saucepan) to keep it warm.

4. **To prepare the Italian meringue,** place the egg whites in the mixer bowl. Stir the ⅓ cup (2½ oz./70 g) sugar into the water in a saucepan. To ensure success, the following two steps must be done simultaneously.

5. **Dissolve the sugar** over low heat, then increase the heat and bring to a boil.

6. **As soon as the syrup** starts to boil, begin whisking the egg whites on high speed. When they hold soft peaks, add the 1 tsp sugar (4 g) and continue whisking until firm peaks form (about 5 minutes in total).

7. **Check the temperature** of the sugar syrup. As soon as it reaches 250°F (121°C), reduce the mixer speed to low and very carefully drizzle the syrup into the whites in a steady stream. Do not let the hot syrup touch the whisk, as it could spray up and burn you. Continue whisking on low speed for 2 minutes.

8. **Whisk one-third of the meringue** into the warm pastry cream to loosen it and, using a flexible spatula, gently fold in the remainder in 2 equal quantities, taking care not to deflate the mixture.

9. **Use the cream immediately** to fill choux puffs (see p. 38) or a Gâteau Saint-Honoré (see p. 214). The cream can also be served on its own in dessert glasses or layered with fresh fruit. Chill and serve on the same day as it is made.

CRÈME D'AMANDE MÉLANGÉE

FRANGIPANE CREAM *

Makes
2¼ lb. (1 kg)

Active time: 15 minutes

Storage: 3–4 days
in the refrigerator or
1 month in the freezer
in an airtight container

INGREDIENTS
1 stick + 3 tbsp
    (6 oz./165 g) butter,
    diced
1½ cups (7 oz./200 g)
    confectioners' sugar
2 cups (7 oz./200 g)
    almond powder
2 eggs (scant ½ cup/
    100 g)
1 large egg yolk (1½ tbsp/
    25 g)
2 tbsp (20 g) cornstarch
4 tsp (20 ml) dark rum
9 oz. (250 g) vanilla pastry
    cream (see p. 66)

EQUIPMENT
Stand mixer fitted with
    the paddle beater

1. **Beat the butter** on medium speed until soft
and creamy.
2. **Sift in the sugar and almond powder** and beat until
incorporated.
3. **Add the eggs** one at a time, followed by the egg yolk,
beating for 30 seconds after each addition. Continue
beating until the mixture is light and smooth. Finally,
incorporate the cornstarch and rum.
4. **Whisk the vanilla pastry cream** until smooth and stir
it into the almond mixture until evenly incorporated.

Chef's Notes
• This recipe makes enough frangipane cream for
about 32 tartlets, or 2 large almond Kings' Cakes,
each serving 8 (see p. 120), and a tart serving 6–8.
• The cream can be prepared up to the end of step 3,
at which stage it is known as almond cream, and stored
in the refrigerator for 1 week in an airtight container.
Let it come to room temperature before adding
the pastry cream to make frangipane cream.
• If freezing the completed frangipane cream, let it thaw
in the refrigerator overnight before using.

PÂTE D'AMANDE À FAIRE CHEZ SOI

HOMEMADE MARZIPAN ★★

Makes
1 lb. 2 oz. (500 g)

Active time: 15 minutes

Storage: Up to 1 week
in the refrigerator,
wrapped airtight

INGREDIENTS
2½ cups (9 oz./250 g)
    almond powder, or
1½ cups (9 oz./250 g)
    blanched whole
    almonds
2 cups minus 1 tbsp
    (9 oz./250 g)
    confectioners' sugar
2 egg whites (¼ cup/60 g),
    lightly whisked with
    a fork

EQUIPMENT
Food processor

1. **In a mixing bowl**, stir together the almond powder or blanched whole almonds, the sugar, and about 1 egg white.
2. **Transfer one-third of the mixture** to the food processor and process until smooth.
3. **Repeat, adding another third**, followed by the remaining third. Gradually add a little more egg white as necessary, to soften the mixture and make it malleable. It must form a ball, but avoid overworking the marzipan or it will become oily.
4. **Let it cool** completely before covering with plastic wrap or placing in an airtight container.

Chef's Notes
• Homemade marzipan has a superior texture and flavor to store-bought. It can be shaped into decorations (see p. 73) or used in recipes such as French Almond Cake (see p. 136), almond and walnut Val d'Isère Tartlets (see p. 306), or Colombier (see p. 114).

CRÈME PÂTISSIÈRE

PASTRY CREAM ★

Makes
1¼ lb. (600 g)

Active time: 15 minutes

Cooking time: 5 minutes

Storage: Up to 2 days
in the refrigerator, covered

INGREDIENTS
1⅔ cups (400 ml) whole
milk
½ Madagascar Bourbon
or Tahitian vanilla bean,
split lengthwise
5 egg yolks (⅓ cup/100 g)
½ cup minus 1½ tbsp
(2¾ oz./80 g) sugar
1½ tbsp (15 g) AP flour
1½ tbsp (15 g) cornstarch

EQUIPMENT
Electric hand beater
and balloon whisk

1. **Pour the milk** into a large saucepan and scrape
in the vanilla seeds. Bring to a simmer.
2. **While the milk is heating**, use the electric hand
beater to whisk the egg yolks and sugar together until
pale and thick.
3. **Sift the flour and cornstarch** together and fold
in gently until just combined.
4. **Whisk one-quarter of the hot milk** into the yolk
mixture to loosen it, then pour it back into the
saucepan, whisking continuously.
5. **Place over medium heat** and let boil for 1 minute,
whisking continuously with the whisk to prevent
the mixture from sticking to the bottom of the pan.
6. **Remove from the heat**, pour into a shallow dish so
that the cream cools quickly, and immediately press
plastic wrap over the surface. Transfer to the refrigerator
when cool.
7. **Whisk until smooth** before using.

Chef's Notes
• The quantities of ingredients can be halved if you
require less pastry cream for the recipe you are
making. However, 10½ oz. (300 g) is the minimum
recommended amount to make, to ensure optimal
results.
• You can flavor the pastry cream with an alcohol
of your choice, if desired. Stir it into the cream at
step 6, before pouring it into a shallow dish to cool.

CRÈME PÂTISSIÈRE CAFÉ DU GUATEMALA

COFFEE PASTRY CREAM ⋆

Makes
1 lb. 2 oz. (500 g)

Active time: 15 minutes

Infusing time: 1 hour

Cooking time: 5 minutes

Storage: Up to 2 days
in the refrigerator, covered

INGREDIENTS
Scant 2 cups (440 ml)
    whole milk, divided
⅓ cup (1 oz./30 g) ground
    coffee, preferably
    Guatemalan
4 egg yolks (scant ⅓ cup/
    80 g)
Scant ⅓ cup (2 oz./60 g)
    sugar
1 tbsp + 1 scant tsp (12 g)
    cornstarch
1½ tbsp (12 g) AP flour
1 tbsp (15 g) butter, diced

EQUIPMENT
Fine-mesh sieve
Electric hand beater
    and balloon whisk

1. **Bring ½ cup (125 ml) of the milk** to a simmer in a large saucepan. Remove from the heat, stir in the ground coffee, cover, and let infuse for 1 hour.
2. **Strain through a fine-mesh sieve**, return to the saucepan, and add the remaining milk. Bring to a simmer.
3. **While the milk is heating**, use the electric hand beater to whisk the egg yolks and sugar together until pale and thick.
4. **Sift the cornstarch and flour** together and gently fold in until just combined.
5. **Whisk one-quarter of the hot milk** into the yolk mixture to loosen it, then pour it back into the saucepan, whisking continuously.
6. **Place over medium heat** and let boil for 1 minute, whisking continuously with the whisk to prevent the mixture from sticking to the bottom of the pan.
7. **Remove from the heat** and gradually whisk in the butter until it has melted and the mixture is smooth.
8. **Pour into a shallow dish** so that the cream cools quickly and immediately press plastic wrap over the surface. Transfer to the refrigerator when cool.
9. **Whisk until smooth** before using.

CRÈME PÂTISSIÈRE CHOCOLAT

CHOCOLATE PASTRY CREAM *

Makes
1 lb. 2 oz. (500 g)

Active time: 15 minutes

Cooking time: 5 minutes

Storage: Up to 2 days
in the refrigerator, covered

INGREDIENTS
1⅓ cups (310 ml) whole
   milk
⅓ cup (2¼ oz./65 g) sugar,
   divided
3 egg yolks (scant ¼ cup/
   60 g)
3 tbsp (1 oz./30 g)
   cornstarch
2 tbsp (15 g) unsweetened
   cocoa powder
2¾ oz. (80 g) dark
   couverture chocolate,
   70% cacao, chopped
1 tbsp + 1 tsp (20 g)
   butter, at room
   temperature, diced

EQUIPMENT
Electric hand beater
   and balloon whisk

1. **Bring the milk** and 5 tsp (20 g) of the sugar
to a simmer in a large saucepan.
2. **While the milk is heating**, use the electric beater
to whisk the egg yolks and the remaining sugar together
until pale and thick.
3. **Sift the cornstarch and cocoa powder** together
and fold in gently until just combined.
4. **Whisk one-quarter of the hot milk** into the yolk
mixture to loosen it, then pour it back into the saucepan,
whisking continuously.
5. **Place over medium heat** and let boil for 1 minute,
whisking continuously with the whisk to prevent
the mixture from sticking to the bottom of the pan.
6. **Remove from the heat** and whisk in the chocolate
and butter until they have melted and the mixture
is smooth.
7. **Pour into a shallow dish** so that the cream cools
quickly and immediately press plastic wrap over
the surface. Transfer to the refrigerator when cool.
8. **Whisk until smooth** before using.

DÉCOR EN CHOCOLAT
CHOCOLATE DECORATIONS ★★

Active time: 5 minutes

Storage: Up to 3 days in the refrigerator, in an airtight container

INGREDIENTS
Dark couverture
    chocolate, chopped

EQUIPMENT
2 rimmed stainless steel
    baking sheets
Instant-read thermometer
Paper piping cone or
    pastry bag and assorted
    tips
Offset spatula
Scraper
Paint roller

Making chocolate nests

1. **Place a stainless steel baking sheet** in the freezer for at least 15 minutes. Cut pieces of plastic wrap slightly larger than the size of the nests you wish to make. Set small bowls or cups (the same number as the nests you are making) upside down on the second baking sheet.
2. **Melt the chocolate** to 104°F (40°C) in a heatproof bowl over a saucepan of barely simmering water (bain-marie), or in a microwave, until it is smooth and glossy.
3. **Spoon the melted chocolate** into a paper piping cone or pastry bag and snip off the end, cutting a hole the desired size of the piped lines of chocolate.
4. **Remove the baking sheet** from the freezer and place on the work surface. Place the pieces of plastic wrap on top, spacing them slightly apart.
5. **Working from left to right**, pipe thin lines of chocolate onto each piece of plastic wrap. Make sure you leave space between the lines so that they do not run together, and avoid piping beyond the edges of the plastic wrap.
6. **Wait about 1 minute** until the chocolate is no longer runny and is starting to set but is still pliable. Carefully lift the piped nests off the baking sheet and place each one over an upturned bowl or cup. You can continue piping nests until the baking sheet is no longer cold.
7. **Very carefully transfer the nests**, still draped over the bowls or cups, onto the baking sheet. Place in the refrigerator and chill until completely set.
8. **Holding the plastic wrap**, gently remove one nest from a bowl or cup, then very carefully pull away the plastic wrap. Repeat with the remaining nests and store them in a single layer in a rigid airtight container. Line the container with clean crumpled plastic wrap or foil before placing the nests in it, so they do not bump against each other and break.

Making chocolate cigarettes

1. **Place a stainless steel baking sheet** in the freezer for 15 minutes (for cigarettes, it should be chilled but not ice cold).
2. **Melt the chocolate** as for the nests, until it is smooth and glossy.
3. **Using the offset spatula**, spread the melted chocolate over the chilled baking sheet in a thin, even layer. Let the chocolate set lightly, until it is firm but not hard. Using even pressure, push the scraper across the chocolate to shave off thin cigarette-shaped rolls.

Making chocolate fans

1. **Heat a baking sheet** in the oven to 120°F (50°C/ Gas Mark ½).
2. **Melt the chocolate** as for the nests, until it is smooth and glossy.
3. **Using an offset spatula** (or a paint roller, if you have one), spread the melted chocolate in a thin, even layer over the heated baking sheet.
4. **As soon as the sheet has cooled**, transfer it to the refrigerator and chill for 1 hour.
5. **Remove from the refrigerator** and let it come to room temperature: the chocolate should still be firm but no longer hard and you should be able to scratch it easily with your fingernail.
6. **With your index finger** pressed down firmly on one corner of the scraper, push the scraper away from you, maintaining even pressure with your finger, so the chocolate is shaved off in a curved fan shape. Repeat to make more fans, working across the width of the sheet for the most attractive results.

DÉCOR EN PASTILLAGE

PASTILLAGE DECORATIONS ★★

Makes
1 lb. (500 g)

Active time: 20 minutes

Storage: Up to 1 month
in an airtight container
in a cool, dark place

INGREDIENTS
3 sheets gelatin
3½ cups (15¾ oz./450 g)
   confectioners' sugar
2 tbsp + 2 tsp (25 g)
   cornstarch + more
   for dusting
2 tsp (10 ml) white vinegar

EQUIPMENT
Cookie cutters
   of your choice
Molds of your choice

1. **Soak the gelatin** in a bowl of cold water until softened.
2. **Sift the sugar and cornstarch** together into a mixing bowl.
3. **Squeeze the gelatin** to remove excess water and melt in a bowl over a pan of barely simmering water (bain-marie) or for about 10 seconds on full power in the microwave.
4. **Stir the gelatin and vinegar** into the sugar and cornstarch using a flexible spatula until combined. Knead with your hands until smooth.
5. **Dust the work surface** with cornstarch and, since pastillage dries out quickly, only work with small pieces at a time, keeping the rest tightly covered with plastic wrap.
6. **Roll out the pastillage** and stamp out shapes using cookie cutters, or cut them out using a knife. You can also shape the pastillage into decorations with your hands, press it into a mold, or drape it over a rolling pin or bowl so it dries in an attractive shape: dust the rolling pin or mold with cornstarch first, to prevent the pastillage from sticking.
7. **Let dry** for at least 24 hours before using or storing.

DÉCOR EN PÂTE D'AMANDE

MARZIPAN DECORATIONS ★

Active time: 15 minutes

Storage: Up to 1 week
in the refrigerator,
in an airtight container

INGREDIENTS
10½ oz. (300 g) marzipan
   made with blanched
   almonds (see p. 63)
Natural paste food
   colorings (see Chef's
   Notes), preferably
   organic, or dehydrated
   fruit or vegetable
   powders
Cornstarch, for dusting

EQUIPMENT (optional)
Cookie cutters
Cookie or marzipan
   stamps
Molds
Marzipan sculpting tools

---

1. **Use your hands** to knead food coloring or powder
into the marzipan, until it is evenly colored to the
desired shade.
2. **Dust the work surface** with cornstarch.
3. **Roll out the marzipan** to the desired thickness,
lifting and rotating it gently after each roll to prevent
it from sticking and cracking. If this happens, gather
the marzipan into a ball and roll it out again.
4. **To make marzipan decorations**, use cookie cutters
to cut out the desired shapes, or decorate with cookie
or marzipan stamps. You can also press the marzipan
into molds and leave it to become firm before turning
it out, or mold it into flowers, small fruits (such
as cherries), or animals, using your hands or marzipan
sculpting tools.

Covering a cake with marzipan (see Chef's Notes)
1. **Before rolling out the marzipan,** spread the cake
with a thin, even layer of buttercream, or brush the top
and sides with warmed apricot jam (push it through
a sieve first to remove any pieces of fruit).
2. **Roll out the marzipan** so it is large enough to cover
the top and sides of the cake.
3. **Curl the rolled-out marzipan** around the rolling pin,
then carefully unroll it over the center of the cake, as if
you were lining a tart pan.
4. **Gently smooth the marzipan** over the top and down
the sides of the cake, taking care not to pleat or crease it.
5. **Trim the base neatly** using a sharp knife.

Chef's Notes
• If using food colorings, choose natural paste colors,
as liquid ones are less strong and may change the texture
of the marzipan, making it too wet.
• 10½ oz. (300 g) marzipan is enough to cover a cake
serving 8.

GLAÇAGE AU CHOCOLAT MAISON

CHOCOLATE ICING *

Makes
12¼ oz. (350 g), enough
to cover a cake serving 8

Active time: 10 minutes

INGREDIENTS
5 oz. (150 g) dark
  chocolate, 55% cacao,
  chopped
Scant 1 cup (4 oz./120 g)
  confectioners' sugar,
  sifted
3 tbsp (1½ oz./60 g)
  butter, diced
5 tbsp (75 ml) water

EQUIPMENT
Palette knife

1. **Melt the chocolate** in a bowl over a saucepan of barely simmering water (bain-marie), stirring with a flexible spatula.
2. **Stir in the confectioners' sugar,** followed by the butter, and continue stirring over the heat until smooth.
3. **Remove from the heat** and stir in the water, 1 tbsp at a time, to cool the icing: it should be lukewarm when you spread it over your cake. If the icing is too warm, it will be too runny; if too cold, it will not cover the sides.
4. **To ice a cake,** place it on a stand slightly smaller than the cake, or on a rack, to make it easier to ice the sides. Using the palette knife, smooth the icing over the top and down the sides of the cake, removing any excess.
5. **Let the icing set** before carefully lifting the cake onto a serving plate using a spatula.

Chef's Notes
• This easy-to-make icing can be used as an alternative to the chocolate glaze on p. 76. It is soft and glossy, so avoid touching it as your fingers will leave marks. Although not as elegant as the glaze, it does add a rich chocolate flavor to homemade pastries and cakes.

GLAÇAGE CHOCOLAT LAIT CAFÉ

MOCHA GLAZE ★

Makes
1 lb. (475 g), enough
to cover a cake serving 8

Active time: 15 minutes

Cooking time: 5 minutes

Chilling time: 24 hours

Storage: Up to 1 month
in the refrigerator
in an airtight container

INGREDIENTS
4¾ oz. (135 g) milk
    couverture chocolate,
    chopped
1½ tsp (6 g) pectin NH
Scant ⅔ cup
    (4¼ oz./120 g) sugar
Generous ¾ cup (200 ml)
    water
2 tsp (15 g) glucose syrup
1¾ tsp (2 g) instant coffee
    powder

EQUIPMENT
Instant-read thermometer
Immersion blender

1. **Place the chocolate** in a heatproof mixing bowl.
2. **Mix together** the pectin and the sugar.
3. **Pour the water** into a saucepan, then whisk
in the pectin and sugar. Bring to a boil, stirring
regularly.
4. **Add the glucose,** return to a boil, and boil for
2 minutes.
5. **Skim off any impurities** from the surface, take off
the heat, and let cool to 160°F (70°C).
6. **Pour over the chocolate,** wait for 2 minutes, then
gently whisk in the coffee powder until incorporated.
7. **Blend for 30 seconds.** taking care not to create air
bubbles. Press plastic wrap over the surface and, when
cooled, chill for 24 hours.
8. **When ready to use,** first ensure the cake you are
coating is well chilled.
9. **Melt the glaze** to 104°F (40°C) in a bowl over
a saucepan of barely simmering water (bain-marie).
10. **Place the cake** on a wire rack over a tray and pour
the glaze over to evenly coat it, tilting the rack slightly
if necessary. Let the glaze set before carefully lifting
the cake onto a serving plate using a spatula.

GLAÇAGE AU CHOCOLAT
CHOCOLATE GLAZE ★

Makes
1 lb. 2 oz. (500 g), enough
to cover a cake serving 8

Active time: 15 minutes

Cooking time: 5 minutes

Chilling time: 24 hours

Storage: Up to 1 month
in the refrigerator
in an airtight container

INGREDIENTS
5¼ oz. (150 g) dark
   couverture chocolate,
   70% cacao, chopped
1 tsp (4 g) pectin NH
¾ cup (5 oz./140 g) sugar
Generous ¾ cup (200 ml)
   water
2 tsp (15 g) glucose syrup

EQUIPMENT
Instant-read thermometer
Immersion blender

1. **Place the chocolate** in a heatproof mixing bowl.
2. **Mix together** the pectin and the sugar.
3. **Pour the water** into a saucepan, then whisk in the pectin and sugar. Bring to a boil, stirring regularly.
4. **Add the glucose,** return to a boil, and boil for 2 minutes.
5. **Skim off any impurities** from the surface, take off the heat, and let cool to 160°F (70°C).
6. **Pour over the chocolate**, wait for 2 minutes, then gently stir with a whisk.
7. **Blend for 30 seconds.** taking care not to create air bubbles. Press plastic wrap over the surface and, when cooled, chill for 24 hours.
8. **When ready to use,** first ensure the cake you are coating is well chilled.
9. **Melt the glaze** to 104°F (40°C) in a bowl over a saucepan of barely simmering water (bain-marie).
10. **Place the cake** on a wire rack over a tray and pour the glaze over to evenly coat it, tilting the rack slightly if necessary. Let the glaze set before carefully lifting the cake onto a serving plate using a spatula.

GLAÇAGE FRAISE
STRAWBERRY GLAZE ⋆

Makes
4½ oz. (130 g)

Active time: 10 minutes

Cooking time: 5 minutes

Storage: Up to 4 days
in the refrigerator
in an airtight container

INGREDIENTS
½ tsp (2 g) pectin NH
1 tbsp (12 g) sugar
2 oz. (60 g) strawberry
   puree
2 oz. (60 g) neutral glaze
   (see p. 81)

---

1. **Mix the pectin** with the sugar.
2. **Pour the strawberry puree** into a saucepan, then whisk in the pectin and sugar.
3. **Bring to a boil** and add the neutral glaze. Bring back to a boil, whisking continuously, and boil for 2 minutes.
4. **Skim off any impurities** from the surface, if necessary, and let cool completely.
5. **Transfer to an airtight container** and store in the refrigerator until ready to use.

Chef's Notes
• You can use this colorful glaze to coat marzipan decorations and make them shine.

GLAÇAGE FRAMBOISE
RASPBERRY GLAZE ★

Makes
4½ oz. (130 g)

Active time: 10 minutes

Cooking time: 5 minutes

Storage: Up to 4 days
in the refrigerator
in an airtight container

INGREDIENTS
½ tsp (2 g) pectin NH
1 tbsp (12 g) sugar
2 oz. (60 g) raspberry
   puree
2 oz. (60 g) neutral glaze
   (see p. 81)

1. **Mix the pectin** with the sugar.
2. **Pour the raspberry puree** into a saucepan, then whisk in the pectin and sugar.
3. **Bring to a boil** and add the neutral glaze. Bring back to a boil, whisking continuously, and boil for 2 minutes.
4. **Skim off any impurities** from the surface, if necessary, and let cool completely.
5. **Transfer to an airtight container** and store in the refrigerator until ready to use.

Chef's Notes
• You can use this colorful glaze to coat marzipan decorations and make them shine.

GLAÇAGE NEUTRE

NEUTRAL GLAZE ★

Makes
1 lb. 2 oz. (500 g), enough
to cover a cake serving 8

Active time: 10 minutes

Cooking time: 5 minutes

Storage: Up to 1 month
in the refrigerator
in an airtight container

INGREDIENTS
4½ tsp (18 g) pectin NH
1⅓ cups (9 oz./250 g)
   sugar, divided
Scant 1 cup (225 ml) water
4 tsp (1 oz./30 g) glucose
   syrup

EQUIPMENT
Instant-read thermometer

1. **Combine the pectin** with half the sugar.
2. **Pour the water** into a saucepan and whisk in the rest
of the sugar.
3. **Bring to a boil,** add the glucose syrup, and bring
back to a boil.
4. **Add the pectin and sugar** and, whisking
continuously, cook for 2 minutes.
5. **Skim off any impurities** from the surface,
if necessary, and let cool completely.
6. **Transfer to an airtight container** and store
in the refrigerator until ready to use.
7. **Before using,** ensure the cake you are glazing is well
chilled.
8. **Melt the glaze** to 104°F (40°C) in a bowl over
a saucepan of barely simmering water (bain-marie).
9. **Place the cake** on a wire rack and pour the glaze over
to evenly coat it, tilting the rack slightly if necessary.
Let the glaze set before carefully lifting the cake
onto a serving plate using a spatula.

Chef's Notes
• This glaze is also known as clear glaze.
• It is particularly good for glazing fruit tarts, as it
preserves the fruit and gives the tart a glistening sheen.

MOUSSE AU CHOCOLAT

CHOCOLATE MOUSSE ★

Makes
12¼ oz. (350 g), to serve 6

Active time: 15 minutes

Chilling time: 2 hours

Storage: Up to 2 days
in the refrigerator or
2 months in the freezer

INGREDIENTS
4½ oz. (125 g) dark
  chocolate, 70% cacao,
  chopped
3 egg whites
  (6½ tbsp/90 g;
  see Chef's Notes)
1 tbsp + 2 tsp (20 g) sugar
5 tbsp (2½ oz./75 g)
  butter, diced
2 egg yolks (2½ tbsp/40 g;
  see Chef's Notes)

EQUIPMENT
Electric hand beater

1. **Melt the chocolate** in a bowl over a saucepan
of barely simmering water (bain-marie), or in
the microwave.
2. **Whisk the egg whites** until they hold soft peaks.
Whisk in the sugar and continue to whisk until they
hold firm peaks.
3. **When the chocolate** has melted, add the butter
one piece at a time, whisking until melted. When all
the butter has been added, whisk in the egg yolks until
incorporated and the mixture is smooth and glossy.
4. **Whisk in one-third of the egg whites** until evenly
combined, then gently fold in the rest using a flexible
spatula. The whites need to be fully incorporated but do
this lightly so as not to deflate the mousse.
5. **Cover and chill** for 2 hours before serving or using.

Chef's Notes
• Prepare the mousse without any delay between
the steps, to ensure it has a light, airy texture.
• Remove the eggs from the refrigerator 1 hour before
starting the recipe as it is important they are at room
temperature.
• As the egg whites and yolks are not cooked in this
recipe, make sure you use eggs that are as fresh
as possible. If you are worried about salmonella risks,
you can use pasteurized eggs.
• If freezing, let thaw overnight in the refrigerator
before serving or using.

MOUSSE AU CHOCOLAT N° 2
CHOCOLATE MOUSSE No. 2 ⋆

Makes
11¾ oz. (330 g), to serve 6

Active time: 20 minutes

Chilling time: 2 hours

Storage: Up to 2 days
in the refrigerator or
2 months in the freezer

INGREDIENTS
4½ oz. (125 g) dark
    chocolate, 70% cacao,
    chopped
2 tbsp (25 g) butter, diced
1 egg yolk (1½ tbsp/20 g;
    see Chef's Notes)
2 egg whites (¼ cup/60 g;
    see Chef's Notes)
2 tbsp (25 g) sugar
⅓ cup (75 ml) heavy
    cream, well chilled

EQUIPMENT
Electric hand beater
Instant-read thermometer

---

1. **Melt the chocolate** in a bowl over a saucepan of barely simmering water (bain-marie), or in the microwave.
2. **Whisk the egg whites** until they hold soft peaks. Whisk in the sugar and continue whisking until they hold firm peaks.
3. **When the chocolate has melted**, add the butter one piece at a time, whisking until melted. When all the butter has been added, whisk in the egg yolk until incorporated and the mixture is smooth and glossy. Cool to 104°F (40°C).
4. **Whip the cream** in a separate bowl until it holds its shape.
5. **Whisk one-third of the egg whites** into the chocolate mixture until evenly combined, then gently fold in the rest using a flexible spatula. The whites need to be fully incorporated but do this lightly so as not to deflate the mousse. Finally, fold in the whipped cream.
6. **Cover and chill** for 2 hours if using as part of another recipe. If serving the mousse on its own, spoon it into individual dishes, cover, and chill for 2 hours.

Chef's Notes
• Prepare the mousse without any delay between the steps, to ensure it has a light, airy texture.
• Remove the eggs from the refrigerator 1 hour before starting the recipe as it is important they are at room temperature.
• As the egg whites and yolk are not cooked in this recipe, make sure you use eggs that are as fresh as possible. If you are worried about salmonella risks, you can use pasteurized eggs.
• If freezing, let thaw overnight in the refrigerator before serving or using.

SAUCE À LA VANILLE

VANILLA CUSTARD SAUCE ★

Makes
12¼ oz. (350 g)

Active time: 25 minutes

Infusing time: 15 minutes

Cooling time: 30 minutes

Storage: Up to 3 days
in the refrigerator

INGREDIENTS
1 cup (250 ml) whole milk
½ Bourbon Madagascar
   vanilla bean, split
   lengthwise
3 egg yolks
   (scant ¼ cup/60 g)
¼ cup (1¾ oz./50 g) sugar

EQUIPMENT
Electric hand beater
Instant-read thermometer
Immersion blender,
   if needed

1. **Place the milk** and split vanilla bean in a saucepan and bring to a boil.
2. **Remove from the heat**, cover, and let infuse for at least 15 minutes. Keep warm.
3. **Fill a large bowl** halfway with cold water and add some ice cubes to it.
4. **Whisk together** the egg yolks and sugar in a mixing bowl. Slowly pour in half the warm vanilla-infused milk, whisking continuously.
5. **Pour the mixture back** into the saucepan and stir constantly over low heat, using a spatula in a figure-eight motion. Take care not to let the mixture come to a boil.
6. **When the custard** reaches about 181°F (83°C) and coats the spatula, remove from the heat and plunge the bottom of the saucepan into the bowl of ice water to prevent the custard cooking any more.
7. **Stir the custard** a few times with the spatula, then let it cool for about 30 minutes, stirring occasionally to prevent a skin from forming.
8. **Remove the vanilla bean** and scrape any remaining seeds into the custard. If necessary, blend until smooth.

Chef's Notes
• After use, rinse the vanilla bean under running water and let it dry completely. The bean can be finely ground with sugar to be added to recipes that require vanilla sugar.

SAUCE AU CARAMEL

CARAMEL SAUCE ★★

Makes
1⅔ cups (400 ml)

Active time: 10 minutes

Cooking time: 10 minutes

Chilling time: 5 minutes

Storage: Up to 4 days
in the refrigerator
in an airtight container

INGREDIENTS
1⅓ cups (9 oz./250 g)
    sugar
1 cup (250 ml) heavy
    cream
Cold milk as needed

EQUIPMENT
Heavy-bottomed
    saucepan with a 2-qt.
    (2-L) capacity
Instant-read thermometer

1. **Make a dry caramel** with the sugar in the large saucepan, following the instructions on p. 46.
2. **Remove from the heat** and set aside for about 5 minutes while you heat the cream.
3. **Bring the cream to a boil** in another saucepan. The temperature of the caramel and the hot cream must be about the same, so that the cream does not curdle when it is added to the caramel.
4. **Slowly pour the hot cream** into the caramel, stirring continuously.
5. **The sauce will thicken** as it cools. If serving it cold, it can be thinned out by stirring in a little cold milk.

Chef's Notes
• The sauce can be served hot or cold, according to personal taste. It can also be used to coat cakes and desserts.

SAUCE AU CHOCOLAT

CHOCOLATE SAUCE ⋆

Makes
1⅔ cups (400 ml)

Active time: 10 minutes

Cooking time: 5 minutes

Storage: Up to 4 days
in the refrigerator
in an airtight container

INGREDIENTS
Scant ½ cup (2 oz./60 g)
    unsweetened
    cocoa powder
Scant cup (6 oz./180 g)
    sugar
Generous ¾ cup (200 ml)
    water
Scant ½ cup
    (3½ oz./100 g) crème
    fraîche

1. **Sift the cocoa powder** into a large heatproof bowl.
2. **Combine the sugar and water** in a large saucepan.
Stir with a whisk over low heat until the sugar dissolves,
and then bring to a boil.
3. **Carefully pour the hot syrup** into the cocoa powder,
whisking continuously as you pour.
4. **Return to the saucepan** and cook over medium heat
until the sauce begins to thicken (about 5 minutes),
whisking continuously to prevent it from sticking
to the bottom of the pan.
5. **Whisking constantly**, add the crème fraiche.
Return to a boil, then remove from the heat.
6. **Serve the sauce** hot or warm, reheating it gently if it
has been refrigerated.

Chef's Notes
• This sauce is delicious drizzled over Savoy Cake
(see p. 124), French Almond Cake (see p. 136),
and ice creams.

SIROP À ENTREMETS

SIMPLE SYRUP ★

Makes
1 cup (250 ml)

Active time: 5 minutes

Cooking time:
A few minutes

Storage: Up to 5 days
in the refrigerator
in a sealed bottle

INGREDIENTS
¾ cup (5 oz./150 g) sugar
¾ cup (175 ml) water

Optional flavorings
3½ oz. (100 g) fruit puree
    of your choice
1–2 tbsp (15–30 ml)
    alcohol of your choice
    (such as Kirsch, rum,
    or Grand Marnier)
Seeds of 1 vanilla bean

1. **Combine the sugar and water** in a large saucepan.
2. **Place over low heat,** stirring until the sugar dissolves.
Increase the heat and bring to a simmer.
3. **Remove from the heat** and let cool.
4. **If adding a flavoring**, whisk it in once the syrup
has cooled.

Chef's Notes
• This basic syrup, made without adding any flavorings,
can be used for soaking sponge cakes.

EVERYDAY PASTRIES AND CAKES

AMANDINES AUX CERISES

CHERRY ALMOND TARTLETS ⋆

Makes
16

Active time: 10 minutes
+ making the shortcrust
pastry and frangipane
cream

Chilling time: 1 hour

Cooking time: 20 minutes

INGREDIENTS
Melted butter for the pans
9 oz. (250 g) shortcrust
  pastry dough
  (see p. 40) or sweet
  shortcrust pastry dough
  (see p. 41)
½ quantity (1 lb. 2 oz./
  500 g) frangipane
  cream (see p. 62)
48 fresh cherries, pitted
  (see Chef's Notes)
Sliced almonds
Confectioners' sugar,
  for dusting (optional)
Cherry or red currant jelly
  (see p. 366), warmed
  (optional)

EQUIPMENT
16 × 2½-in. (6.5-cm) tartlet
  pans
Large rimmed baking
  sheet
3½-in. (9-cm) round
  cookie cutter

1. **Grease the pans** by brushing them with melted butter. Set them on the baking sheet.
2. **Roll out the pastry dough** on a floured surface to a thickness of ⅛ in. (3 mm). Cut out 10 rounds using the cookie cutter. Line them into the tartlet pans, then chill for 1 hour.
3. **Preheat the oven** to 400°F (200°C/Gas Mark 6).
4. **Fill each tartlet shell** with frangipane cream. Place 3 cherries in each one, then scatter sliced almonds over the top.
5. **Place in the oven** and immediately reduce the temperature to 340°F (170°C/Gas Mark 3). Bake for 20 minutes, until golden.
6. **Cool the tartlets** for 10 minutes to firm them up, before removing them from the pans. Cool completely on a wire rack.
7. **Once cooled,** the tartlets can be dusted with confectioners' sugar or brushed with warmed red currant or cherry jelly.

Chef's Notes
• These tartlets can be made all year round using frozen cherries. There is no need to thaw them first.

BOSTOCK AUX AMANDES

ALMOND BRIOCHE TOAST ★

Serves
8

Active time: 30 minutes
+ making the brioche
mousseline and frangipane
cream

Cooking time:
10–12 minutes

INGREDIENTS
Almond syrup
⅔ cup (150 ml) water
¾ cup (5 oz./150 g)
   granulated sugar
⅓ cup (1½ oz./45 g)
   confectioners' sugar
⅓ cup (1¼ oz./35 g)
   almond powder
10 drops orange flower
   water

Almond brioche toast
1 brioche mousseline
   (see p. 100), made
   1–2 days ahead
14 oz. (400 g) frangipane
   cream (see p. 62)
¾ cup (2 oz./60 g) sliced
   almonds
Confectioners' sugar,
   for dusting

EQUIPMENT
Instant-read thermometer
Rimmed baking sheet
   lined with parchment
   paper

1. **To prepare the almond syrup,** place the water and granulated sugar in a saucepan over low heat and stir until the sugar dissolves.
2. **Whisk in the confectioners' sugar** and almond powder. Heat to 176°F (80°C). Maintain this temperature for 15 minutes, stirring frequently with a whisk.
3. **Stir in the orange flower water.** Keep warm until ready to use.
4. **To prepare the almond brioche toast,** preheat the oven to 350°F (180°C/Gas Mark 4).
5. **Slice the brioche** into ½-in. (1.5-cm) thick slices using a bread knife.
6. **Pour the warm almond syrup** into a shallow bowl large enough to dip the brioche slices.

7. **Place one brioche slice** at a time on a slotted spatula and submerge it in the syrup. Transfer to a wire rack set over a sheet of parchment paper, to allow excess syrup to drip off.
8. **Once all the slices** have been dipped, lift them carefully onto the prepared baking sheet. Using a palette knife, spread each slice with an even layer of frangipane cream (about 1¾ oz./50 g per slice).
9. **Sprinkle with the sliced almonds.** Bake for 10 minutes, until golden brown.
10. **Let cool a little,** then dust with confectioners' sugar. Serve warm, with tea or fruit juice.

BRIOCHE BORDELAISE

BORDEAUX BRIOCHE ★★

	INGREDIENTS	Decoration	EQUIPMENT
Serves 8	*Cake* 1 quantity (1¼ lb./600 g) brioche dough (see p. 36), made 1 day ahead	Apple, apricot, or peach jelly (homemade or store-bought), warmed (optional)	Cookie sheet lined with parchment paper
Active time: 1 hour + making the brioche dough		Candied fruit, such as orange, lemon, citron, angelica, ginger	
Rising time: 1½ –2 hours	3½ oz. (100 g) best-quality candied fruit, diced	Raw whole almonds, toasted and roughly chopped	
Cooking time: 30 minutes	Fava bean or trinket (optional)	Crushed pralines	
Storage: Up to 2 days at room temperature in an airtight container	1 egg, lightly beaten Pearl sugar		

1. **On a lightly floured surface,** flatten the dough slightly into a square, using your hand.
2. **Sprinkle the candied fruit** over the dough, pressing down lightly so the fruit sticks. If making for Epiphany, add a fava bean or trinket (see Chef's Notes).
3. **Bring the edges of the dough** into the center to enclose the fruit, then shape into a ball. Place the dough on the cookie sheet and let rest for 5–10 minutes.
4. **Using your thumb,** press a hole in the center and rotate, so the dough stretches into an evenly shaped ring.
5. **Continue stretching until the hole** is about 4 in. (10 cm) in diameter, taking care not to tear it. If necessary, let the dough rest for several minutes between each rotation.
6. **Let rise for 1½–2 hours** in a warm place (about 82°F/28°C), until doubled in volume. Toward the end of the rising time, preheat the oven to 400°F (200°C/ Gas Mark 6).

7. **When the dough has risen**, brush it with the beaten egg. Wet the blades of a pair of kitchen scissors and make decorative diagonal cuts about ⅓ in. (1 cm) deep in the dough, at regular intervals around the ring: if the cuts are too shallow, they will disappear when the brioche bakes; if they are too deep, the dough will collapse. Sprinkle with pearl sugar.
8. **Bake for 30 minutes**, until the brioche is golden brown and sounds hollow when tapped on the base. Keep a close eye on the color and if the brioche browns too quickly, cover it with aluminum foil.
9. **Remove from the oven** and immediately transfer the brioche to a wire rack. For a shiny finish, brush with warmed fruit jelly. Let cool on a wire rack.
10. **Decorate the brioche** with candied fruit, toasted almonds, and crushed pralines.

Chef's Notes
• This "Kings' cake" in the form of a brioche ring decorated with candied fruit is the Bordeaux alternative to the more familiar puff pastry tart filled with frangipane cream that is baked at Epiphany in the rest of France. Traditionally, they both contain a fava bean or trinket.

BRIOCHE MOUSSELINE ★★

Serves
6

Active time: 15 minutes +
making the brioche dough

Rising time: 2–2½ hours

Cooking time:
30–35 minutes

Storage: Up to 2 days
at room temperature or
2 months in the freezer

INGREDIENTS
1 tbsp (20 g) butter for
   the mold
12¾ oz. (360 g) brioche
   dough (see p. 36),
   made 1 day ahead
1 egg, lightly beaten with
   a small pinch of salt

EQUIPMENT
Brioche mousseline mold
   or tall food can with
   a 4½-cup (1-L) capacity

1. **Line the sides of the mold** with a double cylinder of parchment paper twice as tall as the mold, fixing the paper to the sides of the mold with a few dots of butter.
2. **Grease the bottom of the mold** with butter, then thoroughly grease the sides of the parchment paper all the way to the top.
3. **On a lightly floured surface**, flatten the dough slightly into a square, using your hand. Bring the edges into the center, then shape the dough into a ball.
4. **Place the dough in the mold** with the seam uppermost, then press it down firmly with your fist.
5. **Let rise for 2–2½ hours** in a warm place (about 82°F/28°C), until the dough fills three-quarters of the mold. Toward the end of the rising time, preheat the oven to 400°F (200°C/Gas Mark 6).
6. **When the dough has risen**, brush it with the beaten egg. Take care not to brush the parchment paper, or the brioche will stick and will not rise properly. Wet the blades of a pair of kitchen scissors and cut a decorative cross in the top of the dough.
7. **Bake for 30–35 minutes**, until the brioche is golden brown. It is important for the brioche to be fully baked; if underbaked, the sides will buckle as it cools.
8. **Let the brioche cool** slightly in the mold before turning it out onto a wire rack. Serve warm or at room temperature. If storing, cover the brioche tightly with plastic wrap while still warm to keep it moist.

Chef's Notes
• After freezing, let the brioche thaw at room temperature for about 5 hours. Alternatively, let it thaw for 1 hour, then place in a 400°F (200°C/Gas Mark 6) oven for 10 minutes. Serve warm.

BRIOCHE NANTERRE

CLASSIC BRIOCHE ★★

Serves
6

Active time: 15 minutes +
making the brioche dough

Rising time: 2–2½ hours

Cooking time:
30–35 minutes

Storage: Up to 2 days
at room temperature
or 2 months
in the freezer

INGREDIENTS
1 tbsp (20 g) butter,
    for the pan
12¾ oz. (360 g) brioche
    dough (see p. 36),
    made 1 day ahead
1 egg, lightly beaten with
    a small pinch of salt

EQUIPMENT
7- × 3-in. (18- × 8-cm) loaf
    pan, 2½ in. (6 cm) deep

1. **Line the loaf pan** with parchment paper, leaving
a 1¼-in. (3-cm) overhang, and fix it in place with
a few dots of butter. Grease the paper with the butter.
2. **On a lightly floured surface**, divide the dough
into 6 equal pieces, each weighing 2 oz. (60 g). Shape
them into balls, then roll them with the palm of your
hand to elongate into ovals.
3. **Arrange the pieces of dough** in the prepared pan,
leaving an equal amount of space between each one.
4. **Let rise for 2–2½ hours** in a warm place (about
82°F/28°C), until the dough fills three-quarters
of the pan and the pieces of dough are touching.
Toward the end of the rising time, preheat the oven
to 400°F (200°C/Gas Mark 6).
5. **When the dough has risen**, brush it with the beaten
egg. Take care not to brush the parchment paper, or
the brioche will stick and will not rise properly. Wet
the blades of a pair of kitchen scissors and cut a cross
in the top of each piece of dough.
6. **Bake for 30–35 minutes** until golden brown.
It is important for the brioche to be fully baked;
if underbaked, the sides will buckle as it cools.
Keep a close eye on the color and if the top browns
too quickly, cover with aluminum foil.
7. **Let the brioche cool** slightly in the pan before
turning it out onto a wire rack. Serve warm or at room
temperature. If storing, cover the brioche tightly with
plastic wrap while still warm to keep it moist.

Chef's Notes
• After freezing, let the brioche thaw at room
temperature for about 5 hours. Alternatively, let it thaw
for 1 hour, then place in a 400°F (200°C/Gas Mark 6)
oven for 10 minutes. Serve warm.

BRIOCHE PARISIENNE

PARISIAN BRIOCHE ★★

Serves
6

Active time: 10 minutes +
making the brioche dough

Rising time: 1½–2 hours

Cooking time:
30–35 minutes

Storage: Up to 2 days
at room temperature or
2 months in the freezer

INGREDIENTS
1 tbsp (20 g) butter,
  for the mold
12¾ oz. (360 g) brioche
  dough (see p. 36),
  made 1 day ahead
1 egg, lightly beaten with
  a small pinch of salt

EQUIPMENT
Brioche mold with a 3-cup
  (750-ml) capacity

1. **Thoroughly grease the brioche mold** with the butter.
2. **Place the dough** on a lightly floured surface
and divide it into 2 pieces: one weighing 10 oz. (280 g)
for the body, and the other weighing 2¾ oz. (80 g)
for the head.
3. **Gently roll the large piece** between your hands
to shape it into a smooth ball. Place in the mold.
Use the same technique with the smaller piece to form
a pear shape.
4. **Make a small indent** in the center of the larger ball.
Place the smaller piece in the indent, with the narrower
end facing downward. With floured fingers, press gently
so the two pieces stick together.
5. **Let rise for 1½–2 hours** in a warm place (about
82°F/28°C), until doubled in volume. Toward the end
of the rising time, preheat the oven to 400°F (200°C/
Gas Mark 6).
6. **When the dough has risen,** wet the blades of a pair
of kitchen scissors and make four equally spaced cuts
around the top of the larger piece of dough from
the center to the edge: this will allow the brioche
to expand while baking.
7. **Brush with the beaten egg.** Take care not to brush
the mold, or the brioche will stick and will not rise
properly.

8. **Bake for 30–35 minutes,** until golden brown.
It is important for the brioche to be fully baked;
if underbaked, the sides will buckle as it cools.
Keep a close eye on the color and if the top browns
too quickly, cover with aluminum foil.
9. **Let the brioche cool** slightly in the pan, before
turning it out onto a wire rack. If storing, cover
the brioche tightly with plastic wrap while still warm
to keep it moist.

Chef's Notes
• After freezing, let the brioche thaw at room
temperature for about 5 hours. Alternatively, let it thaw
for 1 hour, then place in a 400°F (200°C/Gas Mark 6)
oven for 10 minutes. Serve warm.
• The brioche can be served warm or at room
temperature, either plain or with jam or vanilla custard
sauce (see p. 86) on the side. It can also be filled with
a mousse or cream (see p. 334).

BRIOCHE DE MENTON

MENTON BRIOCHE ★★

Serves
6

Active time: 15 minutes +
making the brioche dough

Rising time: 2 hours

Cooking time:
45–50 minutes

Storage: Up to 3 days
in the refrigerator or
2 months in the freezer

INGREDIENTS

⅔ cup (2 oz./60 g) almond
    powder

Scant ½ cup (2 oz./60 g)
    confectioners' sugar
    + more for dusting

1 extra-large egg white
    (2 tbsp/35 g)

¾ lb. (350 g) brioche
    dough (see p. 36),
    made 1 day ahead

3½ oz. (100 g) best-quality
    candied fruit, diced

EQUIPMENT

10- × 2½- × 2½-in.
    (26- × 6- × 6-cm)
    nonstick loaf pan

1. **Using a flexible spatula,** combine the almond powder, confectioners' sugar, and egg white in a mixing bowl.

2. **Place the dough** on a lightly floured surface and roll it into a rectangle measuring 8 × 10 in. (20 × 25 cm).

3. **Using a palette knife,** spread 3½ oz. (100 g) of the almond powder mixture over the dough in an even layer. Scatter over the diced candied fruit.

4. **Roll the dough up** into a 10-in. (25-cm) log and cut into 5 equal slices. Lay these flat in the loaf pan, leaving a little space between each one to allow for expansion during baking.

5. **Cover the slices** with the remaining almond powder mixture.

6. **Let rise** for about 2 hours in a warm place (about 82°F/28°C), until doubled in volume. Toward the end of the rising time, preheat the oven to 400°F (200°C/ Gas Mark 6).

7. **When the dough has risen,** place it in the oven and immediately reduce the temperature to 340°F (170°C/Gas Mark 3). Bake for 45–50 minutes, until golden brown. Keep a close eye on the color and if the top browns too quickly, cover with aluminum foil.

8. **Turn the brioche out** onto a wire rack and dust with confectioners' sugar. Serve warm or at room temperature.

BRIOCHE POLONAISE ★★★

Serves
8

Active time: 1 hour +
making the Parisian
brioche, pastry cream,
and Italian meringue

Cooking time:
8–10 minutes

INGREDIENTS
1 Parisian brioche
(see p. 104), made
1–2 days ahead
⅔ cup (150 ml) simple
syrup flavored with rum
(see p. 91 and Chef's
Notes)
15¾ oz. (450 g) pastry
cream flavored with rum
(see p. 66 and Chef's
Notes)

3½ oz. (100 g) candied
fruit, diced
1¾ oz. (50 g) whole
candied cherries,
preferably Bigarreaux
1 quantity (6½ oz./190 g)
Italian meringue
(see p. 32), lukewarm
⅔ cup (1¾ oz./50 g) sliced
almonds
⅓ cup (1¾ oz./50 g)
confectioners' sugar

EQUIPMENT
Round cake pan or heavy
cardboard circle slightly
larger than the base
of the brioche

---

1. **Cut off the top** of the brioche and set aside.
Cut the bottom part horizontally into 4 equal slices.
The slices can be lightly toasted, if desired.
2. **Using a pastry brush,** generously soak the crumb side
of the bottom slice with syrup. Set it in the cake pan
or on the cardboard circle, with the crust side facing
downward.
3. **Spread one-quarter** of the pastry cream over
the slice and arrange one-quarter of the candied fruit
and cherries on top. Repeat with the remaining slices,
layering them on top of one another.
4. **Soak the base** of the brioche top with syrup using
a pastry brush. Place on top of the layered slices.
5. **Preheat the oven** to 450°F (240°C/Gas Mark 8).
6. **Spread the assembled stack** with a ½-in. (1-cm) layer
of meringue, using a palette knife, until it is completely
covered. Sprinkle with the sliced almonds, then dust
with the confectioners' sugar.
7. **Bake for 3–5 minutes,** until the meringue is light
gold and crisp. Once the meringue has reached
the desired color, turn the oven off and leave the brioche
inside for an additional 5 minutes to warm through
to the center.

Chef's Notes
• If preferred, kirsch can be used instead of rum
to flavor the syrup and pastry cream. If making
the brioche for children, simply flavor both with
vanilla instead.
• Keen potters can add a modern twist by using their
wheel. Coat the assembled brioche with a thin layer
of meringue, set it on a clean potter's wheel, and,
using a pastry bag fitted with a Saint-Honoré tip,
pipe meringue around the brioche as the wheel turns,
working from the bottom to the top. Sprinkle with
sliced almonds, dust lightly with confectioners' sugar,
and continue with step 7.

BRIOCHES INDIVIDUELLES

INDIVIDUAL PARISIAN BRIOCHES ★★

Makes
18

Active time: 15 minutes +
making the brioche dough

Rising time: 1½ –2 hours

Cooking time: 12 minutes

Storage: Up to 2 months
in the freezer

INGREDIENTS
1 tbsp (20 g) butter,
    melted, for the molds
1 quantity (1¼ lb./600 g)
    brioche dough
    (see p. 36), made 1 day
    ahead
1 egg, lightly beaten with
    a small pinch of salt

EQUIPMENT
18 individual brioche
    molds
Rimmed baking sheet

1. **Lightly grease the molds** by brushing the insides with the melted butter. Set them on a rimmed baking sheet.
2. **Place the dough** on a lightly floured surface and shape it into a loaf. Cut into 18 equal pieces.
3. **Dust the palm of one hand** with flour and roll the dough into balls between the palm and the work surface. Avoid pressing down too hard on the dough or it will stick. Leave the fold that forms under each ball.
4. **Shape the brioche "heads"** by pressing down on each ball with the side of your hand, about one-third of the way along, and gently rolling back and forth, keeping the fold underneath. Take care not to break the dough.
5. **Place upright in the molds** with the "heads" on top. Make a hole in each one by pushing down through the head to the base with your finger.
6. **Let rise for 1½–2 hours** in a warm place (about 82°F/28°C), until doubled in volume. Toward the end of the rising time, preheat the oven to 450°F (230°C/ Gas Mark 8).
7. **When the brioches have risen,** brush with the beaten egg. Take care not to brush the molds, or the brioches will stick and will not rise properly.
8. **Bake for 12 minutes.** Let the brioches cool slightly in the molds, before turning them out onto a wire rack to cool. If storing, cover the brioches tightly with plastic wrap while still warm to keep them moist.

Chef's Notes
• After freezing, refresh the defrosted brioches in a 450°F (230°C/Gas Mark 8) oven for a few minutes before eating.
• These brioches can be served warm or at room temperature, either plain or with jam or vanilla custard sauce (see p. 86).

CAKE AUX FRUITS CONFITS

CANDIED FRUIT CAKE ★

Serves	INGREDIENTS	*For soaking, glazing,*	EQUIPMENT
6	1 stick + 2 tsp	*and decorating*	Loaf pan with a 2-qt. (2-L)
	(4½ oz./125 g) butter,	3 tbsp (45 ml) dark rum	capacity
	diced + more for the pan	2 oz. (50 g) apricot glaze,	Electric hand beater
Active time: 15 minutes	Scant 1 cup (4½ oz./125 g)	warmed	
	confectioners' sugar,	Assorted candied fruit	
Resting time: 1 hour	sifted	and cherries	
	3 eggs (⅔ cup/150 g),		
Cooking time: 45 minutes	at room temperature		
	1¾ cups (5¾ oz./160 g)		
Storage: Up to 1 week	cake flour		
in a dry place, well	1¼ tsp (5 g) baking powder		
wrapped, or 3 months	9 oz. (250 g) assorted		
in the freezer	candied fruit, diced		
	2 oz. (50 g) whole candied		
	cherries, preferably		
	Bigarreaux or Amarena		
	Scant ¼ cup (20 g) sliced		
	almonds		

1. **Lightly grease the loaf pan** with butter and line it with enough parchment paper to leave an overhang.
2. **Whisk together** the butter and confectioners' sugar in a mixing bowl.
3. **Whisk in the eggs**, one by one, until incorporated. If the mixture starts to separate, set the bowl over a saucepan of barely simmering water (bain-marie) and continue whisking. Set aside.
4. **Sift the flour and baking powder** onto a sheet of parchment paper. Add the diced candied fruit and whole cherries, and toss until evenly coated, to prevent the fruit from sinking to the bottom of the pan during baking.
5. **Gently fold the fruit** into the first mixture using a flexible spatula.
6. **Pour the batter** into the pan and sprinkle with the sliced almonds. Let rest for 1 hour in the refrigerator. Preheat the oven to 450°F (240°C/ Gas Mark 8).
7. **Place the cake in the oven** and immediately reduce the temperature to 340°F (170°C/Gas Mark 3). Bake for 45 minutes until golden and the tip of a knife inserted into the center of the cake comes out clean. If the cake browns too quickly, lower the oven temperature to 325°F (160°C).

8. **Remove the cake from the oven** and immediately drizzle the rum over it.
9. **Let the cake cool** for a few minutes in the pan, before turning it out onto a wire rack to cool. If storing, cover the cake with plastic wrap while it is still warm to keep it moist.
10. **Once the cake is cool,** brush it with the warmed apricot glaze. Decorate the top with candied fruit and cherries.

Chef's Notes
• This cake freezes well, so it is worth doubling the quantities of ingredients and baking 2 cakes on the same baking sheet.
• After freezing, let the cake thaw for 24 hours in the refrigerator. Let it come to room temperature before glazing, decorating, and serving.

CAKE AUX FRUITS SECS

DRIED FRUIT CAKE ★

Serves
6

Active time: 30 minutes

Soaking time: 15 minutes

Resting time: 45 minutes

Cooking time: 45–
50 minutes

Storage: Up to 3 days
at room temperature,
wrapped airtight, or
3 months in the freezer

INGREDIENTS
7 tbsp (3½ oz./100 g)
    butter, softened + more
    for the pan
Scant 3 tbsp (25 g) golden
    raisins
⅓ cup (1¾ oz./50 g) whole
    hazelnuts
⅓ cup (1¾ oz./50 g) whole
    blanched almonds
Scant 3 tbsp (25 g) pine
    nuts
Scant ¼ cup (25 g) dried
    apricots
1 cup (4½ oz./125 g)
    AP flour + 1 tsp (3 g)
    for the dried fruit

1 tsp (3 g) baking powder
½ cup (1¾ oz./50 g)
    almond powder
3 eggs (⅔ cup/150 g)
½ cup (4½ oz./125 g)
    brown sugar
Scant ¼ cup (25 g) shelled
    pistachios, finely
    chopped
Scant 2 tbsp (10 g) sliced
    almonds
Melted butter for drawing
    a line down the center
    of the cake

EQUIPMENT
Loaf pan with a 2-cup
    (500-ml) capacity
Cookie sheet
Electric hand beater

1. **Preheat the oven** to 340°F (170°C/Gas Mark 3).
2. **Lightly grease the loaf pan** with butter and line
it with enough parchment paper to leave an overhang.
3. **Soak the raisins** in a bowl of hot water for
15 minutes.
4. **Spread the hazelnuts, almonds, and pine nuts** over
the cookie sheet. Place in the oven for 8–10 minutes,
stirring occasionally, until evenly toasted and fragrant.
Pay close attention, as the pine nuts will toast more
quickly than the other nuts.
5. **Remove the nuts** from the cookie sheet and turn off
the oven. Let the nuts cool, then chop them roughly.
6. **Roughly chop the dried apricots.** Drain the golden
raisins and dry them well. Place both in a bowl and toss
with the 1 tsp flour (3 g) until evenly coated, to prevent
them from sinking to the bottom of the pan during baking.
7. **Sift together** the 1 cup (4½ oz./125 g) flour, baking
powder, and almond powder into a large bowl.
8. **In a separate large bowl,** whisk together the eggs
and brown sugar until pale and thick.
9. **Add the butter and the flour mixture** and stir
with a wooden spoon just until combined. Fold
in the toasted nuts and dried fruit.

10. **Pour the batter** into the loaf pan. Dip the tip
of a knife into melted butter and draw a line down
the center of the batter. Sprinkle over the pistachios
and almonds. Let rest for 45 minutes in the refrigerator.
11. **Preheat the oven** to 450°F (240°C/Gas Mark 8).
12. **Place the cake** in the oven and immediately reduce
the temperature to 340°F (170°C/Gas Mark 3). Bake
for 45 minutes, until the cake is golden and the tip
of a knife inserted into the center comes out clean.
If the cake browns too quickly, lower the oven
temperature to 320°F (160°C).
13. **Let the cake cool** for a few minutes in the pan,
before turning it out onto a wire rack to cool. If storing,
cover the cake with plastic wrap while it is still warm
to keep it moist.

Chef's Notes
• After freezing, let the cake thaw for 24 hours
in the refrigerator. Let it come to room temperature
before serving.

COLOMBIER DE LA PENTECÔTE

COLOMBIER FOR PENTECOST ★★

Serves
6

Active time: 30 minutes +
making the marzipan

Cooking time: 20 minutes

Storage: Up to 24 hours
in the refrigerator,
in a covered container

INGREDIENTS
1 tbsp (20 g) butter,
    melted, for the pan
1 cup (4 oz./100 g) sliced
    almonds, for the pan
7 oz. (200 g) marzipan
    made with raw almonds
    (see p. 63), roughly
    chopped
3 eggs (⅔ cup/150 g)
3 tbsp (1 oz./30 g) AP
    flour, sifted
4 tbsp (2 oz./60 g) butter,
    melted and cooled
3½ oz. (100 g) candied
    fruit, diced
3½ oz. (100 g) candied
    orange peel, chopped

Water icing
¾ cup (3½ oz./100 g)
    confectioners' sugar
2 tbsp (30 ml) water
3 drops rum

EQUIPMENT
9-in. (23-cm) round cake
    pan
Stand mixer fitted with
    the paddle beater

1. **Preheat the oven** to 400°F (200°C/Gas Mark 6).
2. **Generously grease** the bottom and sides of the pan with the 1 tbsp (20 g) melted butter, then cover with the sliced almonds, removing any loose ones. Chill while making the cake batter.
3. **Lay a sheet** of parchment paper over a wire rack.
4. **Beat the marzipan** in the stand mixer on low speed to loosen it. Increase the speed to medium and beat until the marzipan is softened and smooth.
5. **Add the eggs** one by one, beating for 5 minutes after each egg has been added to increase the volume of the mixture. Scrape down the bowl and beater each time to avoid any lumps of marzipan. This will take about 15 minutes.
6. **Add all the flour** at once and fold it in using a flexible spatula. Fold in the butter.
7. **Pour the batter** into the pan, filling it three-quarters full. Scatter over the candied fruit and orange peel.
8. **Bake for 10 minutes**, then reduce the temperature to 350°F (180°C/Gas Mark 4) and bake for an additional 10 minutes, until golden brown. If the cake browns too quickly, lower the temperature to 340°F (170°C/Gas Mark 3).

9. **Remove the cake** from the oven, then immediately place a plate on top and invert it onto the plate. Place the wire rack with parchment paper on top and invert once again, so the cake is sitting on the rack. This must be done carefully as the cake is fragile. Let the cake cool completely on the rack.
10. **To prepare the icing,** stir the confectioners' sugar, water, and rum together until smooth.
11. **Spread the icing** over the cake using a palette knife. Chill until ready to serve.

Chef's Notes
• A colombier (dovecote) cake is traditionally made each year to celebrate the religious festival of Pentecost in Provence, in the south of France.

CROISSANTS ★★

Makes
12–15
(1¼ lb./600 g dough)

Active time: 1 hour

Chilling time: 4–5 hours
(preferably overnight)

Rising time: 4 hours

Cooking time: 15 minutes

Storage: Up to 2 months
in the freezer in a sealed
bag (see Chef's Notes)

INGREDIENTS
Water dough
⅓ oz. (10 g) fresh yeast
   (see Chef's Notes)
1 tbsp (15 ml) lukewarm
   water
2 tbsp (25 g) sugar
1½ tsp (7 g) fine salt
1 tbsp (20 g) butter
¼ cup (60 ml) water
¼ cup (60 ml) whole milk
   + 1 tbsp for the sugar
   and salt
2 cups (9 oz./250 g) bread
   flour

For laminating
1 stick + 1 tbsp
   (4½ oz./130 g) butter,
   at room temperature

1 egg, lightly beaten

EQUIPMENT
Instant-read thermometer
Stand mixer fitted
   with the dough hook
2 silicone baking mats
   (or parchment paper)
Rimmed baking sheet lined
   with parchment paper

---

1. **To prepare the water dough**, dissolve the yeast in the lukewarm water in a small bowl. In a separate bowl, stir the sugar and salt into the 1 tbsp milk until dissolved.

2. **Heat the 1 tbsp (20 g) butter** in a small saucepan with the water and milk, until the butter has melted and the temperature reaches 86°F (30°C).

3. **Sift the flour** into the bowl of the stand mixer. Beat in the sugar/salt/milk mixture on low speed, then the warm butter/milk mixture. Finally, mix in the dissolved yeast.

4. **Continue kneading** until the dough is smooth, comes away from the sides of the bowl, and is just warm to the touch (about 1 minute).

5. **Cover the bowl** with plastic wrap and let the dough rise at room temperature, ideally around 77°F/25°C, until doubled in volume (about 1 hour).

6. **Dust a shallow baking dish** with flour and press out the dough over the base. Cover with plastic wrap and refrigerate for 2–3 hours.

7. **To laminate the dough**, remove the butter from the refrigerator about 30 minutes ahead, so it will be easier to work with. Place between the two silicone baking mats or two sheets of parchment paper, then beat with a rolling pin to make the butter as malleable as the dough. Cut into 2 equal pieces, wrap 1 piece, and return it to the refrigerator.

8. **On a lightly floured surface**, roll the dough into a rectangle three times as long as it is wide.

9. **Cut the butter into small pieces.** Dot these evenly over the bottom two-thirds of the dough: the butter should be slightly softer than the dough at this point. Fold the top third of the dough down over the butter and the bottom third up. Give the folded dough a quarter turn and roll into a rectangle again. Fold in thirds as before. Cover in plastic wrap and chill for at least 2 hours, or, for best results, overnight.

10. **When ready to proceed**, remove the remaining butter from the refrigerator and leave it at room temperature for about 30 minutes. Beat with a rolling pin until malleable, as described in step 7, and repeat the rolling and folding instructions (steps 8–9) with the chilled dough and butter. After giving the dough a quarter turn, in the same direction as before, roll it into a rectangle measuring about 8 × 10 in. (20 × 25 cm). Cover with plastic wrap and chill for 1 hour.

11. **To form the croissants,** roll the dough into a rectangle measuring 6 × 17½ in. (15 × 45 cm), with a thickness of about ⅛ in. (3 mm). Cut into 12–15 triangles with a narrower, 2–3-in. (6–7.5-cm) base.

12. **Roll up each triangle** from the base to the tip. Place on the baking sheet, leaving space between each one. The croissants can now be frozen, if desired (see Chef's Notes).

13. **Brush the croissants** with beaten egg to prevent them drying out while rising. Let rise for about 2 hours in a warm place (about 82°F/28°C), until doubled in volume. Toward the end of the rising time, preheat the oven to 400°F (200°C/Gas Mark 6).

→

CROISSANTS

(CONTINUED)

14. **Brush the croissants** with the remaining beaten egg; brush lightly so as not to deflate them. Bake for 15 minutes until deep golden brown. If necessary, rotate the baking sheet toward the end of the baking time so they brown evenly. Cool on a wire rack.

Chef's Notes
• Croissants are traditionally made using fresh yeast, as it gives the best results. If fresh yeast is unavailable, you can substitute 2¼ tsp (7 g) active dry yeast or 1½ tsp (5 g) instant yeast. Instant yeast must be mixed directly into the flour before any liquid is added, rather than dissolved in the water, which can be omitted.
• If freezing, place the unbaked croissants on the baking sheet in the freezer until solid, then place them in a freezer bag, seal, and return to the freezer. Let them thaw overnight in the refrigerator, on a baking sheet lined with parchment paper, then proceed with steps 13 and 14.

FINANCIERS ★

Makes
about 20

Active time: 15 minutes

Cooking time: 15 minutes

Storage: Up to 8 days in the refrigerator or 3 months in the freezer

INGREDIENTS
Butter for the pan, if needed
½ cup (2¼ oz./65 g) AP flour
2¼ cups (10½ oz./300 g) confectioners' sugar
1 cup (3½ oz./100 g) almond powder
½ cup (1¾ oz./50 g) hazelnut powder
1¾ sticks (7 oz./200 g) butter
6 egg whites (¾ cup/180 g)

EQUIPMENT
Stainless steel or silicone financier pan with 1½- × 3-in. (4- × 8-cm) cavities
Instant-read thermometer (optional)
Fine-mesh sieve
Pastry bag

1. **Preheat the oven** to 450°F (240°C/Gas Mark 8). If using a stainless steel pan, grease it with butter. A silicone pan does not need greasing.
2. **Sift the flour and confectioners' sugar** into a mixing bowl. Mix in the almond powder and hazelnut powder.
3. **Melt the butter** in a saucepan over medium heat. Whisk until it turns golden brown and has a nutty aroma (*beurre noisette*). If using a thermometer, the temperature should reach 300°F–311°F (150°C–155°C).
4. **Take the butter off the heat** and strain it through the fine-mesh sieve into a bowl, to eliminate any impurities. Stir the butter into the dry ingredients using a wooden spoon.

5. **Gradually stir in** the egg whites until smooth.
6. **Transfer the batter** to the pastry bag and snip off the tip of the bag. Pipe the batter into the cavities in the mold (about 1½ oz./40 g per financier), filling them almost to the top but leaving a little space for the financiers to rise.
7. **Bake for 5 minutes**, then reduce the heat to 400°F (200°C/Gas Mark 6) and bake for an additional 10 minutes, until the tip of a knife pushed into the center of a financier comes out clean.
8. **Turn out immediately** onto a wire rack to cool.

GALETTE DES ROIS AUX AMANDES

ALMOND KINGS' CAKE ★★★

Serves	INGREDIENTS	EQUIPMENT
8	1 quantity (1¼ lb./600 g) puff pastry dough, classic (see p. 28) or quick (see p. 29)	Cardboard pastry rulers (optional) Rimmed baking sheet lined with parchment paper
Active time: 25 minutes + making the puff pastry and frangipane cream	14 oz. (400 g) frangipane cream (see p. 62)	
Resting time: 1 hour	1 trinket or dried fava bean (optional)	
Cooking time: 40–45 minutes	1 egg, lightly beaten ⅓ cup (1¾ oz./50 g) confectioners' sugar, or scant ½ cup (100 ml) simple syrup (see p. 91)	
Storage: Up to 2 days in the refrigerator or 2 months in the freezer		

1. **Divide the puff pastry dough** into 2 pieces: one weighing ½ lb. (250 g) and the other ¾ lb. (350 g).
2. **Roll out the smaller piece of dough** on a lightly floured surface to a thickness of ¹⁄₁₆ in. (2 mm), using the pastry rulers, if desired. Cut out a 10-in. (26-cm) circle.
3. **Brush the parchment paper** on the baking sheet lightly with water to prevent the dough shrinking during baking. Curl the dough over the rolling pin and carefully unroll it onto the parchment paper.
4. **Roll the larger piece** of dough to a thickness of ⅛ in. (3 mm). Cut out a circle slightly larger than the first.
5. **Prick the smaller circle** all over using a fork. Using an offset spatula, spread the frangipane cream over it in an even layer, leaving a 1-in. (2.5-cm) border. For a traditional Kings' cake for Epiphany, place a trinket or dried fava bean in the frangipane cream.
6. **Brush the pastry border** lightly with water. Cover with the larger circle, pressing the dough edges together with your fingers to seal them.
7. **Brush the top** of the pastry with some of the beaten egg. Let dry for 15 minutes, then brush again with beaten egg. Chill for 1 hour.

8. **When ready to bake,** preheat the oven to 430°F (220°C/Gas Mark 7). Using the tip of a knife, mark a pinwheel pattern on the pastry top, starting at the center and working outward to the edge (see photograph on facing page). Take care not to cut through the pastry. The cake can now be frozen, if desired (see Chef's Notes).
9. **Bake for 10 minutes,** then reduce the heat to 340°F (170°C/Gas Mark 3) and bake for an additional 30–35 minutes, until the pastry is golden brown.
10. **Dust with the confectioners' sugar,** then place under a broiler for 2 minutes to give the pastry an attractive sheen. Alternatively, brush the top with simple syrup.
11. **Transfer to a rack** and serve warm or at room temperature.

Chef's Notes
• If freezing, place the unbaked cake on the cookie sheet in the freezer for about 12 hours, until solid, then slide it into a freezer bag, seal, and return to the freezer. Let thaw overnight on a baking sheet in the refrigerator, then proceed with steps 9 to 11.

GÂTEAU BASQUE

BASQUE CAKE ★

Serves	INGREDIENTS	Cream filling	EQUIPMENT
6	*Pastry*	4 oz. (110 g) pastry cream	Stand mixer fitted
	1 stick (4 oz./120 g) butter,	(see p. 66)	with the paddle beater
Active time: 30 minutes +	diced + more for the pan	½ cup + 1 tbsp (2 oz./55 g)	8-in. (20-cm) round cake
making the pastry cream	⅓ cup (2¼ oz./65 g)	almond powder	pan
	granulated sugar	Scant ⅓ cup (2 oz./55 g)	
Chilling time: 1 hour	½ cup (2¼ oz./65 g) brown	sugar	
	sugar	½ tsp (1.5 g) cornstarch	
Resting time: 15 minutes	½ tsp (2.5 g) fine salt	Pinch of fine salt	
	2 egg yolks (3 tbsp/40 g)	2 egg yolks (3 tbsp/40 g),	
Cooking time: 30 minutes	1½ cups (6½ oz./185 g) AP	lightly beaten	
	flour, sifted	3½ tbsp (2 oz./55 g)	
Storage: Up to 3 days	1½ tsp (5 g) rice flour	butter	
in the refrigerator,	⅔ tsp (2.5 g) baking	2½ tsp (10 ml) dark rum	
well wrapped	powder		
		1 egg yolk, lightly beaten	

---

1. **To prepare the pastry,** beat the butter, sugars, and salt in the stand mixer on medium speed until smooth. Beat in the egg yolks.

2. **Add the AP flour,** rice flour, and baking powder, and mix briefly to make a smooth dough. Chill the pastry until firm enough to roll out.

3. **To prepare the filling,** whisk the pastry cream in a mixing bowl until smooth. Stir in the almond powder, sugar, cornstarch, and salt, using a wooden spoon.

4. **Add the egg yolks** and stir to incorporate.

5. **Heat the butter** in a small saucepan until it melts and begins to foam. Stir the warm butter and the rum into the mixture.

6. **Preheat the oven** to 340°F (170°C/Gas Mark 3). Grease the cake pan with butter.

7. **Divide the pastry** in half. Roll one piece into a 10-in. (25-cm) circle, about ⅛ in. (4 mm) thick. Line it into the pan, pressing the pastry lightly over the base and up the sides, without stretching it.

8. **Spoon in** the cream filling.

9. **Roll the remaining piece of pastry** into an 8-in. (20-cm) circle, then place over the filling. Dampen the pastry edges and press them together to seal.

10. **Brush the pastry** with beaten egg. Score decorative lines across the top in a crosshatch pattern, using the tip of a knife (see photograph on facing page).

11. **Bake for 30 minutes,** or until the pastry is golden brown. Cool the cake in the pan, before turning it out. Serve at room temperature.

GÂTEAU DE SAVOIE

SAVOY CAKE ★

Serves
6–8

Active time: 15 minutes

Cooking time:
40–45 minutes

Storage: Up to 3 days
at room temperature,
in an airtight container, or
2 months in the freezer

INGREDIENTS
Butter and sugar for
the pan
¾ cup + 2 tbsp
(4 oz./115 g) AP flour
¼ cup (1¼ oz./35 g)
potato starch
6 egg yolks
(scant ½ cup/120 g)
1 cup minus 2½ tbsp
(6 oz./170 g) sugar,
divided
Finely grated zest
and juice of ½ lime
6 egg whites
(¾ cup/180 g)

EQUIPMENT
9½-in. (24-cm) Savoy cake
pan or Bundt pan, 4½ in.
(11 cm) deep
Stand mixer fitted with
the whisk

1. **Grease the pan** with butter and dust with sugar until coated. Chill until ready to use.
2. **Preheat the oven** to 340°F (170°C/Gas Mark 3).
3. **Sift the flour** and potato starch together.
4. **Whisk the egg yolks** with three-quarters of the sugar in the stand mixer on medium speed for 5 minutes, until pale and thick.
5. **Gently fold in** the flour and potato starch, making sure the mixture does not deflate. Fold in the lime zest. Transfer the mixture to a mixing bowl.
6. **Wash and dry the mixer bowl.** Whisk the egg whites on high speed until they hold soft peaks. Gradually whisk in the remaining sugar and lime juice until the whites hold firm peaks.

7. **Quickly stir** one-third of the whites into the yolk mixture until combined, then gently fold in the rest.
8. **Transfer the batter** to the prepared pan and smooth the top with a flexible spatula.
9. **Bake for 40–45 minutes**, until the cake is golden and the tip of a knife inserted into the center comes out clean. If the cake browns too quickly, cover it with aluminum foil.
10. **Once baked,** turn the cake out immediately onto a wire rack and let cool completely.

KOUGLOF ALSACIEN

ALSATIAN KUGELHOPF ★★

Serves
6–8

Active time: 30 minutes +
making the brioche dough

Cooking time: 30 minutes

Storage: Up to 2 months
in the freezer

INGREDIENTS
Brioche dough
(make 1 day ahead)
¼ oz. (7 g) fresh yeast
  (see Chef's Notes)
1½ tsp (7.5 ml) lukewarm
  water
2½ tbsp (1 oz./30 g) sugar
1 tsp (5 g) fine salt
3½ tbsp (50 ml) whole
  milk
Generous 2 cups
  (9 oz./250 g) high
  gluten or bread flour
2 eggs
7 tbsp (3½ oz./100 g)
  butter

To assemble
3 tbsp (50 g) butter,
  for the mold
⅔ cup (3½ oz./100 g)
  whole blanched
  almonds

Decoration
Confectioners' sugar

EQUIPMENT
Stand mixer with
  the dough hook
8-in. (20-cm) kugelhopf
  mold, 5 in. (12 cm) deep
  (6½-cup/1.5-L capacity)

1. **A day ahead,** prepare the brioche dough in the stand mixer, using the ingredients listed above and following the instructions on p. 36 (see Chef's Notes).
2. **The following day,** lightly grease the mold with some of the butter and arrange the almonds in the grooves around the bottom of the mold.
3. **On a lightly floured surface,** flatten the dough into a long rectangle with a thickness of 1½ in. (4 cm). Roll it up, as tightly as possible, into a cylinder.
4. **Shape the dough into a ring,** brush with water where the two ends meet to seal them together, and place in the mold.
5. **Let rise for 2 hours** in a warm place (about 82°F/28°C), until the dough fills a little more than three-quarters of the mold. Toward the end of the rising time, preheat the oven to 400°F (200°C/Gas Mark 6).
6. **When the dough has risen,** bake the kugelhopf for 40–45 minutes, until it is golden brown and the tip of a knife inserted into the center comes out clean. If the top browns too quickly, cover it with aluminum foil.

7. **Let the kugelhopf cool** for a few minutes in the mold. Melt the remaining butter. Turn the kugelhopf out onto a wire rack and quickly brush the melted butter over it.
8. **Let cool completely.** Dust lightly with sifted confectioners' sugar just before serving.

Chef's Notes
• If fresh yeast is unavailable, you can substitute 1½ tsp (5 g) active dry yeast or 1¼ tsp (3.5 g) instant yeast. Instant yeast must be mixed directly into the flour before any liquid is added, rather than dissolved in the water, which can be omitted.
• This recipe contains less butter than the traditional brioche dough recipe on page 36, so is not as rich.
• If freezing the kugelhopf, cover it with plastic wrap while it is still warm to keep it moist. Do not brush it with melted butter. When cool, freeze in an airtight freezer bag.
• After freezing, let the kugelhopf thaw at room temperature for 2 hours, then place in a 300°F (150°C/Gas Mark 2) oven for 10 minutes. Brush with melted butter while still warm.

KOUGLOF LENÔTRE
LENÔTRE KUGELHOPF ★★★

Serves
6

Active time: 45 minutes +
making the brioche dough

Soaking time: 1 hour

Rising time: 2 hours

Cooking time:
40–45 minutes

Storage: Up to 2 months
in the freezer

INGREDIENTS
Rum-soaked raisins
(see Chef's Notes)
Scant ½ cup (100 ml)
    water
½ cup (3½ oz./100 g)
    sugar
¼ cup (60 ml) dark rum
⅔ cup (3½ oz./100 g)
    raisins

To assemble
3 tbsp (1¾ oz./50 g)
    butter, for the mold
    and glazing

⅔ cup (3½ oz./100 g)
    whole blanched
    almonds
12¾ oz. (360 g) brioche
    dough (see p. 36),
    made 1 day ahead

Orange flower syrup
¼ cup (1¾ oz./50 g) sugar
3½ tbsp (50 ml) water
1 tsp (5 ml) orange flower
    water

Decoration
⅓ cup (1¾ oz./50 g)
    confectioners' sugar

EQUIPMENT
8-in. (20-cm) kugelhopf
    mold, 5 in. (12 cm) deep
    (6½-cup/1.5-L capacity)

1. **Combine the water and sugar** in a saucepan and stir over low heat until the sugar dissolves.
2. **Increase the heat** and bring to a boil, stirring frequently. Remove from the heat and let cool slightly. Stir in the rum.
3. **Put the raisins in a bowl** and pour the syrup over them. Let soak for 1 hour, then drain.
4. **To assemble the kugelhopf,** lightly grease the mold with some of the butter and arrange the almonds in the grooves around the bottom of the mold.
5. **Flatten the dough** into a long rectangle. Scatter the raisins over it and roll up the dough, as tightly as possible, into a cylinder.
6. **Shape the dough into a ring,** brush with water where the two ends meet to seal them together, and place in the mold.
7. **Let rise for 2 hours** in a warm place (about 82°F/28°C), until the dough fills a little more than three-quarters of the mold. Toward the end of the rising time, preheat the oven to 400°F (200°C/Gas Mark 6).
8. **When the dough has risen,** bake it for 40–45 minutes, until the kugelhopf is golden brown and the tip of a knife pushed into the center comes out clean.

9. **While the kugelhopf is baking,** make the orange flower syrup. Heat the sugar and water in a saucepan over low heat until the sugar dissolves. Increase the heat, bring to a boil, then cool slightly. Stir in the orange flower water.
10. **When the kugelhopf is nearly baked,** melt the remaining butter. Turn the kugelhopf out onto a wire rack while still hot and quickly brush with the melted butter and orange flower syrup to glaze.
11. **Let cool completely.** Dust lightly with sifted confectioners' sugar just before serving.

Chef's Notes
• The syrup for soaking the raisins can be made several weeks ahead and stored in an airtight container in the refrigerator.
• If freezing the kugelhopf, cover it with plastic wrap while it is still warm to keep it moist. Do not brush it with melted butter or syrup. When cool, freeze in an airtight freezer bag.
• After freezing, let the kugelhopf thaw at room temperature for 2 hours, then place in a 300°F (150°C/Gas Mark 2) oven for 10 minutes. Brush with melted butter and orange flower syrup while still warm.

MIRLITONS

MIRLITON TARTLETS ★★

Makes	INGREDIENTS	3 drops orange flower	EQUIPMENT
15	*Tartlet shells*	water	3½-in. (9-cm) round
	9 oz. (250 g) puff pastry	⅓ cup (2¾ oz./80 g)	cookie cutter
Active time: 15 minutes	dough, classic (see p. 28)	crème fraîche	15 × 2½-in. (6-cm) tartlet
+ making the puff pastry	or quick (see p. 29)	⅓ cup (1 oz./30 g) sliced	pans, about ¾ in. (2 cm)
and frangipane cream		almonds	deep
	Filling	Confectioners' sugar,	Rimmed baking sheet
Chilling time: 2½ hours	2 eggs (scant ½ cup/	for dusting	
	100 g)		
Cooking time: 30 minutes	¼ cup (1¾ oz./50 g)		
	granulated sugar		
	2¾ oz. (80 g) frangipane		
	cream (see p. 62)		
	or a scant ½ cup		
	(1½ oz./40 g) almond		
	powder		
	5 tsp (20 g) vanilla sugar		

1. **To prepare the tartlet shells,** roll out the pastry to a thickness of ¹⁄₁₆ in. (2 mm) on a lightly floured surface.
2. **Cut out 15 circles** using the cookie cutter. Line the pastry circles into the tartlet pans so they stand about ¼ in. (5 mm) above the sides of the pans, to compensate for shrinkage. Chill for 30 minutes.
3. **As the tarts shells** need to be very thin, gently press out the pastry edges using your fingers, then chill for another 30 minutes. Repeat the pressing and chilling once more, so the pastry edges are almost transparent.
4. **Prick the base** of each tartlet with a thin-tined fork. Chill for 1 hour.

5. **Preheat the oven** to 350°F (180°C/Gas Mark 4).
6. **To prepare the filling,** mix together the eggs, granulated sugar, frangipane cream or almond powder, vanilla sugar, and orange flower water in a bowl until smooth. Stir in the crème fraîche.
7. **Spoon the filling** into the tartlet shells, sprinkle with sliced almonds, and dust with confectioners' sugar.
8. **Place on a baking sheet** and bake for 30 minutes, until golden.
9. **Carefully remove the tartlets** from the pans and cool on a wire rack. Serve warm or at room temperature on the day they are made.

PAIN D'ÉPICES DES GÂTINES

LENÔTRE GÂTINES SPICE CAKE ★

Makes
2 cakes, each serving 8

Active time: 30 minutes

Cooking time: 1½ hours

Cooling time: 1 hour

Resting time: Up to 3 days (optional, see Chef's Notes)

Storage: Up to 12 weeks in the refrigerator or 6 months in the freezer

INGREDIENTS
1 stick + 2 tbsp (5¼ oz./150 g) butter, diced + more for the pans
1⅔ cups (400 ml) water
1 cup + 3 tbsp (14 oz./400 g) golden honey
1¼ cups (9 oz./250 g) sugar
2 oranges
1 lemon
1 cup (3½ oz./100 g) sliced almonds
3½ tbsp (50 ml) anise syrup or 1 tbsp anise seeds (see Chef's Notes)

Generous 4¾ cups (1 lb. 3 oz./550 g) whole wheat flour or 5 cups (1 lb. 3 oz./550 g) rye flour
¼ cup (1½ oz./45 g) baking powder

Decoration (optional)
Candied orange peel, cut into thin strips the same length as the width of the cakes
Finely grated orange zest

EQUIPMENT
2 × 12-in. (30-cm) loaf pans
Microplane grater
Stand mixer fitted with the paddle beater

1. **Preheat the oven** to 400°F (200°C/Gas Mark 6). Lightly grease the loaf pans with butter and line them with enough parchment paper to leave an overhang.
2. **Heat the water** in a saucepan. Stir in the honey and sugar until dissolved. Add the butter and stir until it has melted.
3. **Wash and dry** the oranges and lemon. Remove the peel in quarters from one orange and cut it into small dice. Zest the other orange and the lemon, preferably using a Microplane grater, as the zest needs to be very fine. Place the diced peel and zest in a mixing bowl and add the almonds and anise syrup or seeds. Stir to combine.
4. **Sift the flour** and baking powder into the bowl of the stand mixer. With the mixer running on low speed, gradually incorporate the first mixture. Sprinkle in the citrus peel/almond/anise mixture and beat until combined.

5. **Divide the batter** between the pans. Bake for 30 minutes, then reduce the temperature to 340°F (170°C/Gas Mark 3) and bake for an additional 1 hour, or until the tip of a knife pushed into the center of each cake comes out clean. If the cakes brown too quickly, cover them with aluminum foil.
6. **Cool the cakes** in the pans for at least 1 hour, before serving. If possible, let them rest overnight or up to 3 days, still in their pans (see Chef's Notes). If wished, decorate the tops of the cakes with strips of candied orange peel and sprinkle over finely grated zest before serving.

Chef's Notes
• There is no need to grind the anise seeds, as they will disintegrate as the cake bakes.
• Although the spice cakes can be eaten 1 hour after being removed from the oven, they will be easier to slice and their flavors will have had time to develop if they are stored in their pans for 2–3 days.

PAIN DE GÊNES

FRENCH ALMOND CAKE ★

Makes
2 cakes, each serving 6

Active time: 30 minutes +
making the marzipan

Cooking time:
30 minutes

Storage: Up to 4 days
in the refrigerator or
3 months in the freezer,
wrapped airtight

INGREDIENTS
7 tbsp (3½ oz./100 g)
    butter + more for
    the pans
⅔ cup (1¾ oz./50 g) sliced
    almonds
13¼ oz. (375 g) marzipan
    (see p. 63), roughly
    chopped
6 eggs (1¼ cups/280 g)
1½ tbsp (15 g) AP flour
1½ tbsp (15 g)
    potato starch
1 tsp (5 ml) Grand Marnier
1 tsp (5 ml) aged rum

EQUIPMENT
2 × 7-in. (18-cm) round
    cake pans
2 × 7-in. (18-cm) rounds
    of parchment paper
Stand mixer fitted with
    the paddle beater

1. **Preheat the oven** to 400°F (200°C/Gas Mark 6).
Grease the pans with butter and line the bases with
the rounds of parchment paper to prevent the cakes,
which are fragile, from sticking. Press the sliced almonds
around the sides of the pans, removing any that do not
stick.

2. **Beat the marzipan** on slow speed in the bowl
of the stand mixer until malleable and smooth.

3. **Add the eggs**, one by one, and beat for 5 minutes
on medium speed after each addition. Scrape down
the sides of the bowl as needed. The mixture should be
light and airy.

4. **Sift the flour** and potato starch into a bowl.

5. **Melt the butter** in a saucepan until foaming.
Remove from the heat. Whisk in about one-quarter
of the marzipan mixture, then the Grand Marnier
and rum.

6. **Gently fold the flour** and potato starch
into the marzipan mixture in the bowl. Slowly pour
in the butter mixture and fold it in using a spatula.

7. **Divide the batter** between the pans, filling them
three-quarters full.

8. **Bake for 10 minutes**, then reduce the oven
temperature to 350°F (180°C/Gas Mark 4) and bake
for an additional 20 minutes, until the cakes are golden
and the tip of a knife inserted into the center comes out
clean.

9. **Let the cakes cool** completely in the pans before
carefully inverting them onto flat serving plates, with
the parchment paper uppermost. Carefully peel off
the parchment paper.

Chef's Notes

• These cakes can be served with chocolate sauce
(see p. 90) or vanilla custard sauce (see p. 86), or with
a fresh fruit coulis (see p. 51). They are also delicious on
their own, with a cup of tea.

PAINS AU CHOCOLAT
CHOCOLATE CROISSANTS ★★

Makes
15

Active time: 10 minutes
+ making the croissant
dough

Rising time: 2 hours

Cooking time: 18 minutes
for each baking sheet

Storage: Up to 2 months
in the freezer (unbaked),
in a sealed freezer bag

INGREDIENTS
Water dough
⅓ oz. (10 g) fresh yeast
1 tbsp (15 ml) lukewarm
   water
2 tbsp (25 g) sugar
1½ tsp (7 g) fine salt
1 tbsp (20 g) butter
¼ cup (60 ml) water
¼ cup (60 ml) whole milk
   + 1 tbsp for the sugar
   and salt
2¾ cups (9 oz./250 g)
   bread flour

For laminating
1 stick + 1 tbsp
   (4½ oz./130 g) butter

Chocolate filling
30 *pain au chocolat*
   sticks, weighing ⅙ oz.
   (5 g) each, or 15 sticks
   weighing ⅓ oz. (10 g)
   each (see Chef's Notes)

1 egg, lightly beaten

EQUIPMENT
Instant-read thermometer
Stand mixer fitted with
   the dough hook
2 silicone baking mats
   (optional)
2 rimmed baking sheets
   lined with parchment
   paper

---

1. **Using the ingredients** listed above, make a croissant dough following steps 1–10 on p. 116.
2. **Roll the dough** into a rectangle measuring 35 × 6 in. (90 × 15 cm), with a thickness of about ⅛ in. (3 mm), and cut into 15 equal-sized smaller rectangles.
3. **Place 1 large or 2 small chocolate sticks** near the base of each rectangle and roll up the dough around the sticks to enclose them. Divide the croissants between the baking sheets, seam side down, leaving space between each one. The tops can be scored using a bread knife for a decorative effect. The croissants can now be frozen, if desired (see Chef's Notes).
4. **Brush the croissants** with a little beaten egg to prevent them from drying out while rising. Let rise at room temperature for about 2 hours, until doubled in volume. Toward the end of the rising time, preheat the oven to 400°F (200°C/Gas Mark 6).
5. **Lightly brush the tops of one sheet of croissants** with half the remaining beaten egg, taking care not to deflate the dough. Place immediately in the oven and bake for 18 minutes, until deep golden brown. If the croissants are browning too quickly, reduce the heat to 350°F (180°C/Gas Mark 4). Rotate the baking sheet toward the end of the baking time, if necessary, so they brown evenly. Brush the tops of the second sheet of croissants with the remaining beaten egg and bake in the same way.
6. **Cool the croissants** on a wire rack.

Chef's Notes
• Croissants are traditionally made using fresh yeast, as it gives the best results. If fresh yeast is unavailable, you can substitute 2¼ tsp (7 g) active dry yeast or 1¼ tsp (3.5 g) instant yeast. Instant yeast must be mixed directly into the flour before any liquid is added, rather than dissolved in the water, which can be omitted.
• If *pain au chocolat* sticks are unavailable in stores, they can be purchased online from various suppliers.
• If freezing, place the unbaked croissants on the baking sheet in the freezer until solid, then place them in a freezer bag, seal, and return to the freezer. Let them thaw overnight in the refrigerator, on a baking sheet lined with parchment paper, then proceed with steps 4–6.

PAINS AUX RAISINS

RAISIN ROLLS ★★

Makes
10

Active time: 15 minutes +
making the brioche dough
and frangipane or pastry
cream

Soaking time: 15 minutes

Resting time: 1 hour

Rising time: 1½–2 hours

Cooking time:
15–20 minutes

Storage: Up to 1 day
at room temperature
(baked) or 2 months
in the freezer (unbaked),
in a sealed freezer bag

INGREDIENTS
1 cup (250 ml) water
⅓ cup (1¾ oz./50 g) raisins
3½ tbsp (50 ml) dark rum
9 oz. (250 g) brioche
  dough (see p. 36),
  made 1 day ahead
3½ oz. (100 g) frangipane
  cream (see p. 62)
  or pastry cream
  (see p. 66)
1 egg, lightly beaten

Fruit glaze
3 tbsp apricot glaze,
  warmed
or
Sugar glaze
¾ cup (3½ oz./100 g)
  confectioners' sugar
3 drops rum
2 tbsp (30 ml) water

EQUIPMENT
Rimmed baking sheet
  lined with parchment
  paper
10 × 4-in. (10-cm) round
  aluminum or silicone
  cake pans (optional,
  see Chef's Notes)

1. **Bring the water to a boil.** Put the raisins in a heatproof bowl, pour over the boiling water, and let soak for 15 minutes to plump them up.
2. **Drain the raisins,** return them to the bowl, and add the rum. Let soak until ready to use.
3. **On a lightly floured surface,** roll the brioche dough into a rectangle measuring approximately 6 × 10 in. (15 × 25 cm).
4. **Spread the frangipane or pastry cream** over the dough in an even layer.
5. **Drain the raisins** and scatter them over the cream.
6. **Carefully roll up the dough** from one long side, as tightly as possible, into a 10-in. (25-cm) cylinder. Chill for 1 hour.
7. **Cut the cylinder** into 10 equal slices. Lay the slices flat on the baking sheet, leaving space between each one, or place in the cake pans. Tuck the dough ends under the slices so the rolls do not unwind as they bake. They can now be frozen, if desired (see Chef's Notes).

8. **Let rise for 1½–2 hours** at room temperature, until doubled in volume. Toward the end of the rising time, preheat the oven to 400°F (200°C/Gas Mark 6).
9. **Brush the rolls** with a thin layer of beaten egg. Bake for 15–20 minutes, until puffed and golden. Transfer to a rack.
10. **If using apricot glaze,** let the rolls cool slightly, before brushing the glaze over them. If using a sugar glaze, stir together the confectioners' sugar, rum, and water in a bowl until the sugar has dissolved. Cool the rolls before brushing them with the glaze.

Chef's Notes
• If freezing, place the unbaked rolls on the baking sheet in the freezer until solid, then place them in a freezer bag, seal, and return to the freezer. Let them thaw overnight in the refrigerator, on a baking sheet lined with parchment paper, then proceed with steps 8–10.
• Baking the rolls in individual cake pans gives a more even and attractive result.

PETIT PRINCE

LITTLE PRINCE CAKE ★

Serves
6

Active time: 20 minutes

Resting time: 45 minutes

Cooking time: 40 minutes

Storage: Up to 4 days
in the refrigerator or
3 months in the freezer

INGREDIENTS
7 tbsp (3½ oz./100 g)
   butter + more for
   the pan
1 generous cup
   (3½ oz./100 g) cake
   flour
½ tsp (2 g) baking powder
Finely grated zest
   of 1 orange (about
   ⅙ oz./5 g)
¾ cup (3¼ oz./95 g)
   confectioners' sugar,
   divided
Scant ¼ cup (20 g)
   almond powder

⅓ oz. (10 g) high-quality
   candied orange, finely
   chopped
2 small eggs (⅓ cup/90 g)
2 tsp (10 ml) whole milk,
   hot (140°F/60°C)

Grand Marnier syrup
1 tbsp + 1 tsp (20 ml)
   water
1 tbsp + 2 tsp (20 g) sugar
1 tbsp + 1 tsp (20 ml)
   Grand Marnier

Decoration (optional)
6 candied orange slices

EQUIPMENT
6- × 3- × 3-in.
   (15- × 8- × 8-cm)
   loaf pan

1. **Lightly grease the loaf pan** with butter and line with enough parchment paper to leave an overhang.
2. **Sift the flour** and baking powder into a bowl.
3. **In a separate bowl,** combine the orange zest with a generous ½ cup (2¾ oz./75 g) of the confectioners' sugar.
4. **Combine the remaining** 2½ tbsp (20 g) confectioners' sugar with the almond powder in a third bowl.
5. **Melt the butter** in a saucepan until it bubbles gently.
6. **While the butter is melting,** place the finely chopped candied orange in a small bowl. Pour over one-quarter of the melted butter and stir to combine.
7. **Pour the remaining butter** into a mixing bowl. Stir in the confectioners' sugar and zest. Using a flexible spatula, fold in the confectioners' sugar and almond powder, then half the flour and baking powder.
8. **Stir in the butter-coated** candied orange pieces and any butter still left in the bowl. Add the eggs and hot milk and stir to combine.
9. **Fold in the remaining flour** and baking powder until just combined.
10. **Pour the batter** into the prepared pan. Let rest in the refrigerator for 45 minutes.
11. **Preheat the oven** to 400°F (200°C/Gas Mark 6).

12. **Place the cake in the oven** and immediately reduce the temperature to 340°F (170°C/Gas Mark 3). Bake for 35–40 minutes, until the cake is golden and the tip of a knife inserted into the center comes out clean. If the cake browns too quickly, lower the oven temperature to 320°F (160°C).
13. **While the cake is baking,** prepare the Grand Marnier syrup. Heat the water and sugar together until the sugar dissolves. Remove from the heat and let cool slightly. Stir in the Grand Marnier.
14. **Remove the cake** from the oven and immediately brush 3½ tbsp (50 ml) of the Grand Marnier syrup over it. Let the cake cool for a few minutes in the pan, before turning it out onto a wire rack. Let cool completely.
15. **Decorate with candied orange slices,** if desired, before serving.

Chef's Notes
• This cake freezes well, so the ingredients can be doubled or tripled to make several cakes for other occasions.

PITHIVIERS ★★★

Serves
6–8

Active time: 20 minutes
+ making the puff pastry
and almond cream

Resting time: 1 hour

Cooking time:
40–45 minutes

Storage: Up to 2 months
in the freezer (unbaked)

INGREDIENTS
1 quantity (1¼ lb./600 g)
   puff pastry dough,
   classic (see p. 28)
   or quick (see p. 29)
14 oz. (400 g) almond
   cream, Frangipane
   Cream recipe
   (see p. 62)
⅓ cup (1¾ oz./50 g)
   confectioners' sugar
1 egg, lightly beaten

EQUIPMENT
10-in. (26-cm) round plate
Cookie sheet lined with
   parchment paper

1. **Divide the puff pastry dough** in half. Roll each half separately on a lightly floured surface into a square with a thickness of ⅛ in. (3 mm). Place the 10-in. (26-cm) plate upside down on the pastry and cut around it (the trimmings can be saved for another recipe).
2. **Roll one pastry circle** around the rolling pin and carefully unroll it onto the cookie sheet.
3. **Brush the edges lightly** with water to moisten them, leaving a 1-in. (2.5-cm) border.
4. **Spoon the almond cream** into the center and spread it over the dough, leaving a 1¼-in. (3-cm) border.
5. **Cover with the second pastry circle**, with the smoothest side facing up. Press the pastry edges together with your fingertips to seal them.
6. **Brush the top** of the pastry with some of the beaten egg. Let dry for 15 minutes, then brush again with beaten egg. Chill for 1 hour.
7. **When ready to bake,** preheat the oven to 400°F (200°C/Gas Mark 6). Cut half-moon shapes around the pastry using a sharp knife, to create a scalloped edge (see photograph pp. 144–45). Remove the pastry trimmings.

8. **Using the tip of the knife,** mark a pinwheel pattern on the pastry top, starting at the center and working outward to the edge. Take care not to cut through the pastry. The cake can now be frozen, if desired (see Chef's Notes).
9. **Bake for about 15 minutes,** until the pastry puffs up, then reduce the temperature to 340°F (170°C/Gas Mark 3) and bake for an additional 30–35 minutes, until the pastry is golden brown.
10. **Dust with the confectioners' sugar** and place under the broiler for 2 minutes to glaze the pastry. Serve warm.

Chef's Notes
• If freezing, place the unbaked cake on the cookie sheet in the freezer for about 12 hours, until solid, then slide it into a freezer bag, seal, and return to the freezer. Let thaw overnight on a baking sheet in the refrigerator, then proceed with steps 9 and 10.

PITHIVIERS HOLLANDAIS

DUTCH PITHIVIERS ★★★

Serves
6–8

Active time: 20 minutes
+ making the puff pastry
and almond cream

Resting time: 1½ hours

Cooking time: 45 minutes

Storage: Up to 2 months
in the freezer (unbaked)

INGREDIENTS
1 quantity (1¼ lb./600 g)
   puff pastry dough,
   classic (see p. 28) or
   quick (see p. 29)
14 oz. (400 g) almond
   cream, Frangipane
   Cream recipe
   (see p. 62)

Topping
½ cup (3½ oz./100 g)
   granulated sugar
⅓ cup (1 oz./30 g) ground
   almonds
½ egg white (1 tbsp/15 g)
⅓ cup (1¾ oz./50 g)
   confectioners' sugar

EQUIPMENT
9½-in. (24-cm) round plate
Cookie sheet lined with
   parchment paper

---

1. **Divide the puff pastry dough** in half. Roll each half separately on a lightly floured surface into a square with a thickness of ⅛ in. (4 mm). Place the 9½-in. (24-cm) plate upside down on the pastry and cut around it (the trimmings can be saved for another recipe).
2. **Roll one pastry circle** around the rolling pin and carefully unroll it onto the cookie sheet.
3. **Brush the edges lightly** with water to moisten them, leaving a 1-in. (2.5-cm) border.
4. **Spoon the almond cream** into the center and smooth it into a dome shape using a palette knife.
5. **Cover with the second pastry circle** and lightly press it over the filling to exclude any air bubbles. Press the pastry edges together with your fingertips to seal them. Chill for 1 hour.
6. **Remove from the refrigerator** and press around the pastry edges again to flatten them. Chill for an additional 30 minutes.
7. **Preheat the oven** to 400°F (200°C/Gas Mark 6).
8. **To prepare the topping**, mix together the granulated sugar, ground almonds, and egg white until smooth. Spread the topping over the pastry using a palette knife.
9. **Dust generously** with the confectioners' sugar. Mark an asterisk shape on top using the tip of a knife (see photograph pp. 148–49) to divide into 6 or 8 servings. Take care not to cut through the pastry.
10. **Bake for 45 minutes,** until the pastry is puffed and golden. Serve warm.

Chef's Notes
• As an alternative to marking an asterisk shape in the topping, thin strips of pastry (use the trimmings) can be placed in a similar shape over the cake. To help them stick, use the tip of a knife to scrape away the confectioners' sugar before laying the strips over the top. Press down lightly to fix them in place.

ENTREMETS AND GÂTEAUX

AMBASSADEUR

AMBASSADOR CAKE ★★

Serves
8

Active time: 25 minutes
+ making the genoise
sponge and pastry cream

Soaking time: Overnight

Chilling time: 1 hour

Storage: Up to 2 days
in the refrigerator
(undecorated)

INGREDIENTS
1½ oz. (40 g) candied fruit,
   finely chopped
¼ cup (60 ml)
   Grand Marnier
½ quantity (10½ oz./
   300 g) pastry cream
   (see p. 66), divided
8-in. (20-cm) round
   genoise sponge
   (see p. 30), made 1 day
   ahead
1 cup (250 ml)
   simple syrup with
   Grand Marnier
   (see p. 91)
14 oz. (400 g) marzipan
   (see p. 63)

Decoration
Fresh cherries
   (see Chef's Notes)
1 quantity (4½ oz./130 g)
   raspberry glaze, for
   dipping (see p. 80)
Crushed almond candy
   (*dragées*; optional)

EQUIPMENT
8-in. (20-cm) round
   cardboard cake board

1. **A day ahead,** place the candied fruit and Grand Marnier
in a bowl. Let soak overnight.
2. **The following day,** drain the candied fruit. Combine
with half the pastry cream in a bowl. Reserve the rest
of the pastry cream in the refrigerator.
3. **Cut the genoise sponge** into 3 equal layers using
a bread knife. Place the bottom layer on the cardboard
cake board, crust side down. Generously brush
the crumb side with the simple syrup. Cover with half
the candied fruit and pastry cream mixture.
4. **Place the middle layer on top,** brush with syrup,
and cover with the remaining candied fruit and pastry
cream mixture. Place the third layer on top, crust side
up, and brush generously with syrup.
5. **Stir the remaining pastry cream** with a whisk
to loosen it. Using a palette knife, spread the cream over
the cake in a thin layer. Chill for 1 hour.
6. **Roll the marzipan** into a circle large enough to cover
the cake. Curl it over the rolling pin and carefully unroll
over the center of the cake. Gently press the marzipan
across the top and down the sides, taking care not
to crease it. Trim the base neatly using a small sharp
knife. Chill until ready to decorate and serve.
7. **To decorate the cake,** wash and dry the cherries.
Remove some but not all of the stems. Dip
in the raspberry glaze and arrange on top of the cake.
Gently press the crushed almond candy, if using,
onto the sides.

Chef's Notes
• If fresh cherries are unavailable, replace them
with candied whole cherries, preferably Bigarreaux.

BABA AU RHUM

RUM BABA***

Makes
1 baba serving 10

Active time:
15 minutes + making
the baba and pastry
cream, if using

INGREDIENTS
Syrup
1¾ cups (12 oz./350 g)
    sugar
2 cups (500 ml) water
2 tbsp (30 ml) dark rum
    (see Chef's Notes)
    + more for drizzling

1 baked baba (see p. 35)

Glaze
3½ oz. (100 g) warm
    apricot glaze

Filling
14 oz. (400 g) Chantilly
    cream (see p. 50) or
1¼ lb. (600 g) pastry
    cream (see p. 66) or
1¼ lb. (600 g) fresh fruit

Decoration (optional)
Fresh fruit of your choice

EQUIPMENT
Instant-read thermometer
Pastry bag fitted with
    a fluted tip (optional)

---

1. **To make the syrup**, place the sugar and water
in a saucepan over low heat and stir until the sugar
dissolves. Bring to a boil, then remove from the heat.
Let the syrup cool to 122°F (50°C). Stir in the rum.
2. **Place the baba** on a wire rack with a dish underneath
to catch drips. Ladle over the hot syrup until the baba
is thoroughly soaked. Alternatively, place the baba
in a heatproof bowl and pour over the hot syrup,
immersing it until thoroughly soaked. Carefully transfer
the baba to a wire rack with a dish underneath to drain,
taking care not to break it. In both cases, reserve any
syrup that does not soak into the baba, to drizzle over
the cake before serving.
3. **Shortly before serving,** combine the reserved syrup
with an equal quantity of rum. Drizzle over the baba.
4. **To glaze the baba,** brush it all over with the warm
apricot glaze.
5. **Fill the center** with Chantilly or pastry cream: either
spoon the cream into the center or pipe it in rosettes.
Alternatively, fill the center with fresh fruit. Decorate,
if desired, with fresh fruit such as raspberries, cherries,
strawberries, or diced mango.

Chef's Notes
• Instead of rum, the syrup can be flavored with
the same quantity of Grand Marnier or kirsch.

BAGATELLE AUX FRAISES

STRAWBERRY BAGATELLE ★★★

Serves
6–8

Active time: 2 hours +
making the pastry cream

Cooking time: 20 minutes

Chilling time: 2 hours

INGREDIENTS

Almond sponge layer
3 eggs (⅔ cup/150 g)
⅔ cup (2¾ oz./80 g)
  confectioners' sugar,
  sifted
¾ cup + 1 tbsp
  (2¾ oz./80 g) almond
  powder
4 egg whites
  (½ cup/120 g)
¼ cup (1¾ oz./50 g)
  superfine sugar
½ cup (2 oz./60 g) AP
  flour, sifted
1 oz. (30 g) white
  chocolate
1 tsp (5 ml) grape-seed oil

Syrup
3½ tbsp (1½ oz./40 g)
  sugar
3½ tbsp (50 ml) water,
  divided
4 tsp (20 ml) kirsch
4 tsp (20 ml) raspberry
  brandy

Mousseline cream
4½ oz. (125 g) pastry
  cream (see p. 66)
¾ lb. (350 g)
  plain buttercream,
  at room temperature
  (see p. 54)
1 tbsp (15 ml) raspberry
  brandy
2 tsp (10 g) butter,
  melted and cooled

To assemble
1½ lb. (700 g) large
  strawberries
  (such as Charlotte)
3½ oz. (100 g) small,
  sweet strawberries
  (such as Fraises des
  Bois)
5 tsp (20 g) sugar
5¼ oz. (150 g) marzipan,
  colored pale green with
  natural food coloring
  (see p. 63)
Confectioners' sugar,
  for dusting

EQUIPMENT

Rimmed baking sheet
Stand mixer fitted
  with the whisk
5- × 7-in. (12- × 18-cm)
  rectangular pastry
  frame, 1½ in. (4 cm)
  deep
Cardboard rectangle
  measuring 6 × 8 in.
  (15 × 20 cm), or flat
  serving platter
Food processor or blender
Fine-mesh sieve
Embossed rolling
  pin (optional)

1. **Preheat the oven** to 340°F (170°C/Gas Mark 3). Using a pencil, draw 2 rectangles measuring 5 × 7 in. (12 × 18 cm) on a sheet of parchment paper and place on the baking sheet with the pencil marks underneath.
2. **To prepare the sponge layer,** whisk together the eggs, confectioners' sugar, and almond powder on high speed for 10 minutes, until pale, thick, and creamy. Carefully transfer to another bowl without deflating the mixture. Wash and dry the whisk and bowl.
3. **Whisk the egg whites** until they hold soft peaks. Gradually whisk in the superfine sugar until the peaks are firm. Gently fold the two mixtures together, then fold in the flour a little at a time.
4. **Spread the batter** over the 2 marked rectangles and bake for 20 minutes, until light gold in color. Invert onto a wire rack and cool before removing from the parchment. If necessary, neaten the sponge edges with a bread knife.

5. **Melt the white chocolate** in a small bowl over a saucepan of barely simmering water (bain-marie) or in the microwave. Stir in the grape-seed oil. Spread evenly over one of the sponge rectangles. Chill.
6. **To prepare the syrup,** place the sugar and 2 tbsp (30 ml) of the water in a saucepan over low heat and stir until the sugar dissolves. Increase the heat, bring to a boil, then stir in the remaining water, kirsch, and raspberry brandy. Let cool. Cover and chill until using.
7. **To prepare the mousseline cream,** whisk the pastry cream and buttercream in separate bowls until smooth. Whisk the raspberry brandy into the pastry cream, followed by the buttercream and melted butter.
8. **To assemble the cake,** wash and hull the strawberries. Trim the tops of the larger berries so they are evenly sized. Set aside 3½ oz. (100 g) of the least attractive berries to make a coulis and a few of the best ones to use as decoration.

9. **Place the pastry frame** on the cardboard rectangle or flat serving platter. Place the chocolate-coated sponge in the frame, chocolate side down. Brush the sponge with a scant ½ cup (100 ml) of the syrup, then spread with 5¼ oz. (150 g; about one-third) of the mousseline cream.

10. **Cut the large trimmed strawberries** in half vertically and arrange them around the sides of the frame, with their ends pointing upward and the cut sides against the frame. Fill the center with the small strawberries.

11. **Blend the 3½ oz. (100 g) strawberries** set aside for the coulis with the 5 tsp (20 g) sugar until smooth. Strain through a fine-mesh sieve. Spoon between the small strawberries.

12. **Cover with 10½ oz. (300 g)** of the remaining mousseline cream. Set the second sponge layer on top and brush with the remaining syrup. Spread the remaining 2 oz. (50 g) cream evenly over the sponge using a palette knife.

13. **Roll out the marzipan** to a thickness of ¹⁄₁₆ in. (2 mm). Imprint it with a design, either manually or by running an embossed rolling pin over it. Cut the marzipan into a rectangle to fit neatly inside the frame. Place it on top of the cream. Chill for 2 hours.

14. **Just before serving**, carefully lift off the pastry frame. Dust the top of the cake generously with confectioners' sugar. Decorate with the reserved strawberries, cut into portions using a bread knife or chef's knife, and serve with any remaining coulis.

Chef's Notes
• Although the cake needs to be assembled on the day it is served, the different elements can be prepared a day ahead and refrigerated. This will make assembling the cake quicker and easier.

BÛCHE FRAISIER

STRAWBERRY

SPONGE ROULADE LOG ★★★

Serves
10

Active time:
20 minutes + making
the roulade sponge
and Italian meringue

Cooking time:
10 minutes

Storage: Up to 2 days
in the refrigerator

INGREDIENTS
1 sheet roulade sponge
  (see p. 27)
⅔ cup (150 ml) simple
  syrup with kirsch
  (see p. 91)
1½ cups (1 lb./500 g)
  strawberry jam
A dozen large fresh
  strawberries
2 quantities (13 oz./380 g)
  Italian meringue, cold
  (see p. 32)
⅓ cup (1¾ oz./50 g)
  confectioners' sugar

EQUIPMENT
Rimmed baking sheet
  lined with parchment
  paper
Pastry bag fitted with
  a flat basket-weave tip
  (or palette knife)

1. **Preheat the oven** to 450°F (240°C/Gas Mark 8).
2. **Place the sponge on the baking sheet.** Prick all over using a fork, brush with the syrup, and spread with the strawberry jam.
3. **Wash and dry** the strawberries. Trim the tops and bottoms so they are level. Arrange them close together, with the cut sides touching, in a line along one side of the sponge.
4. **Carefully roll the sponge** as tightly as possible around the strawberries, so that they are in the center of the roulade log.
5. **Spoon the meringue** into the pastry bag. Pipe it in lines down the length of the log, until it is completely covered. Alternatively, spread the meringue over the log in a slightly uneven layer about ½ in. (1 cm) thick, using a palette knife.

6. **Draw lines through the meringue** with a wet fork, to resemble the bark of a tree. Dust with the confectioners' sugar.
7. **Place in the oven** for 1–2 minutes, until the meringue is firm and light gold. Alternatively, use a kitchen torch to color the meringue.
8. **Let cool,** then carefully transfer the roulade log to a serving plate.

BÛCHE MARRON

CHESTNUT YULE LOG ★★★

Serves
6

Active time: 3 hours

Cooking time: 20 minutes

Freezing time:
At least 2½ hours

Storage: Up to 2 days
in the refrigerator

INGREDIENTS

Chestnut ganache
2 tsp (10 ml) heavy cream
1 oz. (30 g) milk chocolate,
   chopped
1 tsp (5 g) butter
½ oz. (15 g) *crème de
   marrons* (chestnut
   spread, see Chef's
   Notes)
Scant ¼ tsp (1 ml) whisky
1 oz. (30 g) plain
   buttercream (see p. 54),
   at room temperature

Chestnut sponge layer
5 tsp (10 g) almond
   powder
5 tsp (10 g) chestnut flour
¼ tsp (1 g) baking powder
½ egg (5 tsp/25 g), lightly
   beaten
3¾ tsp (15 g) sugar
2 tsp (10 ml) heavy cream
1 tsp (5 g) butter, melted
   and cooled

Crispy praline layer
⅔ oz. (20 g) milk
   chocolate, chopped
2 tsp (10 g) butter
1 oz. (30 g) plain crêpe
   dentelle cookies or crisp
   lace wafers, crushed
1 oz. (25 g) almond-
   hazelnut praline paste

*Mont Blanc chestnut
cream*
Generous 1 tbsp (20 g)
   butter
2¾ oz. (80 g) *pâte de
   marrons* (chestnut
   paste, see Chef's
   Notes)
1 oz. (30 g) *crème de
   marrons* (chestnut
   spread)
1 tsp (5 ml) whisky

Chestnut spread
1¾ oz. (50 g) *pâte de
   marrons* (chestnut
   paste)
⅓ oz. (10 g) *crème de
   marrons* (chestnut
   spread)

To assemble
1 oz. (30 g) Mont Blanc
   chestnut cream
   (see above)
Scant ½ cup (100 ml)
   simple syrup with
   whisky (see p. 91)
1¼ oz. (35 g) candied
   chestnuts, finely
   chopped
12½ oz. (350 g) chestnut
   mousse, Chocolate and
   Chestnut Charlotte
   recipe (see p. 172)

Milk chocolate glaze
1 sheet gelatin
3 tbsp (1¼ oz./35 g) sugar
Scant 2 tbsp (1½ oz./40 g)
   glucose syrup
4 tsp (20 ml) water
1¼ oz. (35 g) milk
   chocolate, chopped
5 tsp (25 g) condensed
   milk

Decoration
2 dark chocolate panels
   (optional, see Chef's
   Notes)
Finely chopped candied
   chestnuts

EQUIPMENT
7- × 8-in. (18- × 20-cm)
   sheet of food-safe
   acetate
Cookie sheet
Electric hand beater
7- × 2¾- × 2¾-in.
   (18- × 7- × 7-cm)
   Yule log mold
Instant-read thermometer
Pastry bag fitted
   with a vermicelli tip

1. **To prepare the ganache**, heat the cream to a simmer in the microwave. Place the chocolate and butter in a mixing bowl and pour over the hot cream. Wait for 2 minutes, then whisk until smooth.

2. **Whisk in** the *crème de marrons* and whisky, followed by the buttercream. Whisk until the ganache is supple and smooth.

3. **Set the acetate sheet** on the cookie sheet. Spread the ganache evenly over the sheet and chill for several minutes to firm it up. Place the sheet in the log mold with the ganache uppermost. Chill until using.

4. **Preheat the oven** to 340°F (170°C/Gas Mark 3).

5. **To prepare the sponge layer**, sift the almond powder, chestnut flour, and baking powder into a bowl.

6. **In a separate bowl**, mix together the egg, sugar, and cream using a balloon whisk. Stir in the flour mixture, then the butter.

7. **Line the cookie sheet** with parchment paper. Spread the batter over it into a rectangle measuring 2½ × 7 in. (6 × 18 cm). Bake for 15 minutes until light gold. Slide the sponge, still on the parchment paper, onto a wire rack. Let cool completely.

8. **To prepare the praline layer**, melt the chocolate and butter in separate bowls in the microwave. In a mixing bowl, stir together the crêpe dentelle cookies and praline paste using a flexible spatula. Add the melted chocolate and stir until the cookies are coated. Stir in the melted butter.

9. **Line the cookie sheet** with fresh parchment paper. Spread the mixture over it into a rectangle measuring 2½ × 7 in. (6 × 18 cm). Freeze for 30 minutes.

10. **To prepare the Mont Blanc chestnut cream**, stir together the butter and *pâte de marrons* in a mixing bowl until smooth. Incorporate the *crème de marrons*, followed by the whisky. Stir until smooth, then chill until using.

11. **To prepare the chestnut spread**, stir together the *pâte de marrons* and *crème de marrons* until smooth.

12. **Weigh out 1 oz. (30 g)** of the Mont Blanc chestnut cream and spread it evenly over the praline layer. Set the sponge over the chestnut cream and brush with the whisky syrup to soak the sponge. Cover with the chestnut spread and sprinkle with the finely chopped candied chestnuts. Freeze until firm.

13. **When ready to assemble the log**, spoon the chestnut mousse into the mold and spread it up the sides using a palette knife. Remove the praline and chestnut layer from the freezer and center it over the mousse with the praline uppermost. The filling should be smooth and flush with the top of the mold. Freeze for at least 2 hours.

14. **To prepare the milk chocolate glaze**, soak the gelatin in a bowl of cold water until softened. In a saucepan, heat the sugar, glucose syrup, and water to 217°F (103°C). Place the chocolate and condensed milk in a bowl, pour over the hot syrup, and whisk until smooth. Squeeze the gelatin to remove excess water and whisk it in until dissolved. Let the glaze cool to 95°F (35°C), stirring so it cools more quickly.

15. **Remove the log** from the freezer and invert it onto a wire rack set over a large dish. Peel away the acetate sheet and pour the glaze over the cake until evenly coated. Let set for 1 minute. Carefully transfer the log to a serving plate. If decorating the ends with chocolate panels, press these in place.

16. **Spoon the remaining Mont Blanc chestnut cream** into the pastry bag fitted with a vermicelli tip and pipe it in tight swirls over the log. Chill until ready to serve.

17. **Sprinkle with finely chopped candied chestnuts** and serve.

Chef's Notes

• *Crème de marrons* (chestnut spread) and *pâte de marrons* (chestnut paste) are available from specialty shops and online.

• To make the chocolate panels, melt 1¾ oz. (50 g) dark couverture chocolate, 70% cacao, in a bowl over a saucepan of barely simmering water (bain-marie). Pour two-thirds of the chocolate onto a marble slab, spreading it back and forth using an offset spatula, until it is cool but not set. Remove the bowl containing the chocolate at 104°F (40°C) from the bain-marie and stir the chocolate from the marble slab into it. Return the bowl to the bain-marie until the temperature of the chocolate reaches 82°F–86°F (28°C–30°C). Keep it at this temperature. Line a cookie sheet with an acetate sheet. Spread the chocolate thinly over the sheet. When it starts to set but is not yet hard, cut into shapes the same size as the ends of the log, using a sharp knife.

BÛCHE SOUS LA NEIGE

SNOW-COVERED YULE LOG★★★

Makes
2 logs, each serving 6

Active time: 4 hours

Drying time: 4 hours

Freezing time: At least
12 hours

Cooking time: 20 minutes

Storage: see Chef's Notes

INGREDIENTS

Marshmallow snow topping
Neutral oil for greasing
3 sheets gelatin,
    180–200 Bloom
Scant 1 cup (6 oz./180 g)
    granulated sugar
¼ cup (60 ml) water
Scant 1 tbsp (20 g)
    glucose syrup
2 egg whites (¼ cup/60 g)
Scant ¼ cup (1½ oz./45 g)
    superfine sugar
Confectioners' sugar,
    for dusting

Chocolate sponge layer
4 egg yolks (scant ⅓ cup/
    80 g)
½ cup (3½ oz./100 g)
    sugar, divided
4 egg whites
    (½ cup/120 g)
¼ cup (1 oz./30 g)
    unsweetened
    cocoa powder, sifted

Chocolate crémeux insert
2¼ oz. (65 g) dark
    couverture chocolate,
    70% cacao, chopped
Generous ⅓ cup (90 ml)
    whole milk
2 tbsp (30 ml) heavy
    cream, well chilled
2 egg yolks (2½ tbsp/40 g)
3¾ tsp (15 g) sugar
½ quantity (3 oz./80 g)
    chocolate syrup,
    Concerto recipe
    (see p. 174)

Crispy praline layer
1 oz. (25 g) dark chocolate,
    70% cacao, chopped
2 tbsp (25 g) butter
1½ oz. (40 g) shortbread
    cookies, crushed
2 oz. (60 g) plain crêpe
    dentelle cookies or crisp
    lace wafers, crushed
⅓ oz. (10 g) caramel
    shards
4 oz. (110 g) almond
    praline paste

Chocolate ganache layer
3½ oz. (100 g) dark
    chocolate, 50% cacao,
    chopped
Scant ½ cup (100 ml)
    heavy cream

Caramel mousse layer
Scant ½ cup (100 ml)
    heavy cream, well
    chilled + 1 tbsp (15 ml)
1½ egg yolks (2 tbsp/30 g)
1½ tbsp (25 g) liquid
    caramel (see p. 47), hot
1½ oz. (40 g) dark
    couverture chocolate,
    70% cacao, chopped

*Milk chocolate mousse
layer*
Generous ¾ cup (200 ml)
    heavy cream, well
    chilled
2 sheets gelatin,
    180 Bloom
8 oz. (220 g) milk
    couverture chocolate,
    chopped
Scant ½ cup (3¼ oz./90 g)
    sugar
2 tbsp (30 ml) water
5 egg yolks (⅓ cup/100 g)

*Chocolate glaze
(make 1 day ahead)*
1 lb. 5 oz. (600 g)
    chocolate glaze
    (see p. 76)

Decoration
Confectioners' sugar,
    for dusting
Chocolate sponge layer
    trimmings
4 dark chocolate panels
    (optional, see Chef's
    Notes)
Small festive decorations
    (optional)

EQUIPMENT
2–3 rimmed baking sheets
    lined with parchment
    paper
Instant-read thermometer
Electric hand beater
14- × 1½- × 1½-in.
    (36- × 4- × 4-cm) small
    Yule log mold
    or Yule log insert
Fine-mesh sieve
2 × 7- × 8-in. (18- × 20-cm)
    sheets of food-safe
    acetate
Immersion blender
2 × 7- × 3- × 2¾-in.
    (18- × 8- × 7-cm)
    Yule log molds

Marshmallow snow topping

1. **Lightly grease the parchment paper** on one of the baking sheets with neutral oil.

2. **Soak the gelatin** in a bowl of cold water until softened.

3. **Combine the granulated sugar and water** in a saucepan over low heat and stir until the sugar has dissolved. Bring to a boil, stir in the glucose syrup, and cook until the syrup reaches 250°F (121°C).

4. **While the syrup is cooking**, whisk the egg whites on high speed until they hold soft peaks. Add the superfine sugar and continue whisking until the peaks are firm.

5. **Reduce the speed to low** and, whisking continuously, very carefully pour in the hot syrup without letting it hit the whisk. Continue whisking on low speed for about 5 minutes until the meringue is firm and glossy and has cooled to room temperature.

6. **Squeeze the gelatin** to remove excess water. Microwave it on full power for about 5 seconds or until melted. Slowly pour into the meringue and whisk on low speed for 20 seconds to incorporate.

7. **Spread the marshmallow mixture** into a rectangle measuring 8 × 16 in. (20 × 40 cm) on a lined baking sheet. Dust with the confectioners' sugar and let dry at room temperature for 4 hours (see Chef's Notes)

Chocolate sponge layer

1. **Preheat the oven** to 340°F (170°C/Gas Mark 3).

2. **Whisk the egg yolks** and half the sugar until pale and thick.

3. **In a separate bowl**, whisk the egg whites until they hold soft peaks. Gradually beat in the remaining sugar and continue whisking until the peaks are firm.

4. **Fold the egg whites** into the yolk mixture a third at a time, then fold in the cocoa powder.

5. **Spread the batter** into a rectangle measuring 4 × 14 in. (10 × 36 cm) on a lined baking sheet. Bake for 17–20 minutes, until springy to the touch.

6. **Slide onto a wire rack**, still on the parchment paper, and let cool.

7. **Remove the parchment paper** and cut the sponge into 2 rectangles measuring 7 × 1½ in. (18 × 4 cm), reserving the trimmings to decorate the log. Chill until using.

Chocolate crémeux insert

1. **Line the mini log mold** with plastic wrap to make unmolding easier.

2. **Place the chocolate** in a mixing bowl.

3. **Bring the milk and cream** to a simmer in a saucepan.

4. **Meanwhile**, whisk the egg yolks and sugar until pale and thick.

5. **Slowly pour** half the hot milk and cream into the yolks, whisking continuously.

6. **Return the mixture to the saucepan** and stir constantly over low heat, using a spatula in a figure-eight motion. Cook until the custard coats the back of the spatula and reaches 181°F (83°C).

7. **Pour through a fine-mesh sieve** into the chocolate and whisk until smooth.

8. **Pour the crémeux** into the mini log mold. Lay the sponge rectangles on top and press them down lightly so they stick to the crémeux. Brush the chocolate syrup over the sponge rectangles.

9. **Freeze for 2 hours**. Remove the insert from the mold, peel off the plastic wrap, and cut in half. Re-wrap and return to the freezer until using.

Crispy praline layer

1. **Melt the chocolate** to 104°F (40°C) in a bowl over a saucepan of barely simmering water (bain-marie).

2. **In another saucepan**, melt the butter until foaming.

3. **Place the crushed cookies**, caramel shards, and praline paste in a mixing bowl and stir until combined. Stir in the melted chocolate, followed by the butter.

4. **Spread the mixture** into 2 rectangles measuring 2½ × 7 in. (6 × 18 cm) on the lined baking sheet. Freeze until using.

Chocolate ganache layer

1. **Place the acetate sheets** on a baking sheet.

2. **Place the chocolate** in a mixing bowl.

3. **Bring the cream to a simmer** in a saucepan. Wait 1 minute, then pour the cream over the chocolate. Wait for another minute, to allow the chocolate to melt, then blend until smooth using the immersion blender.

4. **Spread the ganache** evenly over the acetate sheets. Chill until using.

Caramel mousse layer

1. **Whip the scant ½ cup (100 ml) cream** until it holds its shape. Chill until using.

2. **Whisk the egg yolks** until creamy, then slowly drizzle in the hot caramel. Whisk until cool.

3. **Place the chocolate** in a mixing bowl. Heat the 1 tbsp (15 ml) cream in a microwave, pour it over the chocolate, and whisk until smooth.

4. **Whisk in the yolk mixture**, then gently fold in the whipped cream.

5. **Spread the mousse** over the ganache on the acetate sheets in an even layer. Place into the log molds, with the mousse uppermost. Chill until using.

SNOW-COVERED YULE LOG

(CONTINUED)

Milk chocolate mousse layer

1. **Whip the cream** until it holds its shape. Chill until using.

2. **Soak the gelatin** in a bowl of cold water until softened.

3. **In a bowl over a saucepan** of barely simmering water (bain-marie), melt the chocolate to 104°F (40°C).

4. **Place the sugar and water** in a saucepan over low heat and stir until the sugar dissolves. Increase the heat, bring to a boil, and cook until the syrup reaches 250°F (120°C).

5. **While the syrup cooks,** whisk the egg yolks until creamy. Whisking constantly, very carefully pour the hot syrup into the eggs. Keep the syrup away from the beaters. Continue whisking for 5 minutes to cool slightly.

6. **Squeeze the gelatin** to remove excess water. Microwave it on full power for 5 seconds or until melted. Whisk into the mixture.

7. **Spoon half the mixture** into the melted chocolate, followed by half the whipped cream. Whisk until smooth. Gently fold in the remaining mixture and cream using a flexible spatula.

Assembling the Yule logs

1. **Remove the molds** from the refrigerator. Divide the chocolate mousse between them.

2. **Carefully place** the frozen chocolate crémeux inserts into the mousse, which should now rise nearly to the tops of the molds. Cover with the praline layers so they are flush with the tops of the molds. Smooth over any mousse that overflows.

3. **Cover with plastic wrap.** Freeze for at least 12 hours (see Chef's Notes).

4. **Reheat the chocolate glaze** to 104°F (40°C) in a bowl over a saucepan of barely simmering water (bain-marie). Stir but make sure not to create any air bubbles.

5. **Remove one or both logs** from the freezer. Unmold onto a wire rack.

6. **Peel away the acetate** and pour the glaze over the log(s) to cover completely. Repeat if necessary. Wait 2 minutes to allow excess glaze to drip off. Transfer the log(s) to a serving plate(s).

7. **Lift the marshmallow snow topping** off the parchment paper. Turn it over onto another sheet of parchment paper dusted with confectioners' sugar. Using sharp kitchen scissors, cut the marshmallow into the required shape and size. Place on top of the log and press gently in place.

8. **To make the chocolate crumb decoration,** sift or crumble the reserved chocolate sponge trimmings. Press the crumbs around the base of the log. If decorating the ends with chocolate panels, press these in place. Refrigerate until ready to serve.

9. **Decorate with small festive decorations,** if wished, and dust over confectioners' sugar "snow."

Chef's Notes

• If making ahead and freezing, do so at step 3 of "Assembling the Yule logs." Remove the log(s) from the freezer in the morning if serving that evening, or the night before if serving at lunchtime. Remove the plastic wrap and glaze as soon as the logs are taken out of the freezer, then let thaw completely in the refrigerator. Decorate once the logs have thawed. The marshmallow snow topping can be made the day before serving.

• To make the chocolate panels, melt 3½ oz. (100 g) dark couverture chocolate, 70% cacao, in a bowl over a saucepan of barely simmering water (bain-marie). Pour two-thirds of the chocolate onto a marble slab, spreading it back and forth using an offset spatula, until it is cool but not set. Remove the bowl containing the chocolate at 104°F (40°C) from the bain-marie and stir the chocolate from the marble slab into it. Return the bowl to the bain-marie until the temperature of the chocolate reaches 82°F–86°F (28°C–30°C). Keep it at this temperature. Line a cookie sheet with an acetate sheet. Spread the chocolate thinly over the sheet. When it starts to set but is not yet hard, cut into shapes the same size as the ends of the log, using a sharp knife.

BÛCHE TRADITION

TRADITIONAL YULE LOG★★★

Serves
6

Active time: 2 hours

Cooking time: 20 minutes

Freezing time: At least
1 hour

INGREDIENTS

Coffee sponge layer
2½ tbsp (25 g) AP flour
Scant ¼ cup (1 oz./30 g)
　confectioners' sugar
Scant ⅓ cup (1 oz./30 g)
　almond powder
1 egg (3½ tbsp/50 g)
Scant 1 tsp (1 g) instant
　coffee powder
1 tsp (5 ml) hot water
2 egg whites (¼ cup/60 g)
5 tsp (20 g) granulated
　sugar

Crispy praline layer
2 tbsp (15 g) whole
　hazelnuts, chopped
2 tbsp (15 g) whole
　almonds, chopped
⅓ oz. (10 g) dark
　chocolate, chopped
2 tsp (10 g) butter
½ oz. (15 g) plain crêpe
　dentelle cookies or crisp
　lace wafers, crushed
1 oz. (30 g) almond praline
　paste

Coffee syrup
Generous ¼ cup (65 ml)
　water
¼ cup (1¾ oz./50 g) sugar
2 tbsp (7 g) instant coffee
　powder or 3¾ tsp (7 g)
　strong-flavored ground
　coffee (preferably
　Guatemalan)

Sponge insert
Coffee syrup (see left)
½ quantity (8¾ oz./245 g)
　praline cream, Paris-
　Brest recipe (see p. 210),
　divided
1 oz. (30 g) caramelized
　hazelnuts, Napoleon
　recipe (see p. 200),
　roughly chopped

Chocolate ganache layer
½ quantity (3½ oz./100 g)
　chocolate ganache,
　Snow-Covered Yule Log
　recipe (see p. 164)

To assemble
⅔ quantity (10½ oz./300 g)
　chocolate mousse,
　Concerto recipe
　(see p. 174)

*Chocolate glaze
(make 1 day ahead)*
1 quantity (1 lb. 2 oz./
　500 g) chocolate glaze
　(see p. 76)

Decoration (optional)
Small Swiss meringue
　kisses or other
　decorations, plain or
　dipped in chocolate
　(see p. 32)

EQUIPMENT
Electric hand beater
Rimmed baking sheet lined
　with parchment paper
Fine-mesh sieve,
　if necessary
7- × 8-in (18- × 20-cm)
　sheet of food-safe
　acetate
Cookie sheet
7- × 3- × 2¾-in.
　(18- × 8- × 7-cm)
　Yule log mold
Pastry bag fitted
　with a plain tip

1. **Preheat the oven** to 340°F (170°C/Gas Mark 3).
2. **To prepare the coffee sponge layer,** sift the flour and confectioners' sugar into a mixing bowl. Stir in the almond powder.
3. **Add the egg** and beat with a spoon or spatula for 5 minutes until smooth. Dissolve the coffee in the hot water and stir in.
4. **Whisk the egg whites** until they hold firm peaks, gradually whisking in the granulated sugar. Gently fold into the batter.
5. **Spread the batter** over the lined baking sheet into a rectangle measuring 7 × 9 in. (18 × 23 cm) using an offset spatula.
6. **Bake for 17–20 minutes,** until springy to the touch. Carefully invert the sponge onto a wire rack. Let cool, then remove the parchment paper. Keep the oven switched on to toast the nuts.

7. **To prepare the crispy praline layer,** spread the hazelnuts and almonds over the baking sheet. Toast in the oven for a few minutes until light brown. Remove from the sheet and let cool.
8. **Melt the chocolate and butter** in separate bowls in the microwave. Stir together the crêpe dentelle cookies, praline paste, and nuts in a mixing bowl using a flexible spatula. Stir in the chocolate, then the butter.
9. **Line the baking sheet** with fresh parchment paper. Spread the praline mixture over it into a rectangle measuring 2½ × 7 in. (6 × 18 cm). Place in the freezer until using.
10. **To prepare the coffee syrup,** place the water and sugar in a saucepan over low heat and stir until the sugar dissolves. Increase the heat and bring to a boil. Remove from the heat and stir in the coffee. If using ground coffee, let infuse for a few minutes, then strain. Keep warm.

11. To prepare the sponge insert, cut the coffee sponge into 2 rectangles measuring 7 × 2¾ in. (18 × 7 cm). Brush with the coffee syrup.

12. Spoon 4¼ oz. (120 g) of the praline cream into the pastry bag fitted with a plain tip and set aside in the refrigerator. Spread the rest over the sponge rectangles. Scatter over the hazelnuts. Place one sponge layer on top of the other. Freeze until using.

13. To prepare the ganache, lay the acetate sheet on the cookie sheet. Using an offset spatula, spread half the ganache at a time over the sheet in an even layer. Chill until using.

14. To assemble the log, line the mold with the acetate sheet, with the ganache uppermost, and fill with two-thirds (7 oz./200 g) of the chocolate mousse.

15. Pipe the reserved praline cream in a line down the center, then cover with a little more chocolate mousse.

16. Carefully place the frozen sponge insert on the mousse, cover with the remaining chocolate mousse, and place the crispy praline layer on top: it should be flush with the top of the mold. Smooth over any excess mousse. Freeze for at least 1 hour.

17. Reheat the chocolate glaze to 104°F (40°C) in a bowl over a saucepan of barely simmering water (bain-marie). Stir but make sure not to create any air bubbles.

18. Remove the Yule log from the freezer. Unmold onto a wire rack and peel away the acetate.

19. Pour the glaze over the log to cover completely. Repeat if necessary. Wait 2 minutes to allow excess glaze to drip off. Draw lines in the glaze with a warm fork to resemble bark. Transfer the log to a serving plate and refrigerate until ready to serve.

20. Just before serving, decorate as wished, with small Swiss meringue kisses or other festive decorations.

CASINO ★★

Makes
2 cakes, each serving 6

Active time: 1¾ hours +
making the sponge spirals

Cooking time: 20 minutes

Infusing time: 15 minutes

Freezing time: 4–5 hours +
overnight

Storage: Up to 1 month
in the freezer
(see Chef's Notes)

INGREDIENTS
Sponge spirals
(make 1 day ahead)
1 quantity (4 layers)
    roulade sponge
    (see p. 27)
10½ oz. (300 g) red
    currant jelly (see p. 366)

Mousse
1½ cups (350 ml) heavy
    cream, well chilled
6 sheets gelatin,
    180–200 Bloom
1⅔ cups (400 ml)
    whole milk
1 vanilla bean, slit
    lengthwise
6 egg yolks
    (scant ½ cup/120 g)
Scant ⅔ cup (4¼ oz./
    120 g) sugar
2 tbsp (30 ml) kirsch

To assemble
½ quantity (9¾ oz./275 g)
    ladyfinger sponge
    batter (see p. 24), piped
    into 2 × 5½-in. (14-cm)
    disks and baked
Apricot glaze, warm

For serving
Raspberry coulis
    (see p. 51), well chilled

EQUIPMENT
Rimmed baking sheet
    lined with parchment
    paper
Electric hand beater
Instant-read thermometer
Fine-mesh sieve
2 × 7-in. (18-cm)
    half-sphere molds
    (see Chef's Notes)

---

1. **A day ahead**, prepare the sponge spirals. Place each roulade sponge layer on a sheet of parchment paper. Divide the red currant jelly between them and spread the jelly in an even layer, using an offset spatula.
2. **Roll up each layer** from one short side as tightly as possible, using the parchment paper. Freeze for about 2 hours, until the rolls are firm enough to be sliced easily.
3. **Using a bread knife,** cut the rolls into ¼-in. (5-mm) slices. Lay the slices flat on the baking sheet. Freeze overnight.
4. **The following day**, prepare the mousse. Whip the cream until it holds its shape and chill until using. Soak the gelatin in a bowl of cold water until softened.
5. **Bring the milk to a boil** in a saucepan. Remove from the heat and scrape in the vanilla bean seeds. Add the bean and let infuse for 15 minutes.

6. **Set a large bowl** over another bowl half-filled with ice water. In a third bowl, whisk the egg yolks and sugar until pale and thick.
7. **Remove the vanilla bean** from the milk and slowly pour half of it into the yolk mixture, whisking continuously. Pour the mixture back into the saucepan. Stir over low heat using a spatula in a figure-eight motion until the temperature reaches about 180°F (82°C) and the custard coats the back of the spatula,.
8. **Squeeze the gelatin** to remove excess water, then whisk into the warm custard until melted. Strain through the fine-mesh sieve into the bowl over ice water to halt the cooking process.

9. **Add the kirsch** and whisk until the custard has cooled to 68°F (20°C). Gently fold in the whipped cream a third at a time, using a flexible spatula.

10. **To assemble the cakes,** line the molds with plastic wrap. Cover with the sponge spirals, packing them tightly together. Take care not to leave any gaps between them or the mousse will seep through.

11. **Spoon in the mousse** to within ½ in. (1 cm) of the top of the molds, supporting the molds by setting them on top of a bowl or saucepan to prevent them tipping over. Set a ladyfinger sponge disk over the mousse, with the crust uppermost. Freeze for 2–3 hours until frozen.

12. **Turn the cakes out** of the molds and peel away the plastic wrap. Brush them all over with warm apricot glaze.

13. **Place carefully onto serving plates** and let thaw in the refrigerator until serving. Serve well chilled, with raspberry coulis.

Chef's Notes

• Using half-sphere molds helps the cakes to hold their shape.

• The cakes can be frozen unglazed. The day before serving, remove them from the freezer and brush with the glaze. Transfer to serving plates. Let thaw in the refrigerator until ready to serve.

CHATAIGNERAIE

CHOCOLATE AND CHESTNUT CHARLOTTE ★★

Serves
8

Active time: 45 minutes
+ making the ladyfingers,
ladyfinger disk,
and chocolate glaze

Chilling time: 1½ hours

Cooking time: 30 minutes

Storage: Up to 1 week
in the refrigerator
(unglazed)

INGREDIENTS
Chestnut mousse
1 cup (250 ml) heavy
 cream
1 sheet gelatin 180 Bloom
5 oz. (140 g) chestnut
 paste
1 tbsp (15 ml) whisky
2½ oz. (70 g) chestnut
 spread

To assemble
6¼-in. (16-cm) disk
 of ladyfinger sponge
½ quantity (3 oz./80 g)
 chocolate syrup,
 Concerto recipe
 (see p. 174)
20 ladyfingers, 2 in. (5 cm)
 long (see p. 24)

Glaze (make 1 day ahead)
14 oz. (400 g)
 chocolate glaze
 (see p. 76 and Chef's
 Notes)

Decoration (optional)
Confectioners' sugar,
 for dusting
2 oz. (60 g) candied
 chestnuts, finely
 chopped

EQUIPMENT
7½-in. (19-cm) round cake
 pan, 1½ in. (4 cm) deep
 (preferably a spring-clip
 pan)
Instant-read thermometer

1. **Line the cake pan** with aluminum foil.
2. **To make the chestnut mousse,** whip the cream until it holds soft peaks.
3. **Soak the gelatin** in a bowl of cold water until softened. Squeeze out the gelatin to remove excess water, then microwave in a bowl on high for 5 seconds or until dissolved.
4. **Work the chestnut paste** and whisky together in a mixing bowl. Stir in the chestnut spread and mix until smooth. Stir in the dissolved gelatin. Gently fold in the whipped cream, a third at a time, until incorporated.
5. **Place the disk of ladyfinger sponge** in the bottom of the pan, then soak with the chocolate syrup. Stand the ladyfingers around the sides of the pan so they are touching. Fill the center with the chestnut mousse and smooth it into a slight dome shape using a palette knife. Chill for at least 1 hour, until the mousse has set.

6. **To glaze the charlotte,** heat the chocolate glaze to 104°F (40°C) in a bowl over a saucepan of barely simmering water (bain-marie). Make sure not to create air bubbles when stirring.
7. **Remove the charlotte** from the refrigerator. Carefully unmold it onto a wire rack. Remove the aluminum foil.
8. **Pour the glaze** over the charlotte. Transfer to a serving plate and chill until the glaze has set.
9. **Just before serving,** dust with confectioners' sugar and sprinkle over finely chopped candied chestnuts, if desired.

Chef's Notes
• The chocolate icing on p. 74 can be used instead of chocolate glaze. Spread half the icing over the chilled charlotte, using a palette knife, then chill briefly until set. Repeat with the remaining icing.

CONCERTO ★★★

Serves
10–12

Active time: 2 hours

Chilling time: 30 minutes

Cooking time: 20 minutes

Freezing time: 1 hour

Storage: Up to 2 days
in the refrigerator (glazed)
or 1 month in the freezer
(unglazed)

INGREDIENTS

*Flourless chocolate
sponge layer*
4 egg yolks (scant ⅓ cup/
    80 g)
½ cup (3½ oz./100 g)
    sugar, divided
4 egg whites (½ cup/
    120 g)
¼ cup (1 oz./30 g)
    unsweetened
    cocoa powder, sifted

Chocolate syrup
¼ cup (2 oz./55 g) sugar
⅓ cup (85 ml) water,
    divided
3 tbsp (20 g)
    unsweetened
    cocoa powder

Crispy praline layer
1 oz. (25 g) dark chocolate,
    70% cacao, chopped
2 tbsp (25 g) butter
2 oz. (60 g) plain crêpe
    dentelle cookies or crisp
    lace wafers, crushed
4 oz. (110 g) almond
    praline paste

Dark chocolate mousse
Scant 1 cup (225 ml) heavy
    cream, well chilled
4½ oz. (130 g) dark
    chocolate, 50% cacao,
    chopped
1½ oz. (45 g) dark
    chocolate, 70% cacao,
    chopped
3½ tbsp (50 ml) whole
    milk

Chocolate glaze
1 quantity (1 lb. 2 oz./
    500 g) chocolate glaze
    (see p. 76)

1. **Preheat the oven** to 340°F (170°C/Gas Mark 3).
2. **To prepare the chocolate sponge layer,** whisk the egg yolks with half the sugar on high speed until pale and thick.
3. **Whisk the egg whites** in a separate bowl until they hold firm peaks, gradually whisking in the remaining sugar.
4. **Gently fold the whites** into the yolk mixture a third at a time, then fold in the cocoa powder until just combined.
5. **Spread the batter** into a rectangle measuring 10¼ × 12½ in. (26 × 32 cm) on the baking sheet.
6. **Bake for 17–20 minutes** until springy to the touch. Invert onto a wire rack and let cool. Peel away the parchment paper and cut the sponge into 2 rectangles measuring 6¼ × 10¼ in. (16 × 26 cm). Chill until using.
7. **To prepare the chocolate syrup,** combine the sugar and half the water in a saucepan and stir over low heat until the sugar dissolves. Increase the heat, bring to a boil, and whisk in the cocoa powder until dissolved. Whisk in the remaining water. Let cool and chill until using.

8. **To prepare the crispy praline layer,** line the baking sheet with fresh parchment paper and set the pastry frame on it.
9. **Melt the chocolate** to 104°F (40°C) in a bowl over a saucepan of barely simmering water (bain-marie). In a separate saucepan, melt the butter.
10. **Place the crêpe dentelle cookies** and praline paste in a bowl and stir together with a wooden spoon. Stir in the melted chocolate, followed by the melted butter.
11. **Spread the mixture** in an even layer into the pastry frame. Set one chocolate sponge layer on top, crust side up, and brush with half the chocolate syrup. Set aside.
12. **To prepare the dark chocolate mousse,** whip the cream until it holds its shape. Chill until using.
13. **Melt the 2 chocolates together** to 104°F (40°C) in a bowl over a saucepan of barely simmering water (bain-marie). In a separate saucepan, heat the milk to 140°F (60°C).
14. **Remove the bowl** of melted chocolate from the saucepan. Add the milk and whisk vigorously until smooth and glossy. Whisk in one-third of the whipped cream, then gently fold in the rest using a flexible spatula.

Decoration (optional)
10- × 2½-in. (26- × 6-cm)
    band of chocolate
    sponge
Unsweetened
    cocoa powder
Cacao nibs

To serve
Vanilla custard sauce
    (see p. 86) or a fresh
    fruit coulis (see p. 51
    and Chef's Notes)

EQUIPMENT
Rimmed baking sheet
    lined with parchment
    paper
Electric hand beater
10- × 6-in. (26- × 16-cm)
    rectangular pastry
    frame, 1½ in. (4 cm)
    deep
Instant-read thermometer

15. **Spread half the mousse** over the sponge layer in the frame, then place the second layer on top. Brush with the remaining chocolate syrup. Spoon over the remaining mousse, smoothing it evenly so it is flush with the sides of the frame. Chill for 30 minutes.
16. **Run a warm knife** around the inside of the frame and lift it off. Freeze for at least 1 hour before glazing.
17. **Heat the chocolate glaze** to 104°F (40°C) in a bowl over a saucepan of barely simmering water (bain-marie). Make sure not to create air bubbles when stirring.
18. **Set the well-chilled cake on a rack.** Pour the glaze over it to cover the top and sides (or just the top, if preferred). Let any excess drip off, then transfer the cake to a serving plate. If desired, decorate with a band of chocolate sponge, dusted with cocoa powder, and a few cacao nibs. Chill until ready to serve.
19. **Serve with vanilla custard sauce** or a fresh fruit coulis.

Chef's Notes
• Red berries, like raspberries, pair particularly well with this chocolate cake.
• This is a challenging cake to make, but is a veritable Lenôtre classic.

CONCORDE ★★★

Serves
10

Active time: 40 minutes

Cooking time: 1 hour

Chilling time: 3 hours

Storage: Up to 24 hours
in the refrigerator

INGREDIENTS

Chocolate meringue
5 tbsp (1¼ oz./35 g)
  unsweetened
  cocoa powder
Generous 1 cup
  (5¼ oz./150 g)
  confectioners' sugar
5 egg whites
  (⅔ cup/150 g)
¾ cup (5 oz./150 g)
  granulated sugar,
  divided

Chocolate mousse
6 oz. (170 g) dark
  chocolate, 70% cacao,
  chopped
4 egg whites (scant ⅔ cup/
  140 g)
2 tbsp (25 g) sugar
7 tbsp (3½ oz./100 g)
  butter, diced
3 egg yolks
  (scant ¼ cup/55 g)

Decoration
Confectioners' sugar,
  for dusting
Unsweetened
  cocoa powder,
  for dusting

EQUIPMENT
2 rimmed baking sheets
Stand mixer fitted
  with the whisk
Pastry bag fitted with
  a coupler + ½-in. (1-cm)
  and ⅛-in. (3-mm)
  plain tips
Oval-shaped cardboard
  base, measuring
  5½ × 10 in. (14 × 26 cm)

---

1. **Preheat the oven** to 300°F (150°C/Gas Mark 2).
2. **Using a pencil**, draw 3 ovals, each measuring approximately 5½ × 10 in. (14 × 26 cm), on 2 sheets of parchment paper. Place them on the baking sheets with the pencil marks underneath.
3. **To prepare the chocolate meringue**, sift the cocoa powder and confectioners' sugar into a bowl.
4. **Whisk the egg whites** on high speed until they hold soft peaks. Add about 2 tbsp (20 g) of the granulated sugar and continue whisking until the peaks are firm (about 5 minutes in total). Whisk in the remaining granulated sugar on low speed.
5. **Gently fold in** the cocoa powder and confectioners' sugar until just combined.
6. **Spoon the meringue** into the pastry bag with a ½-in. (1-cm) tip. Stick the parchment paper to the baking sheets with a dab of meringue in each corner.
7. **Pipe the meringue** in a spiral to fill the ovals, starting at the outer edge and working inward toward the center. Switch to the ⅛-in. (3-mm) tip and pipe the remaining meringue in long thin sticks on the rest of the parchment paper, ensuring they are spaced apart and do not touch.
8. **Bake for about 1 hour**, until dry and crisp but not browned. If the meringue has begun to color after 15 minutes, lower the oven temperature and rotate the baking sheets as needed. The sticks will be ready before the ovals, so watch them closely and remove them with a palette knife when they are done.

When ready, the meringue will detach easily from the parchment paper. If the bases stick, return them to the oven and continue baking. Cool the meringue on a wire rack.

9. **Prepare the chocolate mousse** using the ingredients listed above and following the instructions on p. 82.
10. **Set one meringue oval** on the cardboard base and spread with a layer of mousse, using the palette knife. Place a second oval on top, then spread with another layer of mousse. Place the final oval on top, with the underside uppermost, and press down gently to make it flat. Spread the remaining mousse over the top and sides to coat in a thin, even layer.
11. **Cut the meringue sticks** into short lengths. Arrange them over the top and sides of the cake (see photograph on facing page). Chill for at least 1 hour.
12. **When ready to serve**, sift the confectioners' sugar and cocoa powder over the cake.

Chef's Notes
• The meringue ovals and sticks can be made in advance, if wished. They can be stored in an airtight container for up to 2 weeks.
• This dessert was created by Gaston Lenôtre in the 1970s as a tribute to the legendary Concorde airplane.

ENTREMETS PIGNONS

PINE NUT MOUSSE CAKE***

Makes
2 cakes, each serving
10–12

Active time: 1½ hours +
1 hour the previous day

Cooking time: 20 minutes

Drying time: 24 hours
(optional)

Infusing time: 15 minutes

Freezing time: 2½ hours

Storage: Up to 3 months
in the freezer

INGREDIENTS

*Pine nut and hazelnut
praline paste
(make 1 day ahead)*
¾ cup (3½ oz./100 g)
    pine nuts
¾ cup (3½ oz./100 g)
    whole hazelnuts
⅔ cup (4½ oz./125 g)
    sugar
2½ tbsp (40 ml) water
¼ teaspoon (1 g) fine salt

*Hazelnut streusel
(make 1 day ahead)*
6 tbsp (3 oz./90 g) butter
⅔ cup (3 oz./85 g)
    confectioners' sugar
⅔ cup (2¼ oz./65 g)
    hazelnut powder
Scant ¼ cup (20 g)
    almond powder
½ tsp (2 g) *fleur de sel*
½ cup (2¼ oz./65 g) AP
    flour
2 tbsp (15 g) unsweetened
    cocoa powder

*Chocolate sponge layer
(make 1 day ahead)*
⅓ cup (1¾ oz./50 g) whole
    hazelnuts
2 tbsp (15 g) whole
    almonds
½ cup (2¼ oz./65 g)
    confectioners' sugar
8 egg yolks (scant ⅔ cup/
    160 g)
¾ cup (4 oz./115 g) dark
    brown sugar, divided
⅔ cup + 1 tbsp (3 oz./90 g)
    AP flour
2 tbsp (15 g) unsweetened
    cocoa powder
5 tbsp (2½ oz./70 g)
    butter
6 egg whites (¾ cup/
    180 g)

Crispy praline layer
4 oz. (110 g) dark
    chocolate, 70% cacao,
    chopped
10½ oz. (300 g) hazelnut
    streusel (see left)
1½ oz. (45 g) plain crêpe
    dentelle cookies or crisp
    lace wafers, crushed
Scant ⅔ cup (3 oz./85 g)
    pine nuts
11½ oz. (325 g) pine nut
    and hazelnut praline
    paste (see left)

Chocolate syrup
1 quantity (5¾ oz./160 g)
    chocolate syrup,
    Concerto recipe
    (see p. 174)

Chocolate crémeux
9½ oz. (270 g) dark
    chocolate, 65% cacao
    (preferably Madirofolo),
    chopped
1½ cups (375 ml) whole
    milk
½ cup (125 ml) heavy
    cream
7 egg yolks
    (½ cup/140 g)
¼ cup (1¾ oz./50 g) dark
    brown sugar

Chocolate mousse
2 sheets gelatin,
    180–200 Bloom
2 cups + 3 tbsp (540 ml)
    whipping cream
11 oz. (320 g) dark
    chocolate, 65% cacao
    (preferably Madirofolo),
    chopped
½ cup (125 ml) whole milk
Scant ½ cup (110 ml)
    heavy cream
¼ oz. (8 g) Bourbon
    Madagascar
    vanilla bean, split
    lengthwise
5 egg yolks
    (scant ½ cup/110 g)
3 tbsp (2 oz./60 g) honey

Decoration
Unsweetened
    cocoa powder,
    for dusting
Chocolate decorations
    (optional; see p. 69)

To serve
Vanilla custard sauce
    (see p. 86) or chocolate
    sauce (see p. 90)

EQUIPMENT
2 rimmed baking sheets
Fine-mesh sieve
Instant-read thermometer
Food processor
Stand mixer with paddle
    beater and whisk
14½- × 10½-in. (37- × 27-cm)
    rectangular pastry
    frame, 1½ in. (4 cm)
    deep
14½- × 10½- × 1½- in.
    (37- × 27- × 4-cm) sheet
    of food-safe acetate

Pine nut and hazelnut praline paste (1 day ahead)

1. **Preheat the oven** to 300°F (150°C/Gas Mark 2).
2. **Spread the pine nuts and hazelnuts** over 2 separate unlined baking sheets. Toast for about 15–20 minutes, until lightly browned and fragrant. Keep a close eye on the pine nuts, as they will color more quickly.
3. **Remove from the baking sheets.** Rub the hazelnuts in a dish cloth or against a fine-mesh sieve to remove the skins.
4. **Combine the sugar, water, and salt** in a large saucepan. Heat until the sugar and salt dissolve. Increase the heat, bring to a boil, and boil until the syrup reaches 243°F (117°C). Remove from the heat.
5. **Add the hazelnuts** and stir slowly with a wooden spoon for 30 seconds, until the sugar has a sandy texture. Place over medium heat for 5 minutes, scraping the bottom of the pan, until the sugar has dissolved again. Stir in the pine nuts.
6. **Spread the nut mixture** over a baking sheet lined with parchment paper. Separate the nuts to avoid clumps and let cool for at least 1 hour. If possible, let rest for 24 hours, to dry out completely.
7. **Break apart into small pieces.** Process to a smooth paste in the food processor. This will take time: the nut mixture will be coarse at first, but the longer it is processed, the smoother it will become. Chill in an airtight container until using.

Hazelnut streusel (1 day ahead)

1. **Fit the stand mixer** with the paddle beater. Beat the butter until softened.
2. **Add the confectioners' sugar**, nut powders, and *fleur de sel*. Sift in the AP flour and cocoa powder. Beat briefly to combine.
3. **Line a baking sheet** with parchment paper and spread the mixture over it. Chill for 1 hour.
4. **Preheat the oven** to 325°F (160°C/Gas Mark 3). Bake the streusel mixture for 20 minutes. Let cool completely. Break into small pieces and store in an airtight container until using.

Chocolate sponge layer (1 day ahead)

1. **Preheat the oven** to 350°F (180°C/Gas Mark 4). Line a baking sheet with parchment paper.
2. **Process the hazelnuts**, almonds, and confectioners' sugar in the food processor until finely ground.
3. **Fit the stand mixer** with the whisk. Whisk the egg yolks and 3½ tbsp (1½ oz./45 g) of the brown sugar on high speed, until the mixture is thick, creamy, and falls from the whisk in thick ribbons.

→

PINE NUT MOUSSE CAKE

(CONTINUED)

4. **Add the ground nut mixture**, flour, and cocoa. Fold together until combined.

5. **Melt the butter** to 113°F (45°C), then fold it into the mixture. Transfer to another bowl.

6. **Wash and dry the mixer bowl and whisk.** Whisk the egg whites until they hold soft peaks. Gradually whisk in the remaining brown sugar until firm peaks form. Fold the yolk mixture into the whites a third at a time.

7. **Spread the batter** over the baking sheet into a rectangle the same size as the pastry frame. Bake for 15 minutes, until springy to the touch. Turn out onto a wire rack and let cool, then remove the parchment paper. Cover with plastic wrap and store at room temperature until using.

Crispy praline layer

1. **Line a baking sheet** with fresh parchment paper and set the pastry frame on it.

2. **Melt the chocolate** in a bowl over a saucepan of barely simmering water (bain-marie) to 104°F (40°C).

3. **Combine the hazelnut streusel**, crêpe dentelle cookies, and pine nuts in a mixing bowl. Stir in the praline paste, then the melted chocolate.

4. **Spread the praline mixture** into the pastry frame in an even layer. Set the chocolate sponge on top, crust side up, and brush with the chocolate syrup. Refrigerate until using.

Chocolate crémeux

1. **Place the chocolate** in a bowl. Bring the milk and cream to a boil in a saucepan.

2. **Whisk together** the egg yolks and brown sugar until pale and thick. Slowly pour one-quarter of the hot milk and cream into the yolks, whisking constantly.

3. **Pour back** into the saucepan. Stir constantly over low heat using a spatula in a figure-eight motion, until the custard coats the back of the spatula and reaches 185°F (85°C).

4. **Pour over the chocolate**, wait 2 minutes, then whisk until smooth. Let cool to 140°F (60°C); it can be set over a bowl of ice water to speed up the process.

5. **Weigh out** 7 oz. (200 g) of the crémeux and set it aside in the refrigerator. Spread the rest over the chocolate sponge in the pastry frame. Return the cake to the refrigerator.

Chocolate mousse

1. **Soak the gelatin** in a bowl of cold water until softened.

2. **Whip the whipping cream** until it holds its shape. Refrigerate until using.

3. **Place the chocolate** in a bowl. Bring the milk and heavy cream to a boil with the vanilla bean. Remove from the heat, cover, and let infuse for 15 minutes.

4. **In a separate bowl**, whisk the egg yolks and honey until pale and thick.

5. **Remove the vanilla bean** from the infused milk and scrape in any remaining seeds. Slowly pour one-quarter into the yolks, whisking constantly. Return to the saucepan and cook over low heat. Stir constantly until the custard coats the back of the spatula and reaches 185°F (85°C).

6. **Squeeze the gelatin** to remove excess water, then stir into the custard until melted. Pour over the chocolate, whisking until smooth. Let cool to 95°F (35°C), whisking regularly.

7. **Gently fold in** the chilled whipped cream a third at a time. Pour the mousse over the chocolate crémeux in the frame and smooth it flush with the sides. Freeze for 30 minutes.

8. **Run a knife** around the inside of the frame, and lift it off. Return to the freezer for at least 1½ hours.

Finishing the cake

1. **Spread the reserved chocolate crémeux** over the acetate sheet in an even layer. Let set for 10 minutes in the refrigerator.

2. **Place the crémeux** on the cake, with the acetate sheet uppermost. Freeze for 30 minutes.

3. **Carefully peel off** the acetate sheet. Cut the cake in half, or into the desired size, place on a serving plate, and refrigerate until ready to serve.

4. **Just before serving**, dust with cocoa powder and top with chocolate decorations, if wished. Serve with vanilla custard sauce or chocolate sauce.

FEUILLE D'AUTOMNE

AUTUMN LEAF CAKE ★★★

Serves
8

Active time: 1 hour +
making the meringue
bases

Freezing time: At least
2 hours

Chilling time: 1 hour

Storage: Up to 24 hours
in the refrigerator

INGREDIENTS
Meringue layers
5¼ oz. (150 g) dark
  chocolate, 70% cacao
2 tbsp (30 ml) grape-seed
  oil
3 × 7-in. (18-cm) round
  French meringue bases
  (see p. 33)

To assemble
2 quantities (1½ lb./680 g)
  chocolate mousse
  (see p. 82)

Chocolate collar and fans
5¼ oz. (150 g) dark
  couverture chocolate,
  70% cacao

To serve
Confectioners' sugar,
  for dusting

EQUIPMENT
8¼-in. (21-cm) baking ring,
  2½ in. (6 cm) deep
8¼-in. (21-cm) round
  cardboard cake board
Food-safe acetate
Rimmed stainless steel
  baking sheet
Instant-read thermometer
Paint roller or offset
  spatula
Scraper with a 4-in.
  (10-cm) blade

1. **To prepare the meringue layers,** melt the chocolate in a bowl over a saucepan of barely simmering water (bain-marie). Stir in the grape-seed oil.
2. **Brush over** the meringue bases so they are completely coated to prevent them becoming soft. Chill until the chocolate has set.
3. **To assemble the cake,** set the baking ring on the cardboard cake board. Line the inside of the ring with a strip of acetate. Place one of the meringue bases in the center of the ring.
4. **Fill the space** between the meringue and the ring with mousse, then completely cover the base with about one-third of the remaining mousse. Spread it in an even layer. Repeat with the other meringue bases, finishing with a layer of mousse.
5. **Smooth the mousse** flush with the top of the ring using a palette knife. Freeze the cake for 2 hours.
6. **To prepare the chocolate collar and fans,** heat the baking sheet in the oven to 122°F (50°C).

7. **In a bowl over a saucepan** of barely simmering water (bain-marie), or in the microwave, melt the chocolate to 104°F (40°C), until glossy and smooth. Pour onto the warm baking sheet and spread in an even layer using the paint roller or an offset spatula. Chill for 1 hour.
8. **Remove from the refrigerator** and let come to room temperature, until the chocolate is firm but not set hard: it should be malleable and easy to scratch with a fingernail.
9. **Using a large chef's knife,** cut out a band with a width of 2¾ in. (7 cm) and the same length as the circumference of the cake.
10. **Remove the cake** from the freezer and run a hot, damp sponge around the outside of the baking ring to loosen it. Rotate it slightly and carefully lift off the ring.
11. **Wrap the chocolate collar** around the cake, folding the excess over the top. Hide the join at the back.
12. **Use the rest of the chocolate** to make fans (see p. 69).
13. **Arrange the fans** in concentric circles over the top of the cake. Dust with confectioners' sugar just before serving.

FORÊT NOIRE

BLACK FOREST GÂTEAU ★★★

Serves
8

Active time: 45 minutes

Cooking time: 30 minutes

Chilling time: At least
1 hour

INGREDIENTS

Chocolate genoise sponge
Butter and AP flour for
the pan
3 eggs (⅔ cup/150 g)
Scant ½ cup (3 oz./80 g)
sugar
½ cup (2 oz./60 g) AP flour
1½ tbsp (10 g)
unsweetened
cocoa powder
1 tsp (3 g) baking powder
2 tbsp (20 g) cornstarch
1 tbsp (20 g) clarified
butter, melted
and cooled

To assemble
Generous ¾ cup (200 ml)
simple syrup with kirsch
or Cointreau (see p. 91),
cooled
1 quantity (11½ oz./325 g)
chocolate Chantilly
cream (see p. 193)
7 oz. (200 g) Morello
cherries, halved
and pitted

Chocolate collar
5¼ oz. (150 g) dark
couverture chocolate,
70% cacao

Decoration
7 oz. (200 g) Chantilly
cream (see p. 50)
2¾ oz. (80 g) marzipan
(see p. 63)
6 cherry stems
½ quantity (2¼ oz./65 g)
raspberry glaze
(see p. 80)
Milk chocolate, for shaving
Confectioners' sugar,
for dusting
Chocolate shapes

EQUIPMENT
8-in. (20-cm) round cake
pan, 2 in. (5 cm) deep
8-in. (20-cm) baking ring,
2 in. (5 cm) deep
Pastry bag fitted with
a ¾-in. (2-cm) plain tip

1. **Preheat the oven** to 350°F (180°C/Gas Mark 4). Grease the cake pan with butter and dust with flour.
2. **To prepare the chocolate genoise sponge,** make the genoise batter following the instructions on p. 30. Sift the flour, cocoa powder, baking powder, and cornstarch together and gently fold them into the whisked egg and sugar mixture. Fold in the clarified butter.
3. **Pour the batter** into the pan. Bake for 30 minutes, until springy to the touch. Let cool slightly in the pan, then turn out onto a wire rack while still warm to cool completely.
4. **To assemble the gâteau,** cut the genoise crosswise into 3 equal layers, using a bread knife. Place the bottom layer in the baking ring, crust side down, and brush with one-third of the simple syrup. Cover with one-third of the chocolate Chantilly cream and scatter over half the cherries.
5. **Place the middle genoise layer** on top and brush with syrup. Cover with another layer of chocolate cream and the remaining cherries.
6. **Add the final genoise layer,** crust side up. Brush with the remaining syrup, add the remaining chocolate Chantilly cream, and smooth with a palette knife. Chill for 1 hour.

7. **To make the chocolate collar,** prepare the chocolate as indicated in the Autumn Leaf Cake recipe (see p. 184). Once it has come to room temperature on the baking sheet, cut out a band with a width of 2½ in. (6–7 cm) and the same length as the circumference of the cake.
8. **Run a hot, damp sponge** around the outside of the baking ring to loosen it. Rotate it slightly and carefully lift off the ring. Wrap the chocolate collar around the cake, making sure the two ends meet. Hide the join at the back.
9. **Using the pastry bag,** pipe mounds of Chantilly cream over the top of the cake to cover it. Keep chilled.
10. **Shape the marzipan** into 6 cherry-size balls and push the cherry stems into them. Freeze on a plate lined with plastic wrap for at least 30 minutes.
11. **Heat the raspberry glaze.** Dip the frozen marzipan cherries in the warm glaze until they are coated. Place on paper towel to drain and let cool.
12. **Shave the milk chocolate** into curls using a vegetable peeler.
13. **Remove the cake** from the refrigerator. Scatter the chocolate curls over it, then lightly dust with confectioners' sugar. Decorate with chocolate shapes and arrange the marzipan cherries on top. Serve immediately.

GÂTEAU DE COLETTE

COLETTE'S GÂTEAU ★★

Serves
6

Active time: 1 hour +
making the pastry cream

Cooking time: 20 minutes

INGREDIENTS

Almond-hazelnut dacquoise
3 egg whites
  (6½ tbsp/90 g)
3½ tbsp (1½ oz./40 g)
  sugar
½ cup + 1 tsp (2 oz./55 g)
  hazelnut powder
½ cup + 1 tsp (2 oz./55 g)
  almond powder
1 cup minus 2 tbsp
  (4 oz./110 g)
  confectioners' sugar
1 tbsp (10 g) AP flour

Mousseline cream
⅛ Bourbon Madagascar
  vanilla bean, split
  lengthwise
3½ oz. (100 g) pastry
  cream (see p. 66)
1½ tsp (8 ml) raspberry
  brandy
5¼ oz. (150 g)
  plain buttercream
  (see p. 54), at room
  temperature
1 tsp (5 g) butter, melted
  and cooled

To assemble
¾ lb. (350 g) fresh
  raspberries, washed
  and dried
1 quantity (11½ oz./325 g)
  raspberry coulis
  (see p. 51), divided
1 oz. (25 g) pink almond
  candy (*dragées*),
  roughly chopped
Confectioners' sugar,
  for dusting

EQUIPMENT
Stand mixer fitted
  with the whisk
Cookie sheet lined
  with parchment paper
2 pastry bags, each fitted
  with a ½-in. (1-cm)
  plain tip

1. **Preheat the oven** to 350°F (180°C/Gas Mark 4).
2. **To prepare the almond-hazelnut dacquoise,** whisk the egg whites on high speed until firm peaks form. Gradually whisk in the sugar when the whites start to thicken.
3. **Combine the hazelnut powder,** almond powder, confectioners' sugar, and AP flour. Using a flexible spatula, gently fold them into the meringue a third at a time, until thoroughly combined.
4. **Spread the batter** onto the cookie sheet, into 3 × 6-in. (15-cm) squares, ½ in. (1 cm) thick. Bake for about 20 minutes until dry and crisp. Slide the dacquoise, still on the parchment paper, onto a wire rack. Let cool completely.
5. **To prepare the mousseline cream,** scrape the vanilla bean seeds into the pastry cream and add the raspberry brandy. Whisk until smooth. Add the buttercream and melted butter and whisk again until smooth. Transfer to the pastry bag and keep chilled until using.

6. **To assemble the gâteau,** arrange the raspberries upside down around the edge of 2 of the dacquoise squares, then in equally spaced rows (see photograph on facing page).
7. **Pipe the mousseline cream** between the lines of raspberries, using half the cream on each square.
8. **Weigh out 1¾ oz.** (50 g) of the coulis and transfer it to the second pastry bag. Chill the remaining coulis for serving. Pipe dots of the coulis over the mousseline cream.
9. **Scatter over** the chopped almond candy and carefully place one dacquoise layer on top of the other. Place the third layer on top.
10. **Dust with confectioners' sugar,** decorate with raspberries, and serve with the reserved raspberry coulis.

L'ÉTOILE

ÉTOILE ★★

Serves
6

Active time: 1 hour

Freezing time: At least
1 hour

Cooking time: 20 minutes

INGREDIENTS

Chocolate sponge layer
1½ tbsp (12 g) AP flour
1 tbsp + 1 scant tsp (12 g)
   cornstarch
1 tsp (2 g) unsweetened
   cocoa powder
1 egg yolk (1½ tbsp/20 g)
1 egg white (2 tbsp/30 g)
2½ tbsp (1 oz./30 g) sugar,
   divided

Rum syrup
2½ tbsp (1 oz./30 g) sugar
2 tbsp + 1 tsp (35 ml)
   water
1 tbsp (15 ml) aged dark
   rum

Filling
(prepare just before use)
1 quantity (14 oz./400 g)
   chocolate Chantilly
   cream for the Étoile
   (see p. 192)

Chocolate ganache
1 oz. (25 g) dark chocolate,
   50% cacao, chopped
1 oz. (25 g) dark chocolate,
   70% cacao, chopped
1 tbsp (15 g) butter
2 tbsp + 1 tsp (35 ml)
   whole milk
1 oz. (30 g) plain
   buttercream (see p. 54),
   at room temperature

Decoration
1¾ oz. (50 g) cacao nibs
1½ tbsp (10 g)
   unsweetened
   cocoa powder

EQUIPMENT
Rimmed baking sheet
Electric hand beater
Pastry bag fitted with
   a ½-in. (1-cm) plain tip
9-in. (22-cm) round
   cardboard cake board
9-in. (22-cm) baking ring,
   1¼ in. (3 cm) deep

---

1. Preheat the oven to 350°F (180°C/Gas Mark 4).
2. To prepare the chocolate sponge layer, draw an 8-in.
(20-cm) circle on a sheet of parchment paper, using
a pencil. Set it on the baking sheet with the pencil
marks underneath.
3. Sift the flour, cornstarch, and cocoa powder together.
Whisk the egg yolk with half the sugar until pale
and thick. Gently fold in the dry ingredients.
4. Whisk together the egg white and remaining sugar
until firm peaks form. Gently fold into the yolk mixture
until thoroughly combined.
5. Transfer the batter to the pastry bag. Pipe it in a spiral
to fill the marked circle, starting in the center and
piping outward.
6. Bake for 20 minutes, until risen and springy
to the touch. Slide the sponge, still on the parchment
paper, onto a wire rack. Let cool completely, then
remove from the parchment paper.
7. To prepare the rum syrup, combine the sugar
and water in a saucepan over low heat and stir until
the sugar dissolves. Increase the heat and bring to a boil.
Let cool, then stir in the rum.
8. To assemble the cake, place the cardboard cake board
and baking ring on a serving plate. Place the sponge
layer inside the ring and brush with the rum syrup
to soak.

9. Spread the chocolate Chantilly cream over
the sponge using a palette knife. Smooth the cream
so it is flush with the top of the ring. Freeze for at least
1 hour.
10. To prepare the chocolate ganache, place
both chocolates and the butter in a bowl. Bring
the milk to a simmer and pour over the chocolate.
Wait 2 minutes, then whisk until smooth. Whisk
in the buttercream.
11. Preheat the oven to 325°F (160°C/Gas Mark 3).
Spread the cacao nibs over the baking sheet and toast
in the oven for 10 minutes, until fragrant. Remove
from the sheet and let cool. Roughly chop in the food
processor. Set aside until using.
12. Remove the cake from the freezer. Run a hot, damp
sponge around the outside of the ring to loosen it.
Rotate the ring slightly and carefully lift it off.
13. Whisk the ganache until it is smooth enough
to spread. Using a palette knife, cover the top and sides
of the cake with a thin, even layer of ganache.
14. Generously dust the cake with cocoa powder.
Gently press the roughly chopped cacao nibs around
the sides with your hand. Using a knife, mark lines on
top of the cake from the center to the edge, to resemble
the roads that radiate out from the Arc de Triomphe
on Paris's famous Place de l'Étoile.

CHANTILLY CHOCOLAT POUR L'ÉTOILE

CHOCOLATE CHANTILLY CREAM FOR THE ÉTOILE *

Makes
14 oz. (400 g)

Active time: 15 minutes

Storage: Up to 24 hours
in the refrigerator, covered

INGREDIENTS
Generous ¾ cup (200 ml)
heavy cream,
well chilled
4¼ oz. (120 g) dark
chocolate, 50% cacao,
chopped
1½ oz. (40 g) dark
chocolate, 70% cacao,
chopped
3½ tbsp (50 ml)
whole milk

EQUIPMENT
Stand mixer fitted
with the whisk
Instant-read thermometer

1. **Place the cream** in the bowl of the stand mixer
and chill for at least 1 hour. Chill the whisk at the same
time (see Chef's Notes).
2. **Whip the cream** on medium speed until it starts
to thicken, increase the speed to high, and continue
whipping until the cream holds its shape (about
4 minutes in total). Take care not to overwhip the cream
or it will separate.
3. **Melt both chocolates** in a bowl over a saucepan
of barely simmering water (bain-marie) to 104°F
(40°C).
4. **In another saucepan**, heat the milk to 140°F (60°C).
5. **Take the chocolate off** the bain-marie. Pour the hot
milk over the chocolate, whisking until smooth
and shiny.
6. **Whisk one-third of the whipped cream**
into the chocolate mixture to loosen it, then gently fold
in the rest. Take care not to deflate the cream.
7. **Use immediately**, as indicated in the Étoile cake
recipe (see p. 190).

Chef's Notes
• For best results, the cream, bowl, and whisk must
be very cold, to avoid overwhipping.

CHANTILLY CHOCOLAT

CHOCOLATE CHANTILLY CREAM *

Makes
about 11½ oz. (325 g)

Active time: 15 minutes

Storage: Up to 24 hours
in the refrigerator, covered

INGREDIENTS
Scant 1 cup (225 ml) heavy
    cream, well chilled
1 tsp (4 g) vanilla sugar
3½ oz. (100 g) dark
    chocolate, at least 70%
    cacao, chopped

EQUIPMENT
Stand mixer fitted
    with the whisk
Instant-read thermometer

---

1. **Place the cream and vanilla sugar** in the bowl
of the stand mixer and chill for at least 1 hour.
Chill the whisk at the same time (see Chef's Notes).
2. **Whip the cream** on medium speed until it starts
to thicken, increase the speed to high, and continue
whipping until the cream holds its shape (about
4 minutes in total). Take care not to overwhip the cream
or it will separate.
3. **Melt the chocolate** in a bowl over a saucepan
of barely simmering water (bain-marie). Let cool to
at least 77°F (25°C).
4. **Whisk one-third of the whipped cream**
into the chocolate to loosen it, then gently fold
in the rest. Take care not to deflate the cream.

Chef's Notes
• For best results, the cream, bowl, and whisk must be
very cold, to avoid overwhipping.

MARLY AUX FRAMBOISES

RASPBERRY MARLY ★★★

Serves
4

Active time: 1 hour +
making the pastry cream
and ladyfinger layers

Cooking time: 12 minutes

Chilling time: At least
1 hour

Freezing time: 30 minutes

INGREDIENTS

Raspberry syrup
1½ tbsp (25 ml) simple
syrup (see p. 91)
2 tsp (10 ml) water
1 tsp (5 ml) raspberry brandy
⅓ oz. (10 g) unsweetened
raspberry puree

Mousseline cream
¼ Bourbon Madagascar
vanilla bean, split
lengthwise
3½ oz. (100 g) pastry
cream (see p. 66)
1½ tsp (8 ml) raspberry
brandy
5¼ oz. (150 g)
plain buttercream
(see p. 54), at room
temperature
1 tsp (5 g) butter,
melted and cooled

To assemble
Confectioners' sugar,
for dusting
2 × 4½-in. (12-cm) round
ladyfinger layers,
½ in. (1 cm) thick, made
using ½ quantity
(9¾ oz./275 g)
ladyfinger sponge
batter (see p. 24)
2½ oz. (70 g) fresh
raspberries, washed
and dried
½ quantity (5¾ oz./160 g)
raspberry coulis
(see p. 51)
1¾ oz. (50 g) marzipan
(see p. 63)

Decoration
Edible pink velvet spray
Fresh raspberries
Raspberry glaze
(see p. 80)

EQUIPMENT
Electric hand beater
Pastry bag fitted with
a ½-in. (1-cm) plain tip
2 rimmed baking sheets
5-in. (13-cm) round baking
ring, 1½ in. (4 cm) deep
Embossed rolling pin
Pastry bag or paper
piping cone

1. **To prepare the raspberry syrup,** whisk together
the simple syrup, water, and raspberry brandy.
Pour over the raspberry puree, then whisk to combine.
Keep chilled.
2. **To prepare the mousseline cream,** scrape the seeds
of the vanilla bean into the pastry cream and add
the raspberry brandy. Whisk until smooth. Whisk in
the buttercream and melted butter until smooth. Transfer
to the pastry bag and set aside at room temperature.
3. **To assemble the cake,** line one baking sheet with
parchment paper and set the baking ring on it. Dust
the parchment paper inside the ring with confectioners'
sugar. Center one ladyfinger disk inside, with the crust side
down. Brush with half the raspberry syrup.
4. **Pipe a rope of mousseline cream** between the
ladyfinger layer and the ring. Spread the cream up
the sides of the ring using a small palette knife.
Cover the ladyfinger sponge with a thin layer of cream.
5. **Arrange the raspberries** close together over
the cream, standing them upright. Weigh out about
1 oz. (25 g) of the raspberry coulis and drizzle it
between the raspberries. Chill the remaining coulis.
6. **Cover the berries** with a second layer of mousseline
cream. Place the second ladyfinger disk on top.

Brush with the remaining syrup, then cover with
the remaining cream. Smooth the cream with a palette
knife so it is flush with the top of the ring. Chill for
at least 1 hour.
7. **Roll the marzipan** on a surface dusted with
confectioners' sugar into a strip slightly larger than
1½ × 16½ in. (4 × 42 cm). Imprint a design on
the marzipan by running the embossed rolling pin over
it. Using a bread knife, trim it into a 1½- × 16½-in.
(4- × 42-cm) strip, neatening the edges.
8. **To remove the baking ring,** run a hot, damp sponge
around the outside to loosen it. Rotate the ring slightly
and carefully lift it off. Wrap the marzipan strip around
the cake. Freeze for 30 minutes.
9. **Spray the cake** all over with edible pink velvet.
Transfer to a serving plate.
10. **Arrange raspberries** over the top of the cake,
placing them upright and tightly together. Spoon
the raspberry glaze into a pastry bag or paper piping
cone, snip off the tip, and fill the berries with the glaze.
Chill for at least 1 hour. Remove from the refrigerator
30 minutes before serving. Serve on the same day, with
the remaining raspberry coulis.

MILLEFEUILLE

PUFF PASTRY LAYERS

FOR NAPOLEONS ★★★

Makes
3 layers for 1 Napoleon
(see p. 200)

Active time: 40 minutes +
making the puff pastry

Chilling time: At least
1 hour, preferably
overnight

Cooking time:
20–25 minutes per layer

Storage: Up to 1 day
at room temperature,
in an airtight container

INGREDIENTS
1 quantity (1¼ lb./600 g)
    puff pastry dough,
    either classic (see p. 28)
    or quick (see p. 29),
    well chilled
Generous 1 cup
    (5¼ oz./150 g)
    confectioners' sugar

EQUIPMENT
Cookie sheet lined
    with parchment paper

---

1. **Roll out the pastry dough** on a lightly floured surface (see Chef's Notes), to a thickness of ¹/₁₆ in. (2 mm).
2. **Cut into 3 rectangles**, each measuring 8 × 12 in. (20 × 30 cm).
3. **Loosely fold each rectangle** in half. Cover separately with plastic wrap. Let rest in the refrigerator for at least 1 hour, or preferably overnight.
4. **When ready to bake** the puff pastry layers, preheat the oven to 400°F (200°C/Gas Mark 6). Brush the parchment paper on the cookie sheet with water to dampen it.
5. **Remove one pastry rectangle** from the refrigerator and place it on the baking sheet. Unfold the pastry and prick it all over using a thin-tined fork. Bake for 20–25 minutes, until golden brown.
6. **About 5 minutes** before the end of the baking time, preheat the broiler. Generously dust the pastry with confectioners' sugar. Broil for 1 minute, until caramelized and golden brown. Watch closely, as the sugar will burn easily.
7. **Transfer the pastry** to a wire rack and let cool completely. Repeat with the remaining rectangles.

Chef's Notes
• To prevent the pastry from shrinking when it bakes, lift and drop it back onto the work surface several times during rolling. By doing this, shrinkage occurs on the work surface, not in the oven.

MILLEFEUILLE À LA CRÈME PÂTISSIÈRE

NAPOLEON ★★★

Serves
8–10

Active time: 1 hour +
making the puff pastry
layers and pastry cream

INGREDIENTS
*Caramelized hazelnuts
or almonds (optional;
see Chef's Notes)*
Scant 3 cups
　(17 oz./480 g) whole
　hazelnuts or almonds
1 cup + 1 tbsp (4 oz./115 g)
　sugar, divided
2 tbsp (30 ml) water
2 tsp (10 g) butter, diced

Puff pastry layers
3 puff pastry layers for
　Napoleons (see p. 198),
　baked and cooled

Cream filling
1 lb. 2 oz. (500 g) pastry
　cream (see p. 66),
　well chilled
½ quantity (1 cup/4½ oz./
　125 g) Chantilly cream
　(see p. 50), well chilled

EQUIPMENT
Rimmed baking sheet
　lined with parchment
　paper
Instant-read thermometer
Silicone baking mat
　(or parchment paper)
Pastry bag fitted with
　a ¾-in. (1.5-cm) plain tip

1. **Preheat the oven** to 140°F (60°C/Gas on the lowest setting).
2. **Spread the hazelnuts or almonds** over the baking sheet and dry them out in the oven for 30 minutes. Keep warm.
3. **Combine** a scant ½ cup (3 oz./90 g) of the sugar and the water in a large saucepan and cook over low heat until the sugar dissolves. Increase the heat, bring to a boil, and continue boiling until the syrup reaches 239°F (115°C).
4. **Remove from the heat,** then stir in the nuts with a wooden spoon, until the sugar crystallizes and looks sandy. Return the saucepan to medium-low heat and cook, stirring constantly, until the sugar caramelizes. Remove from the heat.
5. **Scatter the butter over the nuts** to make it easier to separate them. Stir in the remaining 2 tbsp (1 oz./25 g) sugar and turn out immediately onto the silicone mat (or parchment paper). Tap to separate the nuts, then let cool completely. Roughly chop the nuts or leave them whole for decorating.
6. **Whisk the pastry cream** and the Chantilly cream in separate bowls until smooth. Whisk the Chantilly cream into the pastry cream until combined. Spoon into the pastry bag.
7. **To assemble the Napoleon,** place the pastry rectangles on a board, caramelized side up. Pipe mounds of cream around the edge of each rectangle, then fill the center. Carefully place the pastry rectangles on top of one another, with the most attractive layer on top. Scatter over the caramelized nuts.
8. **Serve immediately,** so that the pastry remains crisp.

Chef's Notes
• The Napoleon is traditionally made with 2 layers of pastry cream, but a third layer can be added (as here), sprinkled with caramelized nuts.
• The caramelized nut recipe makes about 1 lb. 2 oz. (500 g), which is the minimum recommended amount to make, to ensure optimal results. The remaining nuts will keep for about 2 weeks in an airtight container in a dry place.
• The sides of the Napoleon can be coated with buttercream (see pp. 54–59) and finely chopped toasted or caramelized hazelnuts and almonds. Bring the buttercream to room temperature and whisk until smooth and spreadable. Using a palette knife, spread the buttercream over the sides in a thin layer. Press the nuts onto the buttercream to fix them in place.

MILLEFEUILLE VAL DE LOIRE

LOIRE VALLEY NAPOLEON ★★★

Serves
8–10

Active time: 20 minutes
+ making the puff pastry
layers and pastry cream

INGREDIENTS
Cream filling
2¾ oz. (75 g) Chantilly
    cream (see p. 50),
    well chilled
¾ lb. (350 g) pastry cream
    (see p. 66), well chilled

To assemble
9 oz. (250 g) fresh
    raspberries
9 oz. (250 g) fresh
    strawberries
3 puff pastry layers for
    Napoleons (see p. 198),
    baked and cooled
½ cup (3½ oz./100 g)
    raspberry jam

Decoration
Fresh strawberries
    and raspberries

EQUIPMENT
Pastry bag fitted with
    a ½-in. (1-cm) plain tip

1. **To prepare the cream filling,** whisk the Chantilly cream and pastry cream in separate bowls until smooth. Fold the Chantilly cream into the pastry cream.
2. **Wash and dry** the berries. Hull the strawberries and slice them thinly.
3. **Select the most attractive** puff pastry rectangle for the top layer.
4. **Place one of the remaining rectangles** on a serving plate.
5. **Spoon the raspberry jam** into the pastry bag. Pipe a line of jam around the edges of the pastry. Arrange half the raspberries side by side over the piped jam, to form a row of berries along each outer edge.

6. **Fill the center** with half the cream filling. Place half the strawberry slices over the cream filling.
7. **Carefully place** another puff pastry rectangle on top and cover as before.
8. **Place the final pastry layer** on top, with the caramelized side uppermost.
9. **Decorate** with whole strawberries and raspberries, fixing them in place with a little jam. Serve immediately, so the pastry remains crisp.

MIROIR CASSIS

BLACK CURRANT MIRROR CAKE ★★★

Serves
8

Active time: 1½ hours
+ making the ladyfinger
sponge base and Italian
meringue

Infusing time: 15 minutes

Freezing time: At least
2 hours

Cooking time: About
10 minutes

Storage: Up to 1 week
in the freezer (unglazed)

INGREDIENTS
Panna cotta cream
Generous ¾ cup (200 ml)
   heavy cream, well
   chilled, divided
1 sheet gelatin,
   180–200 Bloom
2 tbsp (25 g) sugar
1 pinch finely grated lemon
   zest
⅛ vanilla bean, split
   lengthwise
Generous ½ tsp (3 ml)
   Cointreau

Ladyfinger sponge base
5-in. (20-cm) round
   ladyfinger layer
   (see p. 24)
Confectioners' sugar,
   for dusting
1½ tbsp (25 ml) simple
   syrup (see p. 91)
⅓ oz. (10 g) black currant
   puree

Black currant mousse
⅓ cup (80 ml) heavy
   cream, well chilled
3 sheets gelatin
3½ oz. (100 g) black
   currant puree, at about
   77°F (25°C)
2½ oz. (70 g) Italian
   meringue (see p. 32)

Black currant glaze
⅝ tsp (2.5 g) pectin NH
½ cup (3½ oz./100 g)
   sugar, divided
Scant ½ cup (100 ml)
   water
1¾ oz. (50 g) black currant
   puree

Decoration
Pink almond candy
   (*dragées*), roughly
   chopped (see Chef's
   Notes)

EQUIPMENT
7-in (18-cm) baking ring,
   ¾ in. (2 cm) deep
Cookie sheet
Fine-mesh sieve
Instant-read thermometer
8¼-in. (21-cm) baking ring,
   1½ in. (4 cm) deep

1. **To prepare the panna cotta cream,** set the 7-in. (18-cm) baking ring on the cookie sheet. Line with plastic wrap to prevent any mixture leaking out.
2. **Whip half the cream** until it holds its shape. Keep chilled.
3. **Soak the gelatin** in cold water until softened. Combine the remaining cream, sugar, lemon zest, and vanilla bean in a saucepan. Bring to a simmer, then remove from the heat. Cover and let infuse for 15 minutes. Strain through the fine-mesh sieve into a mixing bowl.
4. **Squeeze the gelatin** to remove excess water. Place the gelatin in a small bowl and microwave on high for 5 seconds or until melted. Whisk the melted gelatin into the cream and place the bowl in another bowl half-filled with ice water. Add the Cointreau and stir until cooled to 63°F (17°C).
5. **Remove the bowl** from the cold water bath. Gently fold in the whipped cream. Pour the panna cotta into the baking ring and freeze for at least 1 hour until set.

6. **Remove the baking ring.** Return to the freezer until using.
7. **To prepare the ladyfinger sponge base,** line the cookie sheet with parchment paper and set the 8¼-in. (21-cm) baking ring on it. Place the ladyfinger disk in the center of the ring. Dust the top with confectioners' sugar.
8. **Whisk together** the simple syrup and black currant puree. Brush over the ladyfinger disk. Chill until using.
9. **To prepare the black currant mousse,** whip the cream until it holds its shape. Chill until using.
10. **Soak the gelatin** in a bowl of cold water until softened. Whisk together the black currant puree and meringue until thoroughly combined.
11. **Squeeze the gelatin** to remove excess water and melt it in the microwave. Whisk the melted gelatin into the black currant meringue, then gently fold in the whipped cream, using a flexible spatula.

12. To assemble the cake, cover the ladyfinger sponge with two-thirds of the mousse, spreading it up the sides of the ring with a palette knife. Remove the plastic wrap from the frozen panna cotta disk and place it in the center. Cover with the remaining mousse, smoothing it so it is flush with the top of the ring. Freeze for at least 1 hour.

13. To prepare the black currant glaze, combine the pectin with 2½ tbsp (1 oz./30 g) of the sugar in a bowl. Place the remaining sugar and water in a saucepan over low heat and stir until the sugar dissolves. Increase the heat, bring to a boil, and whisk in the pectin and sugar, then the black currant puree. Still whisking, return to a boil and boil for 1 minute. Let cool to 104°F (40°C) before using.

14. Remove the cake from the freezer. Pour the warm glaze over the top without removing the baking ring. Let the glaze set for a few minutes, then run a hot, damp sponge around the outside of the ring to loosen it. Rotate the ring slightly and carefully lift it off. Chill until ready to serve.

15. Just before serving, press the roughly chopped almond candy into the mousse around the sides of the cake, using your hand. Serve well chilled.

Chef's Notes
• The almond candy can be replaced with small shards of French meringue (see p. 33), either white or colored pink.
• Alternatively, the cake can be coated all over with the glaze. After removing it from the freezer, lift off the ring, set the cake on a wire rack, then pour the warm glaze over it. Smooth the glaze evenly over the top and sides using a palette knife. Let any excess drip off, then carefully transfer the cake to a serving plate.

MOKA AU CAFÉ

MOCHA CAKE ★★★

Serves
8

Active time: 35 minutes
+ making the genoise
sponge and coffee
buttercream

Chilling time: 30 minutes

Storage: Up to 24 hours
in the refrigerator

INGREDIENTS
*Coffee syrup (make 1 day
ahead; see Chef's Notes)*
⅓ cup (2½ oz./75 g) sugar
Scant ½ cup (100 ml)
water
3 tbsp (10 g) instant
coffee powder or
5½ tsp (10 g) full-
bodied ground
coffee (preferably
Guatemalan)

To assemble
8-in. (20-cm) round
genoise sponge
(see p. 30), made 1 day
ahead
1 quantity (1 lb. 2 oz./
500 g) coffee
buttercream (see p. 58),
made 1 day ahead,
at room temperature

Decoration
Caramelized hazelnuts,
Napoleon recipe
(see p. 200), roughly
chopped

EQUIPMENT
Fine-mesh sieve
Electric hand beater
8-in. (20-cm) round
cardboard cake board

1. **To prepare the coffee syrup**, combine the sugar and water in a saucepan over low heat and stir until the sugar dissolves. Increase the heat and bring to a boil, or, if using ground coffee, heat the water to 194°F (90°C).
2. **Remove from the heat** and stir in the coffee. If using ground coffee, cover and let infuse for 5 minutes, then strain through the fine-mesh sieve. Let cool and refrigerate in an airtight container until using.
3. **To assemble the cake**, cut the genoise sponge crosswise into 3 equal layers, using a bread knife.
4. **Whisk the buttercream** until it is soft enough to spread.
5. **Heat the coffee syrup** to lukewarm.
6. **Place the bottom genoise layer** on the cardboard cake board, crust side down. Generously brush the crumb side with coffee syrup. Spread with an even layer of buttercream, using a palette knife. Place the middle genoise layer on top, brush with syrup, and cover with another layer of buttercream. Finish with the final genoise layer, crust side up.

7. **Spread a thin layer** of buttercream over the top and sides of the cake, using a palette knife. Chill for 30 minutes to allow the buttercream to firm up slightly.
8. **Smooth the buttercream** with a palette knife. Using a bread knife, mark wavy lines across the top by moving the blade from side to side as it is drawn across the cake.
9. **To decorate**, press the caramelized hazelnuts into the buttercream around the sides of the cake, using your hand. Chill until ready to serve.

Chef's Notes
• This cake has a pronounced coffee flavor. If a more subtle aroma is preferred, replace the coffee syrup with a generous ¾ cup (200 ml) vanilla-flavored simple syrup (see p. 91).
• Roughly chopped caramelized hazelnuts could also be sprinkled over the buttercream in between the layers, to add a little crunch.

OPÉRA ★★★

Serves
20

Active time: 3 hours +
making the sponge layers

Chilling time: At least
3 hours

Storage: Up to 2 days
in the refrigerator

INGREDIENTS

3 Joconde sponge layers
(see p. 26)

Chocolate coating
1¾ oz. (50 g) dark
    couverture chocolate,
    70% cacao, chopped
1 tsp (5 ml) grape-seed oil

Coffee syrup
¾ cup (5 oz./150 g) sugar
Generous ¾ cup (200 ml)
    water
⅓ cup (20 g) instant
    coffee powder
    or ¼ cup (20 g)
    full-bodied ground
    coffee (preferably
    Guatemalan)

Chocolate ganache layer
5½ oz. (155 g) dark
    chocolate, 55% cacao,
    chopped
1 tbsp (20 g) butter, diced
½ cup (125 ml) heavy
    cream

To assemble
Confectioners' sugar,
    for dusting
1 lb. (450 g) coffee
    buttercream (see p. 58),
    at room temperature

*Opéra chocolate glaze
(prepare just before using)*
9½ oz. (270 g) *pâte à
    glacer brune* (brown
    glazing paste)
2¾ oz. (75 g) dark
    chocolate, 70% cacao,
    chopped
¼ cup (60 ml) grape-seed
    oil

Chocolate icing
1 cup + 1 tbsp (2 oz./55 g)
    sugar
3 tbsp (45 ml) water
3½ oz. (100 g) pure cacao
    paste, chopped

To serve
Vanilla custard sauce
    (see p. 86)

EQUIPMENT

Fine-mesh sieve
14½- × 10½-in.
    (37- × 27-cm)
    rectangular pastry
    frame, 1¼ in. (3 cm)
    deep
Instant-read thermometer
Electric hand beater
Cookie sheet lined
    with parchment paper
Pastry bag fitted with
    a very small round tip
    or paper piping cone

1. **Cut the sponge layers** to fit neatly inside the pastry frame. Set aside.

2. **To prepare the chocolate coating,** melt the chocolate in a bowl over a saucepan of barely simmering water (bain-marie) to 104°F (40°C). Stir in the grape-seed oil until smooth.

3. **Using an offset spatula** or pastry brush, coat the crust side of the sponge layers with the melted chocolate. Chill until using.

4. **To prepare the coffee syrup,** combine the sugar and water in a saucepan over low heat and stir until the sugar dissolves. Increase the heat and bring to a boil, or, if using ground coffee, heat the water to 194°F (90°C).

5. **Remove from the heat** and stir in the coffee. If using ground coffee, cover and let infuse for 5 minutes, then strain through the fine-mesh sieve. Keep warm until using.

6. **To prepare the chocolate ganache layer,** melt the chocolate in a bowl over a saucepan of barely simmering water (bain-marie) to 104°F (40°C), then stir in the butter.

7. **Heat the cream** to 140°F (60°C), pour it over the chocolate, and whisk until smooth. Set aside at room temperature.

8. **To assemble the cake,** set the pastry frame on the cookie sheet. Dust the parchment inside the frame with confectioners' sugar and place a chocolate-coated sponge layer in the frame, chocolate side down. Brush the top with a scant ½ cup (110 ml) coffee syrup.

9. **Whisk the coffee buttercream** until smooth and spreadable. Spoon 10½ oz. (300 g) over the sponge base and spread it into an even layer using an offset spatula.

10. **Place a second sponge layer** on top, crust side down, pressing it down gently with something flat to make sure it is level. Brush with a scant ½ cup (110 ml) coffee syrup. Spread with the chocolate ganache.

11. **Set the third sponge layer** over the ganache and press down gently again. Brush once more with a scant ½ cup (110 ml) syrup. Add the remaining buttercream and smooth it over so it is flush with the frame.

12. **Immediately run a warm knife** around the inside of the frame and carefully lift it off. Either leave the cake whole or cut it in half to make 2 cakes, each serving 10. Chill for 2 hours.

13. **Remove from the refrigerator** and leave at room temperature for 15 minutes before glazing.

14. **Shortly before glazing, prepare the chocolate icing.** Dissolve the sugar in the water over low heat, then bring to a boil. Pour over the cacao paste and whisk until smooth. Let cool slightly while glazing the cake.

15. **To prepare the chocolate glaze,** melt the glazing paste, chocolate, and oil together in a bowl over a saucepan of barely simmering water (bain-marie) to 95°F (35°C).

16. **Place the cake** on a wire rack and, using an offset spatula, coat the top with a thin layer of glaze. You will need to work fast as the glaze sets quickly.

17. **Trim a small amount** off each side of the cake, to remove any excess glaze, using a knife dipped in very hot water. Transfer the cake to a serving plate.

18. **Spoon the chocolate icing** into a pastry bag or piping cone. Snip off the tip if using a cone. Pipe elegant swirls over the top of the cake. Chill until ready to serve.

19. **Serve with vanilla custard sauce** and a cup of good-quality coffee.

PARIS-BREST ★★

Serves
6

Active time: 40 minutes
+ making the choux pastry
and pastry cream

Cooking time: 30 minutes

INGREDIENTS

Choux rings
6 oz. (180 g) choux pastry
dough (see p. 38)
1 egg, lightly beaten
⅔ cup (1¾ oz./50 g) sliced
almonds

Praline cream
(see Chef's Notes)
1 stick + 3 tbsp (5½ oz./
160 g) butter,
well chilled and diced
3 oz. (80 g) almond-
hazelnut praline paste
9 oz. (250 g) pastry cream
(see p. 66)
1 tsp (5 ml) rum or coffee
extract

To assemble
Confectioners' sugar,
for dusting
1 oz. (30 g) hazelnuts,
whole or roughly
chopped
1 oz. (30 g) sliced almonds

EQUIPMENT
2 cookie sheets
Pastry bag fitted
with a ½-in. (1-cm)
plain tip
Stand mixer fitted
with the paddle beater
Pastry bag fitted with
a ¾-in. (2-cm) fluted tip

---

1. **Preheat the oven** to 400°F (200°C/Gas Mark 6).

2. **To prepare the choux rings,** draw an 8-in. (20-cm) circle on 2 sheets of parchment paper, using a pencil. Place on the cookie sheets with the pencil marks underneath.

3. **Transfer the choux pastry dough** to the pastry bag with a ½-in. (1-cm) tip. Pipe 3 rings on the first sheet of parchment: the first around the outline of the drawn circle, the second inside and touching it, and the third on top, in the center where the rings join.

4. **Brush with the beaten egg** and sprinkle with the sliced almonds. On the second sheet, pipe a ring around the inside of the drawn circle.

5. **Place both baking sheets** in the oven and prop the door ajar with the handle of a wooden spoon. Bake for about 15 minutes, until the pastry puffs up, then reduce the temperature to 350°F (180°C/Gas Mark 4) and bake for another 15 minutes, until golden brown and crisp. Avoid adjusting the position of the oven door during baking, as this could make the pastry collapse.

6. **Slide the baked rings,** still on the parchment paper, onto a wire rack to cool.

7. **As soon as the triple ring** is cool enough to handle, cut off the top third using a bread knife. Leave on the rack to cool completely.

8. **To prepare the praline cream,** beat the butter in the stand mixer until smooth but not soft. Add the praline paste and beat for 1 minute on medium speed until combined, scraping down the sides of the bowl to ensure even mixing.

9. **Whisk the pastry cream** until smooth. Beat into the praline mixture a third at a time. Beat for 1 minute each time so the cream becomes light and fluffy. Mix in the rum or coffee extract and transfer to the pastry bag with a fluted tip.

10. **To assemble,** place the choux base on a serving plate, cut side up. Pipe a thick rope of praline cream over it. Place the uncut ring on top and pipe cream around the outside to resemble petals. Pipe the remaining cream in a zigzag pattern on top.

11. **Dust the other half** of the cut ring with confectioners' sugar and place it carefully over the praline cream. Sprinkle with chopped or whole hazelnuts and sliced almonds.

12. **Keep chilled** and serve on the same day.

Chef's Notes

• Instead of praline cream, the Paris-Brest can be filled with chiboust cream (see p. 60).
• The individual choux ring not only adds extra height to the cake, but, more importantly, it provides the perfect balance between pastry and cream.

ROSACE À L'ORANGE / CLAIREFONTAINE

ORANGE UPSIDE-DOWN CAKE ★★

Serves
8

Active time: 30 minutes
+ making the genoise
sponge and pastry cream

Cooking time: 2 hours
20 minutes

Macerating time: At least
24 hours

Chilling time: At least
2 hours

Storage: Up to 24 hours
in the refrigerator

INGREDIENTS
*Candied orange slices
(make 1 day ahead)*
4 oranges, preferably
   organic
1½ cups (10½ oz./300 g)
   sugar
2 cups (500 ml) water

Orange syrup
⅔ cup (150 ml)
   simple syrup with
   Grand Marnier
   (see p. 91)
Juice of ½ orange

Cream filling
10½ oz. (300 g) pastry
   cream (see p. 66)
5¼ oz. (150 g) Chantilly
   cream (see p. 50)

To assemble
Melted butter and sugar
   for the pan
8-in. (20-cm) round
   genoise sponge
   (see p. 30)

EQUIPMENT
Mandoline (optional)
Electric hand beater
9-in. (22-cm) round
   cake pan

1. **Wash the oranges** under cold water and scrub them with a small brush. Using a mandoline or sharp knife, slice the unpeeled oranges into very thin rounds, removing any seeds and discarding the ends.

2. **Combine the sugar and water** in a large saucepan over low heat and stir until the sugar dissolves. Increase the heat, bring to a boil, then lower the heat again. Add the orange slices and simmer, without boiling, for 1–1½ hours, until the slices are very tender. Remove from the heat, cover, and let macerate for 24 hours or longer. Do not drain until ready to use.

3. **To prepare the orange syrup**, whisk together the simple syrup and orange juice.

4. **To prepare the cream filling,** whisk the pastry cream in a mixing bowl until smooth.

5. **Drain the candied orange slices**. Set aside the most attractive and evenly sized slices for decoration. Finely chop the rest and stir them into the pastry cream. Gently fold in the Chantilly cream.

6. **To assemble the cake,** brush the cake pan with melted butter and sprinkle with sugar until coated. Line the base and sides of the pan with the whole orange slices, partially overlapping them. Half-fill the pan with orange cream.

7. **Cut the genoise sponge crosswise** into 2 equal slices using a bread knife. Brush the orange syrup over the crumb sides to soak them.

8. **Place one genoise sponge layer** in the pan over the orange cream, trimming the edges a little, if necessary, to ensure a neat fit. Cover with the remaining orange cream. Place the second genoise sponge layer on top, crust side up.

9. **Place a plate on top** of the cake, to press it down. Chill for at least 2 hours.

10. **To unmold the cake,** immerse the base of the pan briefly in hot water and invert onto a serving plate. Chill until ready to serve.

SAINT HONORÉ CHIBOUST

GÂTEAU SAINT-HONORÉ ★★

Serves
8

Active time:
1 hour 40 minutes + making
the puff and choux pastries

Cooking time:
30 minutes

INGREDIENTS
Pastry base
⅓ quantity (7 oz./200 g)
    puff pastry dough,
    either classic (see p. 28)
    or quick (see p. 29)

1 egg white, lightly beaten
2½ tsp (10 g) sugar
6 oz. (170 g) choux pastry
    dough (see p. 38)

Vanilla pastry cream
1½ cups (350 ml) whole milk
½ vanilla bean, split
    lengthwise and seeds
    scraped
5 egg yolks (⅓ cup/100 g)
Scant ¼ cup (1½ oz./45 g)
    sugar
3 tbsp (1 oz./30 g)
    cornstarch, sifted

Caramel coating
1 cup (7 oz./200 g) sugar
¼ cup (60 ml) water

Chiboust cream (prepare just before use)
11½ oz. (325 g)
    vanilla pastry cream
    (see left)
Italian meringue:
2 sheets gelatin
½ cup (3¾ oz./105 g) sugar
2 tsp (10 ml) water
Generous ¼ cup (2¼ oz./
    65 g) egg white (about
    2 whites + 1 tsp)

EQUIPMENT
Rimmed baking sheet
    lined with parchment
    paper
Pastry bag fitted with
    a coupler + ¾-in.
    (1.5-cm) and ½-in.
    (1-cm) plain tips
Pastry bag fitted with
    an ⅛-in. (3-mm)
    plain tip
Stand mixer fitted with
    the whisk
Instant-read thermometer
Pastry bag fitted with
    a large Saint-Honoré tip
    (see Chef's Notes)

---

1. **Preheat the oven** to 400°F (200°C/Gas Mark 6).
2. **Roll the puff pastry dough** on a lightly floured surface into a 9-in. (24-cm) circle. Place on the baking sheet, prick all over with a fork, then brush with the beaten egg white. Sprinkle over the sugar, which will caramelize as the pastry bakes.
3. **Transfer the choux pastry dough** to the pastry bag with a ¾-in. (1.5-cm) tip. Pipe a ring around the edge of the pastry base, about ¼ in. (5 mm) from the edge. Using the ½-in. (1-cm) tip, pipe 18 choux puffs onto the same baking sheet (see p. 38).
4. **Bake for about 10 minutes**, until the choux pastry puffs up. Reduce the temperature to 350°F (180°C/Gas Mark 4) and continue baking until golden brown (about 20 minutes in total for the puffs and 30 minutes for the base). Transfer to a wire rack when baked. Let cool completely.
5. **While the choux is baking,** prepare the pastry cream, using the ingredients listed above and following the instructions on p. 66. Transfer 7 oz. (200 g) pastry cream to the pastry bag fitted with an ⅛-in. (3-mm) tip, to fill the choux puffs. Reserve the remaining pastry cream for the chiboust cream. Pierce a hole in the side of each choux puff and fill with the pastry cream.
6. **To prepare the caramel coating,** line the baking sheet with fresh parchment paper. Heat the sugar and water gently until the sugar dissolves. Increase the heat and bring to a boil. Boil, without stirring, until a gold caramel is obtained. Remove from the heat.
7. **Dip the tops** of the choux puffs into the caramel, using the tip of a sharp knife to hold each puff, to avoid

burns. Place the dipped puffs on the baking sheet, caramel side down, and let cool (this will only take a few minutes). As soon as the caramel has cooled, stick the puffs around the outer edge of the pastry base with a little more caramel.
8. **Prepare the Italian meringue** for the chiboust cream. Soak the gelatin in a bowl of cold water until softened. Using the quantities of sugar, water, and egg white indicated above and following the instructions on p. 32, make an Italian meringue. Once the temperature of the sugar syrup reaches 250°F (121°C) and it has been whisked in a steady stream into the egg whites, squeeze the gelatin to remove excess water and microwave in a small bowl on full power for 5 seconds, or until melted. With the mixer running, slowly drizzle in the melted gelatin until combined.
9. **Prepare the chiboust cream** by combining the reserved pastry cream with the Italian meringue, following the instructions on p. 60, step 8.
10. **Fill the center** of the pastry base with a layer of the cream, shaping it into a slight dome using a palette knife. Transfer the rest to the pastry bag with the Saint-Honoré tip and pipe on top to resemble petals. Keep chilled and serve on the same day.

Chef's Notes
• It is essential to use a Saint-Honoré tip as it has a wide opening. A smaller tip would crush the delicate chiboust cream.

LE SCHUSS AUX FRUITS

FRUIT SCHUSS ★★★

Serves
10–12

Active time: 1½ hours
+ making the sweet
shortcrust pastry
and ladyfinger batter

Cooking time: 40 minutes

Freezing time: At least
2 hours

INGREDIENTS
Sweet shortcrust layer
8 oz. (225 g) sweet
    shortcrust pastry dough
    (see p. 41)
1¾ oz. (50 g) white
    chocolate, chopped
2 tsp (10 ml) grape-seed
    oil

Ladyfinger layer
½ quantity (9¾ oz./275 g)
    ladyfinger sponge
    batter (see p. 24)

Kirsch syrup
4 tsp (20 ml) kirsch
¼ cup (60 ml) simple
    syrup (see p. 91)

Fromage blanc mousse
4 sheets gelatin,
    180–200 Bloom
1 cup (250 ml) heavy
    cream, well chilled
⅓ cup (2¼ oz./65 g) sugar
4 tsp (20 ml) water

2 egg yolks (2½ tbsp/40 g)
1 cup (8 oz./225 g) full-
    fat fromage blanc
    (see Chef's Notes)

To assemble
⅓ cup (4½ oz./125 g)
    raspberry jam

Chantilly cream
1 cup (250 ml) heavy
    cream, well chilled
5 tsp (20 g) sugar

Decoration
Fresh fruit of your choice
3½ oz. (100 g) caramelized
    almonds, Napoleon
    recipe (see p. 200),
    finely chopped
Apricot glaze, warm
    (optional)

To serve
Fresh fruit coulis,
    well chilled

EQUIPMENT
Cookie sheet lined
    with parchment paper
Stand mixer fitted
    with the whisk
Instant-read thermometer
5- × 7-in. (12- × 18-cm)
    loose-based cake pan,
    1½ in. (4 cm) deep
Thick cardboard base
    slightly larger than
    the pan
Pastry bag fitted
    with a ½-in. (1-cm) tip
    or Saint-Honoré tip

1. **To prepare the sweet shortcrust layer,** roll the pastry dough to a thickness of ⅛ in. (3 mm) on a lightly floured surface. Cut into a rectangle measuring 5 × 7 in. (12 × 18 cm). Transfer to the cookie sheet and chill for 1 hour.
2. **Preheat the oven** to 325°F (160°C/Gas Mark 3). Bake the pastry for 18–20 minutes, until golden. Slide it, still on the parchment, onto a wire rack and let cool completely.
3. **Melt the white chocolate** in a bowl over a saucepan of barely simmering water (bain-marie), then stir in the oil. Let cool but not set. Spread both sides of the pastry with the chocolate until coated. Chill until using.
4. **Preheat the oven** to 340°F (170°C/Gas Mark 3).
5. **To prepare the ladyfinger layer,** draw a rectangle measuring 7 × 9½ in. (18 × 24 cm) on a sheet of parchment paper using a pencil. Place on the cookie sheet with the pencil marks underneath.

6. **Spread the ladyfinger batter** over the rectangle. Bake for 18 minutes, until the sponge is golden underneath. Slide the sponge, still on the parchment, onto a wire rack to cool. Remove from the parchment and cut into 2 rectangles measuring 5 × 7 in. (12 × 18 cm). Chill until using.
7. **To prepare the kirsch syrup,** whisk the kirsch into the simple syrup and refrigerate until using.
8. **To prepare the fromage blanc mousse,** soak the gelatin in a bowl of cold water to soften it. Whip the cream until it holds its shape, then chill until using.
9. **Combine the sugar and water** in a saucepan over low heat and stir until the sugar dissolves. Increase the heat and boil until the temperature reaches 250°F (120°C). Whisk the egg yolks lightly in the stand mixer. Very carefully whisk in the hot syrup in a thin stream (as for making a mayonnaise), making sure the syrup does not hit the whisk. Continue whisking on high speed until thick and creamy and the temperature cools to 86°F (30°C).

10. **Squeeze the gelatin** to remove excess water. Microwave on high in a bowl for 5 seconds or until melted. Whisk the fromage blanc until smooth. Whisk in the egg yolk and syrup mixture, then the gelatin. Fold in the whipped cream a third at a time, using a flexible spatula.

11. **Set the cake pan** on the cookie sheet lined with fresh parchment paper. Place the shortcrust layer in the pan and spread the pastry with the raspberry jam. Set one of the ladyfinger rectangles on top, brush with the kirsch syrup, then pour the mousse over and spread it with a palette knife. Place the second ladyfinger rectangle on top. Freeze for at least 2 hours.

12. **To prepare the Chantilly cream,** whip the cream with the sugar on high speed until the cream holds its shape. Wash and dry the fruit for decoration, cutting larger fruit into smaller pieces as necessary. Remove the cake from the freezer, release it from the pan, and place it on the cardboard base. Arrange the fruit on top, leaving a ¾-in. (1.5-cm) border.

13. **Using a palette knife,** spread the sides of the cake with a layer of Chantilly cream. Spoon the remaining cream into the pastry bag and pipe it attractively around the fruit. Smooth the sides neatly from top to bottom, using a palette knife. Press the finely chopped caramelized almonds into the cream in a thin border around the base of the cake.

14. **Carefully transfer the cake** to a serving plate. If wished, brush the fruit with warm apricot glaze.

15. **Keep chilled** and serve on the same day, with a fresh fruit coulis.

Chef's Notes
• If full-fat fromage blanc is unavailable, Greek yogurt or quark can be substituted.

SINGAPOUR ANANAS ET MANGUE

PINEAPPLE AND
MANGO SINGAPOUR ★★

Serves
8

Active time: 20 minutes +
making the genoise sponge
and marzipan

Cooking time: 5 minutes

Storage: Up to 3 days
in the refrigerator

INGREDIENTS
Fruit filling
1 ripe mango
7 oz. (200 g) fresh
   pineapple (prepared
   weight)
Scant ⅓ cup (2 oz./60 g)
   sugar
3½ tbsp (50 ml) white rum
   (optional)

*Orange-flavored marzipan
collar (optional;
see Chef's Notes)*
About 3 drops (1 g) natural
   orange food coloring
5¼ oz. (150 g) marzipan
   (see p. 63)
Potato starch, for dusting

To assemble
8-in. (20-cm) round
   genoise sponge
   (see p. 30), made 1 day
   ahead
Generous ½ cup
   (7 oz./200 g) apricot
   glaze, warm

Decoration
Coconut flakes
Toasted whole almonds
Finely grated lime zest,
   preferably organic

EQUIPMENT
Rolling pin embossed
   with a honeycomb
   or other design
   (optional)
8-in. (20-cm) round
   cardboard cake board

---

1. **To prepare the fruit filling**, peel the mango, weigh
out 3½ oz. (100 g) of the flesh, and chop it finely.
Finely chop 3½ oz. (100 g) of the pineapple. Reserve
the remaining fruit for decoration.
2. **Combine the chopped mango** and sugar in a saucepan.
Bring to a boil. Simmer for 5 minutes, then stir in
the chopped pineapple and remove from the heat.
Let cool before adding the rum, if using.
3. **To prepare the marzipan collar**, knead the orange
food coloring into the marzipan until it is evenly tinted.
4. **Dust a work surface** and rolling pin with potato starch.
Roll the marzipan into a long rectangle, a little over
24 in. (60 cm) long, with a thickness of ⅛ in. (3 mm).
If using an embossed pin, roll it over the marzipan
to mark it with a design. Trim the band so it measures
3¼ × 24 in. (8 × 60 cm). Set aside until using.
5. **To assemble the cake,** use a bread knife to cut
the genoise sponge crosswise into 2 equal layers.

6. **Place the bottom layer** on the cardboard disk,
crust side down, and spread the mango and pineapple
mixture over it. Place the second genoise layer on top,
crumb side down. Brush the top and sides of the cake
with the warm apricot glaze.
7. **Wrap the marzipan collar** around the cake.
Seal the ends by pinching them together lightly
with your fingers.
8. **Cut the remaining mango and pineapple**
into matchsticks, or other attractive shapes, and pile on
top of the cake. Sprinkle over coconut flakes, almonds,
and lime zest. Chill until ready to serve.

Chef's Notes
• Instead of a marzipan collar, you can press ⅔ cup
(1¾ oz./50 g) sliced almonds or shredded coconut
around the sides of the cake after glazing it.

SUCCÈS PRALINÉ

PRALINE SUCCÈS ★★★

Serves
8

Active time: 20 minutes
+ making the succès
meringue bases

Cooking time: 1 hour
20 minutes

Chilling time: At least
1 hour

Storage: Up to 2 days
in the refrigerator
(undecorated)

INGREDIENTS
1 quantity (1½ lb./
    700 g) hazelnut praline
    buttercream (see p. 59),
    at room temperature
    (see Chef's Notes)
2 × 8-in. (20-cm) succès
    meringue bases
    (see p. 34)

Decoration
1¾ oz. (50 g) caramelized
    almonds, Napoleon
    recipe (see p. 200),
    very finely chopped
¾ cup (3½ oz./100 g)
    confectioners' sugar

EQUIPMENT
Electric hand beater
8-in. (20-cm) round
    cardboard cake board

1. **Whisk the hazelnut praline buttercream** in a mixing bowl until smooth.
2. **Place the most irregular** of the 2 succès bases on the cardboard cake board. Cover with 1¼ lb. (600 g) of the buttercream, using a palette knife to spread it evenly.
3. **Place the second succès base** on top. Press down gently until flat.
4. **Using the palette knife,** spread a thin layer of the remaining buttercream over the cake to cover. Gently press the caramelized almonds around the sides of the cake, using your hand. Chill for at least 1 hour.
5. **Just before serving,** generously dust the top of the cake with the confectioners' sugar.
6. Serve well chilled.

Chef's Notes
• For even more of a gourmet treat, stir finely chopped caramelized almonds into the buttercream.

TARTS, FLANS, AND BAKED DESSERTS

CLAFOUTIS TUTTI FRUTTI

FRUIT CLAFOUTIS TART ★★

Makes
2 tarts, each serving 6

Active time: 10 minutes
+ making the shortcrust
pastry

Chilling time:
1 hour–overnight

Cooking time: 25 minutes

Storage: Up to 1 month
in the freezer (unbaked)

INGREDIENTS

Tart shells
Butter for the pans
10½ oz. (300 g) shortcrust
    pastry dough
    (see p. 40)
1 egg yolk, lightly beaten

Custard filling
1 cup (250 ml) whole milk
Seeds of 1 vanilla bean
Scant ½ cup (3½ oz./
    100 g) crème fraîche
    or ½ cup (120 ml) heavy
    cream
4 eggs (¾ cup + 2 tbsp/
    200 g)
1 cup (7 oz./200 g) sugar
4 drops orange flower
    water

Fruit filling
1 lb. (480 g) fresh fruit,
    washed and dried (see
    Chef's Notes)

EQUIPMENT
2 × 8-in. (20-cm) round
    cake pans (or ceramic
    pie dishes)
Large rimmed baking
    sheet
Pie weights or dried beans

1. **Grease the pans** with butter.
2. **To prepare the tart shells**, cut the pastry dough in half. Roll each half on a lightly floured surface into a circle large enough to line the pans. Press each pastry circle into a pan and chill for at least 1 hour (or overnight).
3. **Set the pans** on the baking sheet. Preheat the oven to 400°F (200°C/Gas Mark 6).
4. **Line the tart shells** with parchment paper and fill with pie weights. Blind-bake for about 10–15 minutes, until the pastry is light gold around the edges. Remove the parchment paper and weights.
5. **Brush the tart shells** with the egg yolk to seal them. Return to the oven for an additional 3–5 minutes, until evenly golden. Let cool.
6. **To prepare the custard filling**, bring the milk and vanilla seeds to a boil in a saucepan. Stir in the cream. Remove from the heat.
7. **Whisk together** the eggs and sugar in a bowl. Slowly pour in the hot milk mixture, whisking nonstop. Whisk in the orange flower water.
8. **Set over a larger bowl** filled halfway with ice water and continue whisking to cool the custard quickly.
9. **Prepare the fresh fruit** as necessary, cutting larger fruits into small dice or thin slices. Divide the fruit between the tart shells. Pour the custard over the fruit, filling the pans three-quarters full.
10. **Bake for 20 minutes** until the custard is just set. Serve warm, at room temperature, or chilled.

Chef's Notes
• Fruit poached in syrup, such as pears (see p. 372), can be used in place of fresh fruit. Drain the fruit from the syrup, pat dry with paper towel, and reduce the quantity of sugar in the custard filling by half.
• If freezing the unbaked tarts, freeze them in their pans on the baking sheet until solid. Remove from the freezer, unmold, wrap airtight, and return to the freezer. When ready to bake, unwrap the frozen tarts and place them back in the tart pans on a baking sheet. Bake from frozen, adding 10–15 minutes to the baking time.

COCHELIN D'ÉVREUX
ÉVREUX APPLE TURNOVER ★★

Serves
8

Active time: 25 minutes +
making the puff pastry

Chilling time: 1 hour

Cooking time: 1 hour
20 minutes

INGREDIENTS

Puff pastry
1 lb. (450 g) puff pastry
  dough, classic
  (see p. 28) or quick
  (see p. 29)
1 egg, lightly beaten

Apple filling
2 lb. (1 kg) tart apples
½ cup (3½ oz./100 g)
  granulated sugar
3½ tbsp (50 ml) water
⅓ cup (2¾ oz./75 g) vanilla
  sugar

EQUIPMENT
2 cookie sheets lined
  with parchment paper

1. **Roll the pastry dough** on a lightly floured surface into a large circle with a thickness of ⅛ in. (3 mm). Prick one half of the circle with a fork—this will form the turnover base. Lift the dough onto a cookie sheet and chill until using.

2. **Preheat the oven** to 340°F (170°C/Gas Mark 3).

3. **To prepare the apple filling,** peel and core the apples. Cut one-third of them into quarters. Place the quartered apples in a saucepan with the granulated sugar and water.

4. **Simmer over low heat** for about 20 minutes, until the apples are very tender and have produced about 1 cup (9 oz./250 g) of compote. Let cool.

5. **Cut the remaining apples** into ¾-in. (1.5-cm) dice, weighing about 1 lb. 2oz. (500 g). Place in a bowl and toss with the vanilla sugar until the apples are coated. Spread them over the baking sheet and bake for 15 minutes. Let cool completely. Mix with the apple compote.

6. **To assemble the turnover,** spread the apple filling over the pricked half of the pastry circle, leaving a ¾ –1¼-in. (2–3-cm) border. Dampen the edges by brushing with a little water.

7. **Fold the other half of the pastry** over the filling to make a half-moon shape. Press the pastry edges firmly together with your fingers to seal. Pinch a decorative ruffle around the edge using your thumb and index finger. Brush the top with the beaten egg. Chill for 1 hour.

8. **Preheat the oven** to 430°F (220°C/Gas Mark 7). Using the tip of a knife, mark a decorative pattern on top. Take care not to cut through the pastry. Cut a small hole in the center to allow steam to escape during baking.

9. **Bake for 10 minutes.** Reduce the oven temperature to 350°F (180°C/Gas Mark 4) and bake for another 25 minutes. Reduce the temperature again to 325°F (160°C/Gas Mark 3) and bake for an additional 10 minutes, until the pastry is puffed and golden brown.

10. **Transfer to a wire rack** and let cool slightly. Serve the turnover hot or warm.

COCOTTE POMME AMANDE

APPLE AND ALMOND COCOTTE ★★

Serves
8

Active time: 45 minutes + making the brioche dough and frangipane cream

Chilling time: 1 hour

Rising time: 1½–1¾ hours

Cooking time:
50 minutes–1 hour

INGREDIENTS

Brioche
14 oz. (400 g) brioche dough (see p. 36), made 1 day ahead

Baked apples
6 firm baking apples (such as Chantecler, Belle de Boskoop, or Golden Delicious)
5 tbsp (2½ oz./75 g) butter, melted
⅓ cup (2¾ oz./75 g) vanilla sugar

To assemble
Butter for the Dutch oven
¾ lb. (350 g) frangipane cream (see p. 62)
1 egg, beaten with a pinch of salt
Sliced almonds

To serve
3½ tbsp (50 ml) rum (optional)
Confectioners' sugar, for dusting
Vanilla ice cream (optional)

EQUIPMENT
1¼-in. (3-cm) round cookie cutter
Cookie sheet lined with parchment paper
Enameled or cast-iron Dutch oven

---

1. **To prepare the brioche rounds**, roll the dough on a lightly floured surface to a thickness of ¼ in. (5 mm). Using the cookie cutter, cut out enough circles to fit around the edge of the Dutch oven with a little space between them. Chill on the cookie sheet, covered with plastic wrap, until using.
2. **Preheat the oven** to 340°F (170°C/Gas Mark 3).
3. **To prepare the baked apples**, peel, halve, and core the apples. Place in a single layer in a baking dish, cut side down. Drizzle over the melted butter and sprinkle with the vanilla sugar.
4. **Bake for 30–35 minutes**, until the apples are tender when pierced with the tip of a knife. Let cool, then chill for 1 hour.

5. **To assemble the cocotte**, lightly grease the Dutch oven with butter. Spoon in the frangipane cream, spreading it in an even layer. Arrange the apples, rounded sides up, over the cream, pressing them down with a spatula to flatten them.
6. **Arrange the brioche slices** around the edge, leaving a little space between them. Brush with the beaten egg and let rise in a warm place for 1½–1¾ hours. Toward the end of the rising time, preheat the oven to 350°F (180°C/Gas Mark 4).
7. **Brush the brioche slices** once more with beaten egg and top each one with a couple of sliced almonds. Bake for 20–25 minutes, until the brioche slices are golden.
8. **Heat the rum**, if using, flambé, and when the flames die down, pour the rum over the brioche slices. Dust with confectioners' sugar and serve warm with vanilla ice cream, if desired.

FAR AUX PRUNEAUX

BRETON PRUNE AND CUSTARD TART *

Serves
8

Active time: 10 minutes

Infusing time: 10 minutes

Cooking time: 45 minutes

Storage: Up to 3 days
in the refrigerator

INGREDIENTS
2 tbsp (25 g) butter and
  AP flour, for the pan
2 cups (500 ml) whole
  milk
½ vanilla bean, split
  lengthwise (see Chef's
  Notes)
⅔ cup (3 oz./80 g)
  AP flour, sifted
¾ cup (4¾ oz./135 g) sugar
5 eggs (1 cup/250 g)
2 tbsp aged rum
7 oz. (200 g) prunes,
  pitted (see Chef's
  Notes)

EQUIPMENT
9½-in. (24-cm) round cake
  pan, 2 in. (5 cm) deep,
  or a ceramic baking dish
Electric hand beater

1. **Preheat the oven** to 400°F (200°C/Gas Mark 6).
Generously grease the cake pan with the butter, then
dust with flour until coated.
2. **Pour the milk** into a saucepan, scrape in the vanilla
seeds, and add the bean. Bring to a simmer, remove
from the heat, and cover. Let infuse for 10 minutes.
Remove the vanilla bean.
3. **Whisk together** the flour, sugar, and eggs. Slowly
whisk in the warm milk, followed by the rum.
4. **Pour into the cake pan** and add the prunes,
distributing them evenly.
5. **Bake for 10 minutes.** Reduce the heat to 340°F
(170°C/Gas Mark 3) and bake for an additional
35 minutes, until the top is golden brown.
6. **Serve warm**, straight from the pan or if preferred,
unmold onto a serving plate.

Chef's Notes
• Instead of a vanilla bean, 1¾ tsp (7 g) vanilla sugar
can be added. Reduce the quantity of sugar in the
ingredients by about 5 tsp (20 g).
• To make the prunes extra moist, soak them unpitted
for 1 hour in hot tea, such as Earl Grey. Drain well
and remove the pits before using.
• The prunes can be replaced with raisins, if desired.

PUDDING ROYAL

BRIOCHE BREAD PUDDING **

Makes
2 desserts, each serving 6

Active time: 15 minutes

Infusing time: 10 minutes

Cooking time: 50 minutes

INGREDIENTS
For the baking dishes
3 tbsp (1¾ oz./50 g)
   butter
2 tbsp (25 g) sugar

Custard
3 cups (750 ml) whole milk
1 Bourbon Madagascar
   vanilla bean, split
   lengthwise
5 eggs (1 cup/250 g)
8 egg yolks (scant ⅔ cup/
   160 g)
1½ cups (10½ oz./300 g)
   sugar

To assemble
9 oz. (250 g) leftover day-
   old brioche
10½ oz. (300 g) assorted
   dried and candied fruit
   (such as golden raisins,
   currants, candied
   cherries)

To serve
Vanilla custard sauce
   (see p. 86), chocolate
   sauce (see p. 90),
   or apricot or raspberry
   coulis (see p. 51)

EQUIPMENT
2 × 9-in. (23-cm) round
   porcelain baking dishes,
   1½ in. (4 cm) deep
Electric hand beater
Large baking pan for the
   bain-marie

1. **Preheat the oven** to 340°F (170°C/Gas Mark 3). Grease the baking dishes with the butter, then sprinkle with the sugar until coated.
2. **To prepare the custard,** pour the milk into a saucepan. Scrape in the vanilla seeds and add the bean.
3. **Bring to a simmer,** then remove from the heat. Cover and let infuse for 10 minutes. Remove the bean.
4. **Whisk the eggs,** egg yolks, and sugar together for 1 minute until frothy. Slowly whisk in the warm milk on low speed.
5. **To assemble the bread pudding,** cut the brioche into approximately ¾-in. (1.5-cm) slices. If necessary, chop the dried and candied fruit into smaller pieces, removing any pits.

6. **Line the bases** of the baking dishes with brioche slices, packing them tightly together. Spoon the fruit over the brioche slices. Cut the remaining brioche into cubes, then scatter them over the fruit in a single layer.
7. **Divide the custard** between the dishes. Place them in the baking pan and pour in enough hot water to come halfway up the sides of the dishes. Carefully transfer to the oven and bake for 50 minutes. Cover with aluminum foil if the tops brown too quickly. Remove from the oven and let cool.
8. **Serve at room temperature** or chilled, with vanilla custard sauce, chocolate sauce, or apricot or raspberry fruit coulis.

LA CHANTELLÉE

BRIOCHE CHEESECAKE ★★

Serves
8

Active time: 15 minutes +
making the brioche dough
and pastry cream

Cooking time: 50 minutes

INGREDIENTS
Butter for the pan
Scant ½ cup (2¾ oz./80 g)
  sugar
Finely grated zest of
  1 lemon, preferably
  organic
7 oz. (200 g) brioche
  dough (see p. 36),
  made 1 day ahead
9 oz. (250 g) pastry cream
  (see p. 66)
9 oz. (250 g) full-fat
  fromage blanc
  (see Chef's Notes)
2 egg yolks (2½ tbsp/40 g)
2 tbsp (20 g) cornstarch
1 pinch salt
4 tbsp (2 oz./60 g) butter,
  melted and cooled
Confectioners' sugar,
  for dusting

EQUIPMENT
9-in. (22-cm) round cake
  pan, 2 in. (5 cm) deep
Electric hand beater

1. **Preheat the oven** to 350°F (180°C/Gas Mark 4).
Grease the pan with butter.
2. **Mix together** the sugar and lemon zest in a mixing
bowl.
3. **Roll the brioche dough** into a circle large enough
to line the pan in a very thin layer.
4. **Place the dough** in the pan. Press over the base and
up the sides of the pan to the top. Do not let the dough
rise.
5. **Add the pastry cream**, fromage blanc, egg yolks,
cornstarch, and salt to the sugar and lemon zest.
Whisk on high speed until combined.
6. **Whisk in** the melted butter, then pour into the pan
to fill it completely.
7. **Bake for 50 minutes**, until puffed and golden.
Dust generously with confectioners' sugar. Let cool
completely before unmolding. Serve cold.

Chef's Notes
• If full-fat fromage blanc is unavailable, Greek yogurt
or quark can be substituted.

TARTE LINZER RHUBARBE FRAMBOISE

RASPBERRY AND RHUBARB LINZER TORTE ★★

Serves
6

Active time: 25 minutes
+ making the shortcrust
pastry and frangipane
cream

Cooking time: 1¾ hours

Chilling time: 1½ hours

INGREDIENTS

Raspberry crumble
2 tbsp (25 g) butter, diced
2 tbsp (25 g) sugar
1 small pinch salt
1½ tbsp (12 g)
    confectioners' sugar
2 tbsp (12 g) almond
    powder
2½ tbsp (25 g) AP flour
Generous 1 tbsp (10 g)
    raspberry powder

Tart base
Butter for the pan
9 oz. (250 g) sweet
    shortcrust pastry dough
    (see p. 41)
7 oz. (200 g) frangipane
    cream (see p. 62)

Rhubarb jam
1 lb. (500 g) fresh rhubarb
1 cup + 1 tbsp (4 oz./115 g)
    sugar
1⅔ cups (385 ml) water
4 tsp (20 ml) beet juice

Candied rhubarb
1 stalk fresh rhubarb
Scant ½ cup (100 ml) pan
    juices from making
    the rhubarb jam

To assemble
Generous 2 tbsp
    (2 oz./50 g) raspberry
    jam

Decoration
5 oz. (150 g) fresh
    raspberries
Confectioners' sugar,
    for dusting

EQUIPMENT
Cookie sheet lined with
    parchment paper
8½-in. (22-cm) baking
    ring or tart pan with
    a removable base

---

1. **To prepare the raspberry crumble**, work the butter, sugar, and salt together in a mixing bowl using your fingers or a spatula, until combined. Add the confectioners' sugar and almond powder. Sift in the flour and raspberry powder. Work the ingredients together to make a crumble.

2. **Spread the crumble** over the cookie sheet. Chill for 1 hour. Toward the end of the chilling time, preheat the oven to 300°F (150°C/Gas Mark 2). Bake the crumble for 20 minutes. Remove from the cookie sheet, let cool completely, then reserve in a dry place.

3. **While the raspberry crumble is chilling**, prepare the tart shell. Lightly grease the inside of the baking ring or tart pan with butter. Line the cookie sheet with fresh parchment paper, then set the ring or pan on it.

4. **On a lightly floured surface**, roll the pastry dough into a circle large enough to line the ring or pan. Place the dough in the ring or pan, pressing it over the base and up the sides. Pinch around the top to make a border. Fill with the frangipane cream. Chill until baking.

5. **To prepare the rhubarb jam**, preheat the oven to 200°F (100°C/Gas Mark ¼). Wash and trim the rhubarb. Cut the stalks into 1¼-in. (3-cm) lengths. Place in the baking dish. Heat the sugar, water, and beet juice in a saucepan over low heat until the sugar dissolves. Bring to a boil, then carefully pour the hot syrup over the rhubarb.

6. **Bake for 20 minutes.** Drain, reserving the juices: there should be about a generous 1 cup (275 ml). Set aside a scant ½ cup (100 ml) to make the candied rhubarb.

Classic Linzer Torte (see p. 236)

7. **Transfer the rhubarb** to a skillet. Cook over low heat until the rhubarb is very tender, deglazing the pan 2–3 times with the remaining ¾ cup (175 ml) of juices. Transfer to a dish and press plastic wrap over the surface. Cool, then chill until using.

8. **To prepare the candied rhubarb,** increase the oven temperature to 250°F (120°C/Gas Mark ½). Wash and trim the rhubarb and cut the stalk into thirds. Place in a small baking dish and pour over the reserved scant ½ cup (100 ml) juices. Bake for 15–20 minutes until the rhubarb is tender.

9. **Cover the dish** with plastic wrap and poke a few holes in the wrap to allow steam to escape. Cool, then chill until using.

10. **Preheat the oven** to 400°F (200°C/Gas Mark 6). Place the tart in the oven and immediately reduce the temperature to 350°F (180°C/Gas Mark 4). Bake for 30–35 minutes, until the pastry is golden. Let cool slightly, then slide the tart off the cookie sheet onto a wire rack. When cool, remove the ring. Transfer to a serving plate.

11. **Drain the candied rhubarb** on paper towel to absorb any excess liquid. Spread the raspberry jam over the frangipane cream, followed by the rhubarb jam. Scatter the raspberry crumble on top. Chill until serving.

12. **When ready to serve,** arrange fresh raspberries over the crumble. Dust with confectioners' sugar and decorate with the candied rhubarb.

LINZER TARTE

CLASSIC LINZER TORTE ★

Makes
2 tortes, each serving 8

Active time: 25 minutes

Chilling time: 1 hour

Cooking time: 20 minutes

Storage: Up to 4 days

INGREDIENTS
Pastry crust
2 sticks + 4 tbsp
  (10 oz./280 g) butter,
  diced + more for the
  rings
2½ cups (10½ oz./300 g)
  AP flour
½ cup (1¾ oz./50 g)
  almond powder
⅓ cup (1¾ oz./50 g)
  confectioners' sugar
¾ tsp (2 g) ground
  cinnamon
1 tbsp rum
6 hard-boiled egg yolks

Filling
1½ cups (1 lb. 2 oz./500 g)
  raspberry jam with
  seeds
Generous ¾ cup
  (7 oz./200 g) apple
  compote (see p. 348),
  made with tart apples

EQUIPMENT
Fine-mesh sieve
2 × 9-in. (23-cm) baking
  rings (see Chef's Notes)
Cookie sheet lined with
  parchment paper
Fluted pastry wheel
  (or a ruler and knife)

1. **To prepare the pastry crust**, place the butter, flour, almond powder, confectioners' sugar, cinnamon, and rum in a mixing bowl. Press the egg yolks through a fine-mesh sieve into the bowl.

2. **Stir with a flexible spatula** to bring the ingredients together, making sure not to overwork them. Cover with plastic wrap, then chill for at least 1 hour (see Chef's Notes).

3. **Preheat the oven** to 430°F (220°C/Gas Mark 7). Lightly butter the baking rings and set them on the cookie sheet.

4. **Cut about** 14 oz. (400 g) of the dough in half. Roll each half on a lightly floured surface into circles large enough to line the rings. Press the dough over the base of each ring and up the sides, pinching around the top to make a border. Place in the refrigerator to firm up.

5. **To prepare the filling,** stir the raspberry jam and apple compote together. Divide between the baking rings, spreading it in an even layer. Knead the remaining dough lightly with your hands to make it a little more elastic and easier to use. Roll it to a thickness of ¼ in. (5 mm) or less on a lightly floured surface. Cut into strips measuring ¾ in. (1.5 cm) in width, using the fluted pastry wheel or a ruler and knife.

6. **Place the strips** over the tarts, arranging them in a crisscross lattice pattern. Trim them to the correct length. Dampen the ends of the strips to stick them to the pastry edges, pressing them lightly to fix them in place.

7. **Bake for 20 minutes**, until the pastry is golden.

8. **Let cool slightly.** Transfer the tarts to serving plates and lift off the rings. Serve warm or at room temperature.

Chef's Notes

• The dough is much crumblier than standard pastry, so baking rings rather than tart pans are recommended, as they are easier to remove.

• The unbaked dough can be stored in the refrigerator, covered in plastic wrap, for up to 2 days.

TARTE AUX ABRICOTS

APRICOT TART *

Serves
8

Active time: 35 minutes
+ making the shortcrust
pastry and frangipane
cream

Chilling time: 1 hour

Cooking time:
25–30 minutes

INGREDIENTS
Butter for the pan
10½ oz. (300 g) shortcrust
    pastry dough
    (see p. 40)
1¾ oz. (50 g) crushed
    plain cookie crumbs
7 oz. (200 g) frangipane
    cream (see p. 62)
2 lb. (1 kg) ripe fresh
    apricots, or canned
    apricot halves in syrup,
    well drained

Scant ⅓ cup (2 oz./60 g)
    sugar
2¾ oz. (80 g) apricot
    glaze, warm
⅔ cup (1¾ oz./50 g) sliced
    almonds, lightly toasted
Confectioners' sugar, for
    dusting

EQUIPMENT
10-in. (26-cm) tart pan,
    1¼ in. (3 cm) deep

1. **Lightly grease** the tart pan with butter.
2. **On a lightly floured surface,** roll the pastry dough very thinly into a large circle. Line it into the tart pan, then chill for at least 1 hour.
3. **Preheat the oven** to 400°F (200°C/Gas Mark 6).
4. **Scatter the cookie crumbs** over the base of the tart shell. Spread over the frangipane cream.
5. **If using fresh apricots,** wash and dry them. Cut them in half and remove the pits.
6. **Arrange the apricot halves,** cut sides up over the frangipane cream, placing them tightly together and overlapping them slightly. Sprinkle with the sugar.

7. **Bake for 10 minutes.** Reduce the oven temperature to 350°F (180°C/Gas Mark 4) and bake for another 25–30 minutes, until the filling is set and the edges of the apricots are nicely golden.
8. **Transfer the tart to a wire rack** to cool slightly. Brush the top with the warm apricot glaze and scatter over the almonds.
9. **Dust round the edge** with confectioners' sugar just before serving. Serve warm or cold, as soon as possible after baking.

TARTE AUX MIRABELLES

MIRABELLE PLUM TART ★★

Serves
8

Active time: 20 minutes
+ making the shortcrust
pastry and frangipane
cream

Cooking time: 35 minutes

Storage: 24 hours
in the refrigerator
(see Chef's Notes)

INGREDIENTS
3 tbsp (1¾ oz./50 g)
   butter + more for the
   pan
1 lb. (450 g) shortcrust
   pastry dough
   (see p. 40)
1¼ lb. (600 g) mirabelle
   plums (see Chef's
   Notes), fresh or canned
   in syrup and well
   drained

Scant ⅓ cup (2 oz./60 g)
   sugar
3 tbsp (45 ml) mirabelle
   or plum brandy
¾ lb. (350 g) frangipane
   cream (see p. 62)
1 egg, lightly beaten

EQUIPMENT
10-in. (26-cm) tart pan
Fluted pastry wheel
   (or a ruler and knife)

1. **Lightly grease the tart pan** with butter. Weigh out 3½ oz. (100 g) of the pastry dough for decoration. Cover with plastic wrap and chill until using.
2. **Roll the remaining dough thinly** into a large circle on a lightly floured surface. Line it into the tart pan. Chill until using.
3. **If using fresh plums,** wash and dry them. Cut the plums in half and remove the pits.
4. **Melt the butter and sugar** in a large skillet over medium-high heat, omitting the sugar if using canned plums. Add the plums and cook for about 5 minutes, until lightly caramelized on the edges.
5. **Add the brandy** and flambé. When the flames die down, remove from the heat. Let cool.
6. **Preheat the oven** to 430°F (220°C/Gas Mark 7).
7. **Spread the frangipane cream** over the base of the tart shell in an even layer. Cover with the plums, packing them tightly together.
8. **Roll the pastry dough** reserved for decoration to a thickness of about ¼ in. (5 mm) on a lightly floured surface. Cut into strips measuring ¾ in. (1.5 cm) in width, using the fluted pastry wheel or a ruler and knife.

9. **Place the strips** over the tart, arranging them in a crisscross lattice pattern. Trim them to the correct length. Dampen the ends of the strips to stick them to the pastry edges, pressing them lightly to fix them in place.
10. **Brush the pastry strips** with the beaten egg. Place the tart in the oven and immediately lower the temperature to 350°F (180°C/Gas Mark 4). Bake for about 35 minutes, until the pastry is golden; check the color toward the end of the baking time.
11. **Remove from the pan** while still warm. Serve as soon as possible after baking.

Chef's Notes
• Although the tart can be cooled and stored in the refrigerator for 24 hours, it is best eaten warm, as soon as possible after baking.
• Mirabelle plums are the size of cherries, golden in color, and exceptionally sweet. They are available in cans. However, if fresh plums are preferred and mirabelles are not available, substitute a small, sweet variety such as Sugar Baby or cherry plums.

TARTE AUX ORANGES CONFITES

CANDIED ORANGE TART ★★

Serves	INGREDIENTS	Tart shell	EQUIPMENT
8	*Candied orange slices (make 1 day ahead)*	Butter for the pan	10-in. (26-cm) tart pan
	3 oranges, preferably organic	10½ oz. (300 g) sweet shortcrust pastry dough (see p. 41)	Pie weights or dried beans
Active time: 55 minutes + making the candied orange slices, pastry cream, and shortcrust pastry	1¼ cups (300 ml) water	1 egg yolk, lightly beaten	Kitchen torch (optional)
	1¼ cups (8½ oz./240 g) sugar		
Macerating time: Overnight	*Orange pastry cream*	*Orange cream filling*	
	14 oz. (400 g) pastry cream (see p. 66), warm	Candied orange slices (see left)	
Cooking time: 20–25 minutes	Juice of ½ orange	Scant ½ cup (100 ml) heavy cream, well chilled	
		Orange pastry cream (see left)	
		Decoration	
		Granulated sugar, for sprinkling	

1. **A day ahead, prepare the candied orange slices.** Wash and dry the oranges. Cut them into very thin slices, without peeling them. Remove the seeds and discard the ends.
2. **Heat the water and sugar** in a saucepan and stir until the sugar dissolves. Add the orange slices, bring to a simmer over low heat, then let simmer for 15 minutes. Transfer to a covered container. Let macerate overnight.
3. **The following day, prepare the orange pastry cream.** Place the warm pastry cream in a mixing bowl and whisk in the orange juice. Let cool, then chill until using.
4. **Preheat the oven** to 400°F (200°C/Gas Mark 6). Lightly grease the tart pan with butter.
5. **To prepare the tart shell,** roll the pastry dough thinly into a large circle on a lightly floured surface. Line the dough into the tart pan, pressing it over the base and up the sides. Line with parchment paper, fill with pie weights, and blind-bake for 20 minutes.
6. **Remove the parchment paper** and weights. Brush the tart shell with the egg yolk to seal it. Return the tart shell to the oven for an additional 3–5 minutes, until evenly golden. Let cool on a wire rack.
7. **To prepare the orange cream filling,** chill the bowl and use the cream straight from the refrigerator (see Chef's Notes).

8. **Drain the candied orange slices,** weigh out 2½ oz. (70 g) of the smallest and least attractive ones, and chop these finely. Whip the cream until it holds its shape.
9. **Whisk the orange pastry cream** to loosen it. Fold in the whipped cream using a flexible spatula, then the finely chopped candied orange slices.
10. **To assemble the tart,** roughly chop 10 of the remaining candied orange slices, saving the most attractive slices for decoration. Scatter the chopped candied orange over the base of the tart shell. Cover with the orange cream filling, spreading it in an even layer.
11. **Sprinkle the top of the tart** with granulated sugar, if desired. Caramelize the sugar using a kitchen torch, or place briefly under a broiler, watching closely to make sure the sugar does not burn. Top with the reserved orange slices. Chill until ready to serve.

Chef's Notes
• If the cream and bowl are well chilled, the cream will be easier to whip.

TARTE BOURDALOUE AUX POIRES

FRENCH PEAR TART ★

Serves
6

Active time:
15 minutes + making
the shortcrust pastry,
frangipane cream,
and macarons

Chilling time:
1 hour

Cooking time:
35–40 minutes

INGREDIENTS
Tart shell
Butter for the baking ring
9 oz. (250 g) sweet
    shortcrust pastry dough
    (see p. 41) or shortcrust
    pastry dough (see p. 40)

Filling
9 oz. (250 g) frangipane
    cream (see p. 62)
4 pears, preferably
    Bartlett (Williams),
    cooked in syrup
    (see p. 372) or canned,
    well drained

Glaze
Pear jelly, homemade
    or store-bought, warm

Decoration
Confectioners' sugar,
    for dusting
6 mini vanilla macarons
    (see p. 407)
Toasted almonds, finely
    chopped

EQUIPMENT
9-in. (22-cm) baking ring,
    ¾ in. (2 cm) deep
Cookie sheet lined
    with parchment paper

1. **Grease the baking ring** with butter. Set it on the cookie sheet.
2. **To prepare the tart shell**, roll the pastry dough thinly into a 10½-in. (27-cm) circle on a lightly floured surface. Line it into the ring. Chill for 1 hour.
3. **Preheat the oven** to 400°F (200°C/Gas Mark 6).
4. **Spread the frangipane cream** over the base of the tart shell in an even layer.
5. **Cut 3 of the pears** in half lengthwise and remove the cores. Arrange the pear halves in a star pattern over the frangipane cream, rounded sides up, with their narrow ends pointing toward the center.
6. **Leave the fourth pear whole**, with the stalk attached, and place it upright in the center of the tart. Cover the stalk with aluminum foil to prevent it from burning.
7. **Place the tart in the oven** and immediately lower the temperature to 350°F (180°C/Gas Mark 4). Bake for 35–40 minutes, until the cream turns a golden color.
8. **Remove from the oven** and let cool. Remove the baking ring.
9. **Brush the warm pear jelly** over the pears to glaze them.
10. **Dust round the edge** of the tart with confectioners' sugar. Top each pear half with a mini macaron. Sprinkle with the chopped almonds and serve immediately.

TARTELETTE COUP DE SOLEIL
SUN-KISSED TARTLETS ★★★

Makes
10

Active time: 15 minutes
+ making the shortcrust
pastry and pastry cream

Chilling time: 1 hour

Cooking time: 15 minutes

INGREDIENTS
¾ lb. (350 g) sweet
   shortcrust pastry dough
   (see p. 41), made 1 day
   ahead
1 egg yolk, lightly beaten
7 oz. (200 g) pears, fresh
   or in syrup (see Chef's
   Notes)
1 lb. 2 oz. (500 g) pastry
   cream (see p. 66),
   chilled
¼ cup (1¾ oz./50 g) sugar

EQUIPMENT
10 × 3-in. (8-cm) round
   tartlet pans or baking
   rings
Cookie sheet lined
   with parchment paper
Pie weights or dried beans
Caramelizing iron
   or kitchen torch

1. **On a lightly floured surface,** roll the pastry dough to a thickness of about ⅛ in. (3 mm). Place the pans or rings on the cookie sheet. Line them with the dough, prick the bases with a fork, then chill for 1 hour.
2. **Preheat the oven** to 400°F (200°C/Gas Mark 6).
3. **Line the tartlet shells** with parchment paper and fill with pie weights. Place in the oven and immediately lower the temperature to 325°F (160°C/Gas Mark 3). Blind-bake for 20 minutes.
4. **Remove the parchment paper and weights.** Brush the tartlet shells with the egg yolk to seal them. Bake for an additional 3–5 minutes, until evenly golden. Let cool, then unmold.
5. **If using fresh pears,** peel, core, and cut them into thin slices. If using pears in syrup, drain them well before slicing thinly.
6. **Whisk the pastry cream** until smooth. Spread it over the base of each tartlet shell in a thin, even layer. Arrange the pear slices on top, then cover with the remaining pastry cream. Using a small offset spatula, smooth the cream to shape it into a slight dome over the fruit.
7. **Sprinkle with the sugar** and caramelize using a hot caramelizing iron or kitchen torch (see Chef's Notes). Serve the tartlets immediately.

Chef's Notes
• Many different fruits can be used, whether fresh or preserved in syrup. Peaches, pineapple, bananas, cherries, strawberries, and raspberries all work well. If using apricots or red currants, ones in syrup work best because, when fresh, these fruits tend to be too tart for this recipe.
• If using a kitchen torch to caramelize the sugar, take care to keep the flame away from the pastry. The sugar could also be caramelized under a broiler, but the pastry must be protected with a strip of aluminum foil to prevent it from burning.

TARTELETTE AUX ABRICOTS

APRICOT TARTLETS ★

Makes
10

Active time: 10 minutes
+ making the shortcrust
pastry

Cooking time: 25 minutes

INGREDIENTS
¾ lb. (350 g) sweet
shortcrust pastry dough
(see p. 41) or shortcrust
pastry dough (see p. 40)
1 oz. (25 g) crushed cookie
crumbs
30–40 pitted apricot
halves, fresh or in syrup
1 cup (7 oz./200 g) sugar
(omit if using apricots
in syrup)

Glaze
3½ oz. (100 g) apricot
glaze or neutral glaze
(see p. 81), warm

Decoration
Lightly toasted blanched
almonds, roughly
chopped

EQUIPMENT
10 × 3-in. (8-cm) tartlet
pans or baking rings,
¾ in. (1.5 cm) deep
Cookie sheet lined with
parchment paper

1. **Preheat the oven** to 400°F (200°C/Gas Mark 6).
2. **On a lightly floured surface**, roll out the pastry
dough to a thickness of about ⅛ in. (3 mm). Place the
pans or rings on the cookie sheet. Line them with the
dough.
3. **Sprinkle the cookie crumbs** over the base of the
tartlet shells to absorb any excess juice from the apricots.
4. **Arrange fresh apricot halves** over the cookie crumbs,
rounded sides up, overlapping them slightly. Sprinkle
with the sugar. If using apricots in syrup, drain them
well before placing them over the crumbs.
5. **Bake for 25 minutes**, until the pastry is golden.
Let cool slightly, then unmold.
6. **Brush the tops** with the warm glaze while the tartlets
are still hot. Sprinkle with the almonds. Serve on the
same day as the tartlets are made.

TARTE CHOCOLAT BANANE

CHOCOLATE AND BANANA TART ★★★

Serves
6

Active time: 1½ hours
+ making the Italian
meringue, shortcrust
pastry, and chocolate
crémeux

Freezing time: 1 hour

Chilling time: 1½ hours

Cooking time:
30–35 minutes

INGREDIENTS

Banana mousse layer
Scant ½ cup (100 ml)
  heavy cream, well
  chilled
1½ sheets gelatin,
  180–200 Bloom
2 bananas, peeled and
  mashed with a fork
1 tsp (5 ml) lemon juice
2¾ oz. (80 g) Italian
  meringue (see p. 32),
  warm

Tart shell
Butter for the baking ring
9 oz. (250 g) sweet
  shortcrust pastry dough
  (see p. 41)
1 egg yolk, lightly beaten
1¾ oz. (50 g) dark
  couverture chocolate,
  70% cacao, chopped
½ tsp (2.5 ml) grape-seed
  oil

Chocolate crémeux layer
2 quantities (1 lb. 1 oz./
  480 g) chocolate
  crémeux, Snow-Covered
  Yule Log recipe
  (see p. 164)
2¼ oz. (60 g) neutral glaze
  (see p. 81), warm

Decoration
1 small banana, preferably
  Lady Finger
Sugar, for sprinkling

EQUIPMENT
Electric hand beater
7-in. (18-cm) baking ring,
  ¾ in. (1.5 cm) deep
2 cookie sheets lined
  with parchment paper
10½-in. (27-cm) baking
  ring, 1 in. (2.5 cm) deep
Pie weights or dried beans
Instant-read thermometer
Pastry bag fitted with
  a Saint-Honoré tip
Kitchen torch (optional)

1. **To prepare the banana mousse layer**, whip the cream until it holds its shape. Chill until using.
Soak the gelatin in a bowl of cold water until softened. In a mixing bowl, whisk together the mashed bananas and lemon juice.
2. **Whisk half the warm Italian meringue** into the mashed bananas. Squeeze the gelatin to remove excess water. Microwave on high in a small bowl for 5 seconds, or until melted. Whisk the gelatin into the banana and meringue mixture. Fold in the other half of the meringue, using a flexible spatula. Finally, fold in the whipped cream.
3. **Set the 7-in. (18-cm) baking ring** on one of the cookie sheets. Spoon the banana mousse into the ring and smooth it level, so it is flush with the top of the ring. Freeze for at least 1 hour.

4. **Grease the 10½-in. (27-cm) baking ring** with butter. Set it on the other cookie sheet.
5. **To prepare the tart shell**, roll the pastry dough on a lightly floured surface into a 10½-in. (27-cm) circle with a thickness of about ⅛ in. (3 mm). Line it into the ring. Chill for at least 1 hour.
6. **Preheat the oven** to 340°F (170°C/Gas Mark 3). Line the tart shell with parchment paper and fill with pie weights. Blind-bake for 20–25 minutes.
7. **Remove the parchment paper** and weights and brush the pastry with the egg yolk to seal it. Return to the oven for an additional 3–5 minutes, until evenly golden. Transfer to a wire rack. Let cool, then remove the ring.
8. **Melt the chocolate** in a bowl over a saucepan of barely simmering water (bain-marie) until the temperature reaches 104°F (40°C). Stir in the grape-seed oil until smooth. Brush the melted chocolate over the pastry. Chill until set.

9. **To prepare the chocolate crémeux layer**, spread 9 oz. (250 g) of the chocolate crémeux over the base of the tart shell in an even layer. Chill for 30 minutes. Chill the remaining crémeux on a plate covered with plastic wrap.

10. **To assemble the tart**, remove the banana mousse from the freezer. Run a thin-bladed knife around the inside of the ring and lift it off. Cover with a thin layer of warmed neutral glaze. Place the mousse in the center of the tart shell, over the chocolate crémeux.

11. **Spoon the remaining crémeux** into the pastry bag and pipe it around the edge of the tart to resemble small petals. Chill until serving.

12. **Just before serving,** cut the small banana in half lengthwise. Place one half, cut side up, on a cookie sheet and sprinkle with sugar. Caramelize with the kitchen torch or under a broiler. Place both halves of the banana on the tart and serve.

Chef's Notes
• For an alternative decoration, caramelize one half of the small banana as above and place it in the ring in step 3, before spooning in the banana mousse and freezing. The caramelized banana will be encased in the mousse.

TARTE CITRON MERINGUÉE

LEMON MERINGUE TART ★★

Serves
8

Active time: 1 hour +
making the shortcrust
pastry

Macerating time:
Overnight

Chilling time: 1 hour

Cooking time:
45–50 minutes

INGREDIENTS

*Lemon sugar
(make 1 day ahead)*
1 cup minus 2 tbsp
   (6 oz./165 g) sugar
Finely grated zest of
   4 lemons, preferably
   organic

Tart shell
10½ oz. (300 g) sweet
   shortcrust pastry dough
   (see p. 41)
1 egg yolk (1½ tbsp/20 g),
   lightly beaten

Lemon crémeux
2 sheets gelatin
Juice of 4 lemons
   (scant ½ cup/100 ml)
2 tsp (10 ml) yuzu or lime
   juice
Lemon sugar (see above)
3 eggs (⅔ cup/150 g)
1 egg yolk (1½ tbsp/20 g)
1 stick (4 oz./120 g) butter,
   diced

Italian meringue
3 small egg whites
   (⅓ cup/75 g)
⅔ cup (4½ oz./125 g)
   sugar
2 tbsp (30 ml) water
1 tsp (4 g) sugar
1 tbsp (15 ml) lime juice

Lemon jelly
½ sheet gelatin
2 tbsp (30 ml) lemon juice
2½ tsp (10 g) sugar

Decoration
1–2 lemons, segmented,
   or very thinly sliced
   candied lemon slices
Fine strips of lemon zest

EQUIPMENT

10-in. (26-cm) baking ring,
   1 in. (2.5 cm) deep
Cookie sheet lined with
   parchment paper
Pie weights or dried beans
Instant-read thermometer
Immersion blender
Pastry bag fitted with a ¾-in.
   (1.5-cm) fluted tip

1. **A day ahead, prepare the lemon sugar.** Stir the sugar and lemon zest together. Chill overnight in a covered container to allow the flavors to develop. Reserve a scant ½ cup (100 ml) of the juice from the lemons to make the crémeux.

2. **The following day**, prepare the tart shell. Set the baking ring on the cookie sheet. Roll out the pastry dough on a lightly floured surface to a thickness of about ⅛ in. (3 mm). Line it into the ring and chill for 1 hour.

3. **Preheat the oven** to 400°F (200°C/Gas Mark 6). Line the tart shell with parchment paper and fill with pie weights. Place the tart in the oven and immediately lower the temperature to 350°F (180°C/Gas Mark 4). Blind-bake for 30 minutes.

4. **Remove the parchment paper** and weights. Brush the tart shell with the egg yolk to seal it. Return it to the oven for 3–5 minutes, until evenly golden. Transfer to a wire rack to cool, then remove the ring.

5. **To prepare the lemon crémeux**, soak the gelatin in a bowl of cold water until softened. Pour the reserved lemon juice and yuzu or lime juice into a saucepan, add the lemon sugar, then whisk in the eggs and egg yolk. Heat until the mixture reaches 192°F (89°C), whisking constantly. Remove from the heat. Squeeze the gelatin to remove excess water, then whisk it into the hot mixture until melted.

6. **Pour into a mixing bowl.** Set over a larger bowl filled halfway with ice water and continue whisking until the crémeux cools to 104°F (40°C). Add the butter, one piece at a time, then process with the immersion blender until smooth.

7. **Pour the crémeux** into the tart shell and smooth it into an even layer. Chill until using.

8. **Prepare the Italian meringue** using the quantities given above, following the instructions on p. 32. Whisk the lime juice into the egg whites when they hold firm peaks. Spoon the warm meringue into the pastry bag.

9. **To prepare the lemon jelly**, soak the gelatin in a bowl of cold water until softened. Heat the lemon juice and sugar in a saucepan until the temperature reaches 140°F (60°C), stirring to dissolve the sugar. Squeeze the gelatin to remove excess water and whisk it into the hot syrup until melted. Pour into a shallow dish and chill until using. The jelly should be starting to thicken but not be completely set when it is spooned over the tart.

10. **Preheat the broiler.** Cut a circle of parchment paper the size of the area in the center of the tart that will not be piped with meringue. Place the circle in the center of the tart and, starting at the outside edge, pipe a tight spiral of meringue over the lemon crémeux, finishing when you reach the edge of the parchment circle.

11. **Place the tart** under the broiler for a few minutes, until the meringue is lightly scorched.

12. **Arrange the lemon segments** or candied lemon slices in the center of the tart. Scatter over the strips of lemon zest, then spoon over the jelly.

13. **Chill and serve** on the same day as the tart is made.

TARTE FEUILLETÉE ÉLÉONORE
ÉLÉONORE'S APPLE TART *

Serves
6

Active time: 15 minutes +
making the puff pastry

Cooking time: 20 minutes

INGREDIENTS
7 oz. (200 g) puff pastry
    dough, classic (see p. 28)
    or quick (see p. 29)
5 even-sized baking apples
    (see Chef's Notes)
Scant ½ cup (3½ oz./
    100 g) apple compote
    (see p. 348 and Chef's
    Notes)
Scant ¼ cup (1 oz./30 g)
    confectioners' sugar,
    divided
4 tbsp (2 oz./60 g) butter,
    diced

To serve (optional)
Crème fraîche

EQUIPMENT
Cookie sheet lined
    with parchment paper
Fine-mesh sieve

1. Preheat the oven to 400°F (200°C/Gas Mark 6).
2. On a lightly floured surface, roll out the pastry dough into a square with a thickness of ⅛ in. (3 mm).
3. Trim the dough to shape it into a circle.
Place the trimmings in the center. Roll out the dough again to a thickness of ⅛ in (3 mm). Place it on the cookie sheet, then cut into a 10-in. (26-cm) circle. The trimmings can be used for another recipe.
4. Peel and core the apples. Cut each one into 8 wedges. Spread a thin layer of apple compote over the pastry, leaving a 1¼-in. (3-cm) border around the edge.
5. Arrange the apple wedges over the compote in concentric circles. Pack them tightly together, working from the outside toward the center and overlapping the circles. Dust with half of the confectioners' sugar. Dot the butter over the top.

6. Place the tart in the oven and immediately lower the temperature to 350°F (180°C/Gas Mark 4). Bake for 25 minutes. Reduce the heat to 340°F (170°C/Gas Mark 3) 5 minutes before the end of the baking time. The pastry and apples should be golden.
7. Remove from the oven. Dust immediately with the remaining confectioners' sugar to make the apples glisten.
8. Serve warm and, if desired, top each slice with a spoonful of crème fraîche.

Chef's Notes
• Chantecler apples are perfect for this tart, as they keep their shape when baked. Other varieties such as Golden Delicious or Belle de Boskoop can be substituted if Chantecler are not available.
• If very sweet apples are used for the wedges, make the compote with tart apples to counterbalance the sweetness.

TARTE FOLLEMENT ANANAS

EXCEEDINGLY PINEAPPLE TART ★★

Serves
6

Active time: 1 hour

Cooking time: 40 minutes

Infusing time: 15 minutes

Chilling time: 1 hour

INGREDIENTS

Gluten-free pastry crust
Neutral oil for the pan
4 tbsp (2½ oz./65 g)
  butter
⅓ cup (1¾ oz./50 g)
  confectioners' sugar
1 small pinch fine salt
1 tbsp (15 ml) whole milk
2 tbsp (20 g) rice flour
2½ tbsp (25 g)
  potato starch
2½ tbsp (25 g) cornstarch
¼ tsp (1 g) gluten-free
  baking powder
1 egg yolk (1½ tbsp/20 g),
  lightly beaten

Coconut dacquoise
2 egg whites (¼ cup/60 g)
3¾ tsp (15 g) granulated
  sugar
⅓ cup (1½ oz./40 g)
  confectioners' sugar,
  sifted
¼ cup (25 g) almond
  powder
3 tbsp (15 g) shredded
  coconut

Passion fruit jelly
¼ sheet gelatin
1 oz. (30 g) passion fruit
  puree or 2 tbsp (30 ml)
  passion fruit juice
1 tsp (4 g) sugar

Vanilla crémeux
1 sheet gelatin
¾ cup (175 ml) heavy
  cream
¼ Bourbon Madagascar
  vanilla bean, split
  lengthwise
2 egg yolks (2½ tbsp/40 g)
5 tsp (20 g) sugar
2 tbsp (1 oz./30 g) butter,
  diced

Pineapple topping
10½ oz. (300 g) fresh
  pineapple
½ oz. (15 g) neutral glaze
  (see p. 81), warm

Decoration
Confectioners' sugar,
  for dusting
Finely grated zest of
  1 lime, preferably
  organic
Toasted coconut shavings

EQUIPMENT
9-in. (22-cm) tart pan,
  1¼ in. (3 cm) deep
Instant-read thermometer
Electric hand beater
Pastry bag fitted with
  a ½-in. (1-cm) plain tip
Immersion blender
Rimmed baking sheet

1. **Preheat the oven** to 340°F (170°C/Gas Mark 3). Grease the tart pan with neutral oil.

2. **To prepare the pastry crust**, melt the butter in a small saucepan until it reaches 140°F (60°C). Whisk in the confectioners' sugar and salt. Heat the milk to 140°F (60°C) in another saucepan (or microwave) and whisk into the melted butter and sugar.

3. **Sift the rice flour**, potato starch, cornstarch, and baking powder into a mixing bowl. Add the mixture from the saucepan, then fold everything together using a flexible spatula. Stir in the egg yolk. Pour into the tart pan.

4. **Bake for 20 minutes.** Let cool in the pan. Keep the oven switched on for the coconut dacquoise.

5. **To prepare the dacquoise**, whisk the egg whites until they hold soft peaks. Gradually whisk in the granulated sugar until the peaks are firm. Combine the confectioners' sugar, almond powder, and shredded coconut in a bowl and, using a flexible spatula, gently fold them into the meringue.

6. **Spoon the meringue** into the pastry bag. Pipe it in a spiral over the base of the tart crust to cover it. Pipe a raised border of meringue around the edge just inside the rim of the pan.

7. **Bake for 25 minutes**, until the dacquoise is dry and lightly golden. Let cool slightly in the pan, then unmold onto a wire rack. Let cool.

8. **To prepare the passion fruit jelly**, soak the gelatin in a bowl of cold water until softened. Heat the passion fruit puree or juice and sugar in a saucepan until the temperature reaches 140°F (60°C). Squeeze the gelatin to remove excess water and whisk it into the hot mixture until melted. Set aside the jelly until using.

9. **To prepare the vanilla crémeux**, soak the gelatin in a bowl of cold water until softened. Heat the cream and vanilla bean in a saucepan, then bring to a simmer. Remove from the heat, cover, and let infuse for 15 minutes. Remove the vanilla bean, scraping any remaining seeds into the cream.

10. **Whisk together the egg yolks** and sugar until pale and thick. Pour over half the warm cream, whisking constantly, then return the mixture to the saucepan. Stir continuously over low heat, using a spatula in a figure-eight motion, until the temperature of the custard reaches 181°F (83°C).

11. **Squeeze the gelatin** to remove excess water. Whisk it into the hot custard until melted. Set the saucepan over a bowl filled halfway with ice water and cool the custard to 104°F (40°C), whisking frequently. Add the butter and process with the immersion blender until smooth.

12. **Pour half the crémeux** over the coconut dacquoise, spreading it in an even layer. Cover with the passion fruit jelly, then the remaining crémeux. Chill for 1 hour.

13. **To prepare the topping**, peel, core, and cut the pineapple crosswise into ½-in. (1-cm) slices. Cut the slices into matchsticks or wedges. Spread out the pineapple on the baking sheet and dry it out for 5 minutes in a 400°F (200°C/Gas Mark 6) oven (see Chef's Notes).

14. **Let cool**, then arrange the pineapple over the center of the tart. Brush with a thin coating of glaze.

15. **Just before serving**, dust round the edges of the tart with confectioners' sugar. Sprinkle the lime zest and toasted coconut shavings over the pineapple. Serve chilled.

Chef's Notes
• Drying out the pineapple in the oven will avoid too much juice leaking into the tart.
• The lime zest garnish will add a wonderful freshness to the tart.

TARTE NORMANDE GLACE ROYALE

ICED NORMANDY APPLE PIE *

Serves
6–8

Active time: 15 minutes
+ making the shortcrust
pastry

Cooking time: 40 minutes

INGREDIENTS
Apple filling
1¼ lb. (600 g) firm baking
    apples (preferably King
    of the Pippins)
3 tbsp (1¾ oz./50 g)
    butter
½ cup minus 1½ tbsp
    (2¾ oz./80 g) vanilla
    sugar

Tart shell
¾ lb. (350 g) shortcrust
    pastry dough
    (see p. 40)

Royal icing
½ egg white (15 g)
Scant 1 cup (4½ oz./125 g)
    confectioners' sugar
3 drops lemon juice

Decoration
Pastry trimmings
Sliced almonds

EQUIPMENT
10-in. (26-cm) tart pan
    with a removable base,
    1½ in. (4 cm) deep

1. **To prepare the apple filling**, peel and core the apples. Cut them into thick slices.
2. **Melt the butter** in a skillet and stir in the vanilla sugar. Add the apples and sauté for 5 minutes, until lightly caramelized. Remove from the pan and let cool completely.
3. **To prepare the tart shell,** divide the pastry dough into two pieces, one slightly larger than the other.
4. **On a lightly floured surface,** roll the larger piece of dough into a 12-in. (30-cm) circle with a thickness of about ⅛ in. (3 mm). Line the dough into the tart pan, pressing it over the base and up the sides. Reserve the trimmings for decoration. Prick the base all over with a fork. Arrange the apples on top.
5. **Roll the remaining dough** into a 10-in. (26-cm) circle with a thickness of about ⅛ in. (3 mm). Dampen the edges of the dough in the tart pan and place the circle of pastry over the apples. Press the edges together to seal, then lightly press the pastry circle to make the top as flat as possible.
6. **Preheat the oven** to 400°F (200°C/Gas Mark 6).
7. **To prepare the royal icing,** whisk the confectioners' sugar and egg white together in a bowl for 2 minutes, until frothy. Stir in the lemon juice. Using a small offset spatula, spread an even layer of the icing over the top of the pie.

8. **Before the icing has set,** roll out the reserved pastry dough trimmings and cut into 3 strips measuring ½ in. (1 cm) in width. Dampen the underside of the strips and place them on top of the pie (see photo on facing page). Place a few sliced almonds between each strip.
9. **Bake for 40 minutes,** until the icing is pale gold. As soon as the icing has dried out, cover the pie with aluminum foil to prevent the icing from burning. The oven door could also be propped open with the handle of a wooden spoon.
10. **Unmold the pie while still warm.** Serve immediately.

Chef's Notes
• This pie is best eaten when freshly baked. If desired, it can be stored at room temperature and served later on the same day. Reheat in a low oven before serving.

TARTE NOUGAT POMME

APPLE AND ALMOND TART ★

Serves	INGREDIENTS	5 tbsp (3 oz./80 g) butter,	EQUIPMENT
6	*Almond topping*	melted	9-in. (22-cm) baking ring,
	(make 3 days ahead)	½ cup minus 1½ tbsp	1¼ in. (3 cm) deep
	2 extra-large egg whites	(2¾ oz./80 g) vanilla	Cookie sheet lined with
Active time: 45 minutes	(⅓ cup/70 g)	sugar	parchment paper
+ making the almond	⅓ cup (2½ oz./70 g) sugar		Pie weights or dried beans
topping, baked apples,	Generous ¾ cup (2½ oz./	*Tart shell*	
and shortcrust pastry	70 g) sliced almonds	Butter for the baking ring	
		10½ oz. (300 g) sweet	
Soaking time: 3 days	*Baked apples*	shortcrust pastry dough	
	(make 1 day ahead)	(see p. 41)	
Cooking time: 1 hour	2¾ lb. (1.2 kg) firm	1 egg yolk, lightly beaten	
20 minutes	baking apples (such as		
	Chantecler or Belle de	*Decoration*	
Storage: Up to 24 hours	Boskoop)	Confectioners' sugar,	
in the refrigerator		for dusting	

1. **Start preparing the almond topping 3 days ahead.** In a bowl, whisk together the egg whites and sugar for a few seconds to dissolve the sugar. Stir in the almonds using a fork until thoroughly coated. Keep covered in the refrigerator, stirring each morning and evening for 3 days to allow the almonds to absorb the syrup.

2. **A day ahead, prepare the baked apples.** Preheat the oven to 340°F (170°C/Gas Mark 3).

3. **Peel, halve, and core** the apples. Place them side by side in a baking dish, cut sides down. Pour the melted butter over them, then sprinkle with the vanilla sugar.

4. **Bake for 30 minutes,** until the apples are tender and can be pierced easily with the tip of a knife. Let cool. Keep covered in the refrigerator overnight.

5. **The following day, prepare the tart shell.** Preheat the oven to 325°F (160°C/Gas Mark 3). Lightly grease the inside of the baking ring with butter. Set it on the cookie sheet.

6. **On a lightly floured surface,** roll the pastry dough into a 12-in. (30-cm) circle with a thickness of about ⅛ in. (3–4 mm). Line it into the ring, pinching the top edge with your fingers to make a slight ridge. Trim off any excess dough.

7. **Line the tart shell with parchment paper,** fill with pie weights, and blind-bake for 20 minutes. Remove the parchment paper and weights and bake for an additional 5 minutes, until evenly golden. Brush the pastry with the egg yolk and return the tart shell to the oven for 3–5 minutes to seal it. Let cool slightly. Increase the oven temperature to 340°F (170°C/Gas Mark 3–4).

8. **Arrange the apples** cut sides down in the tart shell, packing them tightly together and filling any gaps with the smallest pieces. Press down on the apples so they form a slight dome.

9. **Drain the almonds** from any remaining syrup. Spread them over the apples in an even layer, using a palette knife. Bake for 20 minutes, until golden.

10. **Slide the tart** onto a wire rack. Let cool for a few minutes, then run a knife around the inside of the ring and lift it off.

11. **Just before serving,** dust round the edges of the tart with confectioners' sugar. Serve warm.

Chef's Notes
• If keeping the tart until the next day, let cool, then store it in the refrigerator. Reheat in a low oven before dusting with confectioners' sugar and serving.

TARTE TATIN ★

Serves
10

Active time: 10 minutes +
making the puff pastry

Cooking time: 40 minutes

INGREDIENTS
6 oz. (180 g) puff pastry
    dough, classic (see p. 28)
    or quick (see p. 29)
3 lb. (1.25 kg) tart, firm
    baking apples (such as
    Chantecler, Braeburn, or
    Belle de Boskoop)
1 stick (4 oz./120 g) butter
1⅓ cups (9½ oz./270 g)
    sugar

EQUIPMENT
Cookie sheet lined
    with parchment paper
9½-in. (24-cm) burner-
    and oven-safe round
    pan or skillet, preferably
    enameled cast iron

1. On a lightly floured surface, roll the pastry dough into a 10-in. (26-cm) circle with a thickness of 1/16 in. (2 mm). Place the dough on the cookie sheet, then prick it all over with a fork. Chill until using.

2. Preheat the oven to 430°F (220°C/Gas Mark 7).

3. Peel, halve, and core the apples, removing all the seeds. Place the butter and sugar in the pan or skillet and heat until the butter has melted and the sugar has dissolved.

4. Place the apple halves vertically in the melted butter and sugar, packing them tightly together. At this point, the apples will be taller than the sides of the pan.

5. Return the pan to the heat. Let simmer over low heat for about 20 minutes, until the apples have softened and the butter and sugar have turned into a light golden caramel.

6. Place in the oven for 5 minutes, so the apples collapse slightly.

7. Remove from the oven and carefully place the pastry dough over them. Tuck any dough that hangs over the edges down the sides, between the apples and the pan.

8. Return to the oven, reduce the heat to 400°F (200°C/Gas Mark 6), and bake for another 15 minutes, until the pastry is puffed and golden.

9. Place a serving plate with a rim, to catch any caramel that runs out, on top of the tart, then carefully upturn it. Lift off the pan. Serve warm.

TARTE AUX 5 NOIX

FIVE-NUT TART *

Serves	INGREDIENTS	Five-Nut Filling	EQUIPMENT
6	*Caramelized pecans*	3 small eggs (½ cup/130 g)	Rimmed baking sheet
	(see Chef's Notes)	⅔ cup (4¾ oz./135 g)	lined with parchment
	4 cups (17 oz./480 g)	brown sugar	paper
Active time: 35 minutes	pecan halves	⅛ tsp (0.5 g) fine salt	Instant-read thermometer
+ making the shortcrust	1 cup + 1 tbsp (4 oz./115 g)	¼ tsp (1 ml) pure vanilla	Silicone baking mat (or
pastry	sugar, divided	extract	parchment paper)
	2 tbsp (30 ml) water	3 tbsp (2 oz./60 g) maple	9-in. (22-cm) baking ring,
Chilling time: 1 hour	2 tsp (10 g) butter, diced	syrup	¾ in. (2 cm) deep
		3 tbsp (2 oz./60 g) honey	Cookie sheet lined with
	Tart shell	5 tbsp (2½ oz./70 g)	parchment paper
Cooking time: 30–	Butter for the baking ring	butter, melted and	
35 minutes	9 oz. (250 g) sweet	cooled	
	shortcrust pastry dough	9 oz. (250 g) assorted	
Storage: Up to 2 days	(see p. 41)	nuts (walnuts, pecans,	
at room temperature or		cashews, Macadamia,	
5 days in the refrigerator		and Brazil), chopped	
		Decoration	
		Confectioners' sugar,	
		for dusting	

1. **Preheat the oven** to 140°F (60°C/Gas on the lowest setting).
2. **Spread the pecans** over the baking sheet and dry them out in the oven for 30 minutes. Keep warm.
3. **Combine** a scant ½ cup (3 oz./90 g) of the sugar and the water in a large saucepan and cook over low heat until the sugar dissolves. Increase the heat, bring to a boil, and continue boiling until the syrup reaches 239°F (115°C).
4. **Remove from the heat**, then stir in the pecans with a wooden spoon, until the sugar crystallizes and looks sandy. Return the saucepan to medium-low heat and cook, stirring constantly, until the sugar caramelizes. Remove from the heat.
5. **Scatter the butter** over the pecans to make it easier to separate them. Stir in the remaining 2 tbsp (1 oz./25 g) sugar and turn out immediately onto the silicone mat (or parchment paper). Tap to separate the pecans, then let cool completely. Set aside ⅓ cup (1½ oz./40 g) to decorate the tart.
6. **Grease the baking ring** with butter. Set it on the cookie sheet.
7. **To prepare the tart shell**, roll the pastry dough on a lightly floured surface into a 10½-in. (27-cm) circle

with a thickness of about ⅛ in. (3 mm). Line the dough into the ring, pressing it over the base and up the sides. Chill for 1 hour.
8. **Preheat the oven** to 340°F (170°C/Gas Mark 3).
9. **To prepare the filling**, whisk together the eggs, brown sugar, salt, vanilla extract, maple syrup, and honey in a mixing bowl. Whisk in the melted butter.
10. **Spread the chopped nuts** over the base of the tart shell. Pour over the egg mixture, filling the ring to within ¹⁄₁₆ in. (2 mm) of the rim.
11. **Bake for 30–35 minutes**, until golden brown.
12. **Slide the tart** onto a wire rack. Let cool for several minutes. Run a knife around the inside of the ring and lift it off. Let cool completely.
13. **Just before serving**, dust round the edges of the tart with confectioners' sugar and decorate with the reserved caramelized pecans.

Chef's Notes
• The caramelized pecan recipe makes about 1 lb. 2 oz. (500 g), which is the minimum recommended amount to make, to ensure optimal results. The remaining nuts will keep for about 2 weeks in an airtight container in a dry place.

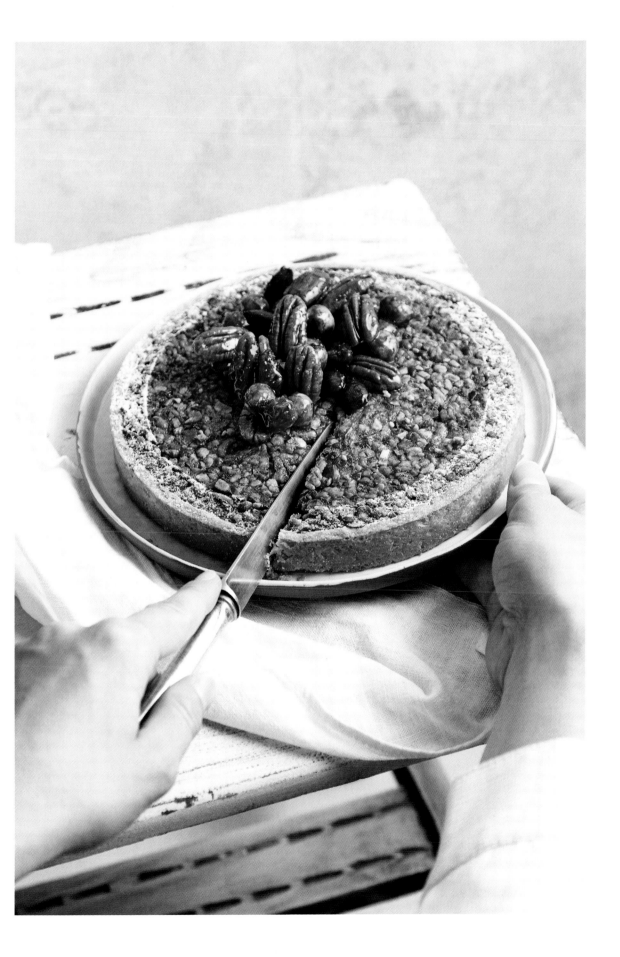

INDIVIDUAL PASTRIES AND TARTLETS

CHOCOLATINES ★★

Makes
10

Active time: 30 minutes
+ making the succès
meringue bases,
chocolate mousse,
and chocolate icing

Chilling time: 2 hours

Storage: Up to 24 hours

INGREDIENTS
30 × 2½-in. (6-cm) succès
meringue bases
(see p. 34 and Chef's
Notes), made 1 day
ahead
1 quantity (12¼ oz./350 g)
chocolate mousse
(see p. 82)
3½ oz. (100 g) chocolate
glaze (see p. 76)
Unsweetened cocoa
powder, for dusting

EQUIPMENT
10 × 2½-in. (6-cm) metal
baking rings, 1¼ in.
(3 cm) deep, or 2½-in.
(6-cm) round plastic
dessert cups
Cookie sheet, lined
with parchment paper
if using rings

1. **Set the rings** or dessert cups on the cookie sheet.
2. **Place a meringue base** in each ring or cup. Using
a palette knife, spread with a layer of chocolate mousse.
Place a second meringue layer on top, then cover with
the remaining mousse.
3. **Clean the palette knife**, dip it in water, and smooth
the mousse so it is flush with the top of each ring.
Chill for 1 hour.
4. **Reheat the chocolate glaze** to 104°F (40°C) in a bowl
over a saucepan of barely simmering water (bain-marie).
Make sure not to create any air bubbles when stirring.
5. **Remove the chocolatines** from the refrigerator. Pour
a thin layer of glaze over the top of each one. Chill for
at least 30 minutes, to allow the glaze to set.
6. **Run a hot, damp sponge** around the outside of the
rings to loosen them. Rotate slightly, then carefully lift
off the rings. If using plastic cups, immerse the bases
briefly in hot water, before unmolding the chocolatines.
Chill for at least 30 minutes.
7. **Before serving,** place a third succès base on each
chocolatine. Dust with cocoa powder.

Chef's Notes
• The succès base recipe on p. 34 makes about 40 small
bases. Only 30 are needed for the chocolatines, but the
remaining bases can be stored in an airtight container
for up to 2 weeks.
• The bases can be made in advance. The mousse,
however, should be made on the day the chocolatines
are assembled.
• Instead of using glaze, the chocolatines can be dusted
with ⅓ cup (1¾ oz./50 g) confectioners' sugar sifted
with 3 tbsp (20 g) unsweetened cocoa powder.

CHOUX PRALINÉS
PRALINE CHOUX PUFFS ⋆

Makes
10

Active time: 30 minutes + making the choux pastry and pastry cream

Cooking time: 30 minutes

INGREDIENTS
Choux puffs
9 oz. (250 g) choux pastry dough (see p. 38 and Chef's Notes)
3 oz. (80 g) chopped almonds

Praline pastry cream
1¾ oz. (50 g) almond praline paste
⅓ quantity (7 oz./200 g) pastry cream (see p. 66)
7 tbsp (3½ oz./100 g) butter, softened and diced

Decoration
⅓ cup (1¾ oz./50 g) confectioners' sugar, for dusting

EQUIPMENT
2 pastry bags fitted with ¾-in. (1.5-cm) and ½-in. (1-cm) plain tips
Cookie sheet lined with parchment paper
Electric hand beater

---

1. **Preheat the oven** to 430°F (220°C/Gas Mark 7).
2. **To make the choux puffs,** spoon the choux pastry dough into the pastry bag with a ¾-in. (1.5-cm) tip. Pipe 10 mounds, 1½ in. (4 cm) in diameter, onto the cookie sheet, leaving space between them so they have room to rise in the oven.
3. **Sprinkle with the almonds.** Place in the oven, propping the door ajar with the handle of a wooden spoon. Bake for 30 minutes, until golden and crisp on the outside but still soft in the center. Let cool on a wire rack.
4. **To prepare the praline pastry cream,** whisk the praline paste into the pastry cream. Whisk in the butter until light and creamy. Transfer to the pastry bag with the ½-in. (1-cm) tip.
5. **Cut a small slit** in the side of each puff with the tip of a knife. Pipe the cream into the puffs to fill them.
6. **Sift over the confectioners' sugar** and chill until ready to serve. Serve on the same day as the puffs are made.

Chef's Notes
• Although choux pastry dough must be used as soon as it is made, it freezes well once baked. Bake extra puffs or éclairs with any leftover pastry and freeze them, unfilled.

COLISÉES ★★

Makes	INGREDIENTS	To serve	EQUIPMENT

Makes
10

Active time: 30 minutes + making the succès meringue bases, hazelnut praline buttercream, and chocolate glaze

Chilling time: 1½ hours

Storage: Up to 24 hours in the refrigerator

INGREDIENTS

⅔ cup (3½ oz./100 g) golden raisins (sultanas)

2 tbsp (30 ml) aged rum, hot

20 × 2½-in. (6-cm) succès meringue bases (see p. 34), made 1 day ahead

¾ lb. (350 g) hazelnut praline buttercream (see p. 59)

10½ oz. (300 g) chocolate glaze (see p. 76 and Chef's Notes)

To serve

Unsweetened cocoa powder, for dusting

Chopped almonds

EQUIPMENT

10 × 2½-in. (6-cm) metal baking rings, 1¼ in. (3 cm) deep, or 2½-in. (6-cm) round plastic dessert cups

Cookie sheet, lined with parchment paper if using rings

Instant-read thermometer

---

1. **Soak the raisins** in the hot rum until softened. Drain well.

2. **Set the baking rings or cups** on the cookie sheet. Place a meringue base in each one.

3. **Whisk the praline buttercream** until smooth and spread half of it over the bases. Sprinkle with the rum-soaked raisins. Place a second meringue base on top, pressing down gently to make sure the layers are level.

4. **Cover with the remaining buttercream.** Using a palette knife, smooth the buttercream so it is flush with the tops of the rings or cups. Chill for 1 hour.

5. **Remove the cakes** from the refrigerator. Run a hot, damp sponge around the outside of the rings to loosen them. Rotate slightly, then carefully lift off the rings. If using plastic cups, immerse the bases briefly in hot water, then invert the cakes onto a rack.

6. **Melt the glaze** in a bowl over a saucepan of barely simmering water (bain-marie), until the temperature reaches 104°F (40°C). Pour the glaze over the cakes to evenly coat them. Chill for at least 30 minutes, to allow the glaze to set.

7. **Sift a generous dusting of cocoa powder** onto serving plates, then scatter over chopped almonds. Carefully place a colisée on each plate. It is preferable to serve the colisées on the day they are made. If serving them the following day, they must be kept chilled.

Chef's Notes

• The chocolate glaze on p. 76 can be replaced by the glaze in the Opéra cake recipe (see p. 208), which should be prepared just before using.

ÉCLAIR GOURMAND CITRON

LEMON MERINGUE ÉCLAIRS **

Makes
10

Active time: 45 minutes +
making the choux pastry,
lemon crémeux and
decorations

Cooking time: 35 minutes

Chilling time: 30 minutes

INGREDIENTS
Éclairs
10½ oz. (300 g) choux
   pastry dough
   (see p. 38)
A little milk

Lemon compote
2 sheets gelatin,
   180–200 Bloom
9 oz. (260 g) seedless
   lemons, preferably
   organic
½ cup (120 ml) lemon
   juice
¾ cup (5 oz./150 g) sugar
Salt

To assemble
10½ oz. (300 g) lemon
   crémeux, Lemon
   Meringue Tart recipe
   (see p. 250 and Chef's
   Notes)

Decoration
A few ladyfingers
   (see p. 24), cut
   into evenly sized cubes
Confectioners' sugar,
   for dusting
French meringue kisses
   (see p. 33)
Candied lemon slices,
   cut into small triangles
Baby licorice greens
   (optional)

EQUIPMENT
2 pastry bags fitted with
   ¾-in. (1.5-cm) and ½-in.
   (1-cm) plain tips
Cookie sheet lined
   with parchment paper
Immersion blender

1. **Preheat the oven** to 430°F (220°C/Gas Mark 7).
2. **To make the éclairs,** spoon the choux pastry dough into the pastry bag with a ¾-in. (1.5-cm) tip. Pipe 10 × 6-in. (15-cm) logs onto the cookie sheet.
3. **Dip a fork** in the milk, then run the tines down the top of each éclair lengthwise to create ridges.
4. **Place in the oven,** prop the door ajar with the handle of a wooden spoon, and bake for 15 minutes. Reduce the oven temperature to 400°F (200°C/Gas Mark 6) and bake for an additional 20 minutes, until the éclairs are golden and crisp on the outside but still soft in the center. Transfer to a wire rack to cool.
5. **To prepare the lemon compote,** soak the gelatin in a bowl of cold water until softened.
6. **Wash and dry the lemons,** then slice them very thinly. Blanch the slices in boiling salted water for 12 minutes, then drain.
7. **Heat the lemon juice and sugar** in a saucepan until the sugar dissolves. Bring to a boil, add the lemon slices, and remove from the heat. Process with the immersion blender until almost smooth and there are only a few tiny pieces of lemon left.
8. **Squeeze the gelatin** to remove excess water. Stir it into the lemon compote until melted. Pour into a shallow dish, then chill for 30 minutes. The compote should have a consistency similar to that of marmalade, so it can be spread.

9. **To assemble the éclairs,** cut the top third off each éclair using a bread knife. Spread a thin ¼-in. (5-mm) layer of lemon compote over the bases, then replace the éclair tops. Spoon about 10½ oz. (300 g) of the lemon crémeux into the pastry bag with the ½-in. (1-cm) tip. Pipe small mounds in a staggered line on top of each éclair, leaving a little space between them.
10. **Dust the ladyfinger cubes** with confectioners' sugar, then arrange them alternately over the crémeux with the meringue kisses and candied lemon triangles. Finish with a few baby licorice greens, if using.
11. **Chill and serve** on the same day.

Chef's Notes
• The lemon crémeux recipe on p. 250 will make more than is needed to fill the éclairs. The remaining crémeux can be stored in the refrigerator for up to 3 days, or in the freezer for up to 1 month.

ÉCLAIR AU CHOCOLAT / ÉCLAIR AU CAFÉ

CHOCOLATE OR COFFEE ÉCLAIRS ⋆

Makes
10

Active time: 30 minutes
+ making the choux
pastry, pastry cream, and
chocolate icing

Cooking time: 30 minutes

INGREDIENTS
Éclairs
9 oz. (250 g) choux pastry
dough (see p. 38)

Filling
14 oz. (400 g) chocolate
pastry cream (see p. 68)
or coffee pastry cream
(see p. 67), or half
and half

Chocolate icing
1 quantity (12¼ oz./350 g)
chocolate icing
(see p. 74 and Chef's
Notes)

Coffee icing
10½ oz. (300 g) white
poured fondant
(see Chef's Notes)
About 10 drops (5 g)
coffee essence, Coffee
Buttercream recipe
(see p. 58), or
store-bought

Decoration (optional)
Dark chocolate, grated
Coffee powder, for
dusting

EQUIPMENT
2 pastry bags fitted with
¾-in. (1.5-cm) and ¼-in.
(6-mm) or ⅛-in. (3-mm)
plain tips
Cookie sheet lined with
parchment paper
Instant-read thermometer

---

1. **Preheat the oven** to 430°F (220°C/Gas Mark 7).
2. **To make the éclairs**, spoon the choux pastry dough into the pastry bag with a ¾-in. (1.5-cm) tip. Pipe 10 × 6-in. (15-cm) logs onto the cookie sheet.
3. **Place in the oven**, prop the door ajar with the handle of a wooden spoon, and bake for 15 minutes. Reduce the oven temperature to 400°F (200°C/Gas Mark 6) and bake for an additional 20 minutes, until the éclairs are golden and crisp on the outside but still soft in the center. Transfer to a wire rack to cool.
4. **Fill the éclairs** with chocolate or coffee pastry cream, or half and half. To fill them, slit the éclairs lengthwise using a bread knife, without cutting all the way through, and pipe in the pastry cream using the pastry bag with a ¼-in. (6-mm) tip. Alternatively, make 3 holes in the base of each éclair and, using the pastry bag with an ⅛-in. (3-mm) tip, pipe the cream in through the holes. If using this second method, serve the éclairs in paper liners or on a serving plate.
5. **Ice the éclairs** with the icing that matches the filling. If using chocolate icing, ensure it is just lukewarm and not too runny. Using a small offset spatula, cover the top of each éclair with the chocolate icing. If desired, sprinkle with grated dark chocolate before the icing sets.

6. **To make the coffee icing**, stir together the white fondant and coffee essence until combined. Heat in a large saucepan over low heat, until the temperature reaches 86°F (30°C). Using a small offset spatula, cover the top of each éclair with the coffee icing, or dip the top of each éclair in the icing to coat.
7. **Chill and serve** on the same day the éclairs are made. Immediately before serving, dust the coffee éclairs with coffee powder, if desired.

Chef's Notes
• For a glossier finish, the chocolate glaze on p. 76 can be used instead of the chocolate icing on p. 74. The glaze must be used almost completely cold.
• Unlike rolled fondant, which is rolled out thinly and used to cover cakes, poured (or liquid) fondant is softer and has a pourable consistency. It can be purchased ready to use from cake decorating stores or online.

ÉCLAIR CROQUEMBOUCHE
CROQUEMBOUCHE ÉCLAIRS **

Makes
10

Active time: 30 minutes +
making the choux pastry
and pastry cream

Cooking time: 35 minutes

INGREDIENTS
Éclairs
10½ oz. (300 g) choux
    pastry dough
    (see p. 38)
A little milk

Filling
½ quantity (10½ oz./
    300 g) pastry cream
    (see p. 66), well chilled
¾ cup (180 ml) heavy
    cream, well chilled
1 tbsp + 2 tsp (20 g) sugar

Caramel topping
1 cup (7 oz./200 g) sugar
¼ cup (60 ml) water
3 drops lemon juice

Decoration
Pearl sugar

EQUIPMENT
2 pastry bags fitted with
    a ¾-in. (1.5-cm) fluted
    tip or plain tip and
    a Saint-Honoré tip
Cookie sheet lined
    with parchment paper
Electric hand beater

1. **Preheat the oven** to 430°F (220°C/Gas Mark 7).
2. **To make the éclairs,** spoon the choux pastry dough into the pastry bag with a fluted or plain tip. Pipe 10 × 6-in. (15-cm) logs onto the cookie sheet.
3. **If a plain tip has been used,** dip a fork in the milk, then run the tines down the top of each éclair lengthwise to create ridges.
4. **Place in the oven,** prop the door ajar with the handle of a wooden spoon, and bake for 15 minutes. Reduce the oven temperature to 400°F (200°C/Gas Mark 6) and bake for an additional 20 minutes, until the éclairs are golden and crisp on the outside but still soft in the center. Transfer to a wire rack to cool.
5. **To prepare the filling,** whisk the pastry cream in a mixing bowl placed over a bowl of very cold water, until smooth.
6. **Whip the cream** and sugar together in another bowl, until the cream holds its shape. Fold into the pastry cream, using a flexible spatula. Chill until using.
7. **To prepare the caramel topping,** line the cookie sheet with fresh parchment paper. Heat the sugar and water in a saucepan that is wider than the length of the éclairs, until the sugar dissolves. Increase the heat, then bring to a boil. Boil, without stirring, until the syrup turns a golden caramel. Stir in the lemon juice, then remove from the heat.

8. **Very carefully dip** the tops of the éclairs into the hot caramel, allowing the excess to drip back into the saucepan. Place on the cookie sheet, caramel side up. Sprinkle with pearl sugar. Let the caramel cool and set.
9. **To fill the éclairs,** cut off the top of each one just below the caramel, using a bread knife. Set the tops aside.
10. **Spoon the filling** into the pastry bag with a Saint-Honoré tip. Pipe the filling attractively over the éclair bases. Chill the bases and store the caramel-coated tops in a cool, dry place.
11. **Immediately before serving,** carefully place the tops back on the bases. Serve the éclairs on the same day as they are made.

GLAÇAGE EXOTIQUE
PASSION FRUIT GLAZE ★

Makes
about 1 lb. 2 oz. (500 g)

Active time: 10 minutes

Cooking time: 5 minutes

Storage: Up to 4 days
in the refrigerator
in an airtight container

INGREDIENTS
2 tbsp (25 g) sugar
½ tsp (2 g) pectin NH
1 oz. (30 g) passion fruit
    puree
Generous ½ cup (135ml)
    water
Scant 1 tbsp (20 g)
    glucose syrup
10 oz. (280 g) neutral
    glaze (see p. 81)
Few drops of natural
    lemon-yellow food
    coloring

EQUIPMENT
Instant-read thermometer

1. **Mix half the sugar** with the pectin in a bowl.
2. **Heat the passion fruit puree** with the water and the rest of the sugar, until the temperature reaches 140°F (60°C).
3. **Pour the mixture** over the sugar and pectin, whisking continuously. Return to the saucepan, then bring to a boil, continuing to whisk.
4. **Add the glucose syrup,** bring back to a boil, then boil for 3 minutes. Whisk in the neutral glaze and yellow coloring.
5. **Chill quickly** by sitting the base of the saucepan in a bowl of water filled halfway with ice.
6. **When cold,** store in the refrigerator in an airtight container or a bowl with plastic wrap pressed over the surface.

Chef's Notes
• This glaze is excellent for coating an entremets flavored with coconut, mango, pineapple, or vanilla, as it will infuse the dessert with an exotic fragrance.

MERINGUE À LA CHANTILLY

MERINGUES
WITH CHANTILLY CREAM ★

Serves
10

Active time: 10 minutes +
making the meringues and
Chantilly cream

Storage: Up to 2 hours
in the refrigerator

INGREDIENTS
About 2 quantities
(1 lb. 2 oz./500 g)
Chantilly cream
(see p. 50),
well chilled
20 oval-shaped French
meringue shells
(see p. 33)

EQUIPMENT
Pastry bag fitted with
a ¾-in. (2-cm) fluted tip
10 small serving dishes
or paper liners

1. **Spoon the cream** into the pastry bag.
2. **Place 2 meringue shells** in each serving dish or paper
liner. Place them on their sides, with their flat sides
facing, leaving a space between them.
3. **Holding the shells** in place with one hand, fill the
centers with piped cream. Alternatively, pipe the cream
in attractive swirls over the base of one meringue.
Lightly press the other meringue on top to sandwich
the shells together. Repeat with the remaining pairs
of meringue shells.
4. **Serve immediately**, if possible. The cream-filled
meringues can be refrigerated for up to 2 hours,
but will soften if they are stored for longer.

MOELLEUX AU CHOCOLAT

CHOCOLATE LAVA CAKES *

Makes	INGREDIENTS	To serve	EQUIPMENT
8	*Lava cakes*	Raspberry coulis	8 × 2-in. (5-cm) round cake
	3 tbsp (1¾ oz./50 g)	(see p. 51)	pans or ramekins, 2½ in.
Active time: 15 minutes	butter, for the pans		(6 cm) deep
	1⅓ cups (3½ oz./100 g)		Rimmed baking sheet
	sliced almonds		Instant-read thermometer
Chilling time: 30 minutes	¾ cup + 2 tbsp (3½ oz./		
	100 g) AP flour		
Cooking time: 10 minutes	1 tsp (4 g) baking powder		
	6 oz. (170 g) dark chocolate,		
	70% cacao, chopped		
	1 stick + 1 tbsp (4½ oz./		
	130 g) butter, diced		
	½ cup (3⅓ oz./95 g) sugar		
	2 extra-large eggs (½ cup/		
	130 g)		

1. **To prepare the lava cakes,** generously grease the pans or ramekins with the 3 tbsp (1¾ oz./50 g) butter. Coat the bases and sides with sliced almonds. Chill on the baking sheet until using.
2. **Sift the flour** and baking powder into a bowl.
3. **Melt the chocolate** in a bowl over a saucepan of barely simmering water (bain-marie) until the temperature reaches 104°F (40°C). Remove the bowl from the heat, then whisk in the 1 stick + 1 tbsp (4½ oz./130 g) butter until smooth.
4. **Whisk in the sugar,** followed by the eggs, one at a time, until incorporated. Stir in the flour and baking powder until just combined. Ensure you do not overmix.

5. **Pour the mixture into the pans** to fill them three-quarters full. Chill for 30 minutes.
6. **Preheat the oven** to 410°F (210°C/Gas Mark 6–7). Place the cakes in the oven, then reduce the temperature to 400°F (200°C/Gas Mark 6). Bake for 10 minutes, until the cakes feel firm on top but the centers are still soft.
7. **Wait for a few minutes** before carefully inverting the cakes onto serving plates. If this is done too soon after they come out of the oven, they could break when unmolded.
8. **Serve immediately,** with raspberry coulis on the side.

MONT-BLANC

INDIVIDUAL MONT-BLANC ✴✴

Makes
10

Active time: 30 minutes
+ making the French
meringue and shortcrust
pastry

Cooking time: 12 minutes

Chilling time: 2 hours

INGREDIENTS

Meringue disks
1 quantity (1 lb./465 g)
French meringue (see
p. 33 and Chef's Notes)

Shortcrust bases
9 oz. (250 g) sweet
shortcrust pastry dough
(see p. 41 and Chef's
Notes)

Chestnut cream
7 oz. (200 g) *crème de
marrons* (chestnut spread)
2 tbsp (30 ml) rum or milk,
as needed

Chantilly cream
1¾ cups (400 ml) crème
fraîche (see Chef's
Notes), well chilled
½ cup (120 ml) whole milk,
well chilled
2½ tbsp (1 oz./30 g) sugar

To assemble
Confectioners' sugar,
for dusting
Candied chestnuts, finely
chopped

To serve
Chocolate sauce
(see p. 90), warm

EQUIPMENT
Large cookie sheet
Pastry bag fitted with
a ¾-in. (2-cm) plain tip
3-in. (8-cm) round cookie
cutter
Pastry bag fitted with
a coupler + a ½-in.
(1.5-cm) plain tip and
a ¹⁄₁₆-in. (2-mm) plain or
vermicelli tip
Pastry bag fitted with
a ¾-in. (2-cm) fluted tip

1. Preheat the oven to 300°F (150°C/Gas Mark 2).
2. To prepare the meringue disks, draw 10 × 3-in.
(8-cm) circles on a sheet of parchment paper, using
a pencil. Place on the cookie sheet with the pencil lines
underneath.
3. Spoon the meringue into the pastry bag with the
¾-in. (2-cm) plain tip. Starting in the center and
working toward the outer edge, pipe tight spirals over
the marked circles.
4. Bake for about 1¼ hours, until dry and pale golden.
Watch carefully to ensure they do not color too much.
Remove from the oven and let cool on a wire rack.
5. Increase the oven temperature to 400°F (200°C/
Gas Mark 6). Line the cookie sheet with fresh
parchment paper.
6. To prepare the shortcrust bases, roll the pastry
dough to a thickness of ¼ in. (5 mm) on a lightly
floured surface. Cut out 10 × 3-in. (8-cm) disks using
the cutter. Place on the cookie sheet and prick all over
with a fork.
7. Bake for 10 minutes, until golden. Let cool on a wire
rack.
8. To prepare the chestnut cream, thin the *crème de
marrons* with the rum or milk, so it is soft enough
to pipe. Transfer to the pastry bag with the coupler and
fit the ½-in. (1.5-cm) tip.
9. To prepare the Chantilly cream, whip together the
crème fraîche, milk, and sugar until the cream holds its
shape. Spoon into the pastry bag with the ¾-in. (2-cm)
fluted tip.

10. To assemble the Mont-Blanc, pipe a layer of
chestnut cream over each shortcrust base. Pipe a swirl
of Chantilly cream and place a meringue disk on top.
Dust generously with confectioners' sugar.
11. Place the ¹⁄₁₆-in. (2-mm) plain or vermicelli tip on
the pastry bag containing the chestnut cream and pipe
the cream in long strands over the meringue.
12. Sprinkle with the chopped candied chestnuts.
Chill for several hours. Serve with warm chocolate sauce.

Chef's Notes
• 1 quantity of French meringue will make more bases
than needed. Pipe the remaining meringue into kisses
or other shapes, then bake and store them for another
occasion. Alternatively, use the full quantity of meringue
to make the Mont-Blanc with two layers of meringue,
instead of a pastry layer. To do this, pipe out 20 ovals
of meringue, measuring approximately 2¾ × 1½ in.
(7 × 3.5 cm), then bake as indicated above.
Pipe mounds of chestnut cream over half the ovals.
Cover with layers of Chantilly cream and strands of
chestnut cream. Top with the remaining meringues.
• If preferred, the Mont-Blanc can also be made
without the meringue layer. Simply pipe a layer
of chestnut cream over each pastry base, followed
by an elegant peak of Chantilly cream. Dust generously
with confectioners' sugar to resemble snow.
• If crème fraîche is unavailable, replace the crème
fraîche and whole milk with 2 cups (500 ml) heavy
cream.

PUITS D'AMOUR

WELLS OF LOVE ★★

Makes	INGREDIENTS	To assemble	EQUIPMENT
10	*Puff pastry wells*	1 lb. (450 g) pastry cream	2-in. (5-cm) round cookie
	10½ oz. (300 g) puff	(see p. 66) or chiboust	cutter
Active time: 30 minutes	pastry dough, classic	cream (see p. 60)	1¼-in. (3-cm) round cookie
+ making the puff pastry	(see p. 28) or quick	½ cup (3½ oz./100 g)	cutter
and pastry cream or	(see p. 29)	sugar	Cookie sheet lined
chiboust cream			with parchment paper
	Caramel coating		Caramelizing iron
Chilling time: 1 hour	1 cup (7 oz./200 g) sugar		or broiler
	¼ cup (60 ml) water		
Cooking time: 20 minutes	3 drops lemon juice		

1. **To prepare the puff pastry wells,** roll the pastry dough on a lightly floured surface to a thickness of ¼ in. (5 mm).
2. **Cut out 20 disks** using the 2-in. (5-cm) cutter. Cut out the centers of 10 of the disks using the 1¼-in. (3-cm) cutter.
3. **Lightly brush with water** the underside of the 10 pastry disks with the centers cut out. Lay them on top of the 10 complete disks, ensuring the edges are aligned.
4. **Place on the cookie sheet,** then chill for 1 hour.
5. **Preheat the oven** to 350°F (180°C/Gas Mark 4). Bake for about 20 minutes, until puffed and golden. If the pastry centers have risen, cut them out using the tip of a knife, so there is room to fill the "wells" with cream. Transfer to a wire rack to cool.
6. **To prepare the caramel coating,** line the cookie sheet with fresh parchment paper. Heat the sugar and water in a saucepan until the sugar dissolves. Increase the heat and bring to a boil. Boil, without stirring, until the syrup turns a golden caramel. Stir in the lemon juice, then remove from the heat.
7. **Dip the tops of the pastry wells** very carefully into the hot caramel. Place them, dipped side down, on the cookie sheet to cool completely.
8. **To assemble the wells,** fill the pastry centers with pastry cream or chiboust cream, smoothing it into a slight dome. Chill until ready to serve, which should preferably be on the same day.
9. **Just before serving,** sprinkle the cream with the ½ cup (3½ oz./100 g) sugar and caramelize using a caramelizing iron or under a broiler. Watch carefully to ensure the sugar does not burn. Serve immediately.

SALAMBO

SALAMBO CHOUX PUFFS *

Makes
10

Active time: 30 minutes +
making the choux pastry
and pastry cream

Cooking time: 30 minutes

INGREDIENTS
Choux puffs
9 oz. (250 g) choux pastry
  dough (see p. 38)

Rum pastry cream
14 oz. (400 g) pastry
  cream (see p. 66), cold
2 tbsp (30 ml) aged rum
  or another alcohol

Caramel coating
⅔ cup (4½ oz./125 g)
  sugar
3 tbsp (45 ml) water
3 drops lemon juice

EQUIPMENT
Pastry bag fitted with
  a ¾-in. (1.5-cm) plain tip
Cookie sheet lined with
  parchment paper
Pastry bag fitted with
  an ⅛-in. (3-mm)
  plain tip
Silicone baking mat

1. **Preheat the oven** to 430°F (220°C/Gas Mark 7).
2. **To make the choux puffs,** spoon the choux pastry
dough into the pastry bag with the ¾-in. (1.5-cm)
tip. Pipe 10 ovals measuring 1¼ × 2¾ in. (3 × 7 cm)
onto the cookie sheet.
3. **Place in the oven,** propping the door ajar with the
handle of a wooden spoon, and bake for 30 minutes,
until the puffs are crisp and golden on the outside
but still soft in the center. Let cool on a wire rack.
4. **To prepare the rum pastry cream,** whisk together
the pastry cream and rum until smooth. Transfer
to the pastry bag with an ⅛-in. (3-mm) tip.
5. **Make a hole** in the base of each choux puff using
the tip of a knife. Fill with the pastry cream.
6. **To prepare the caramel coating,** lay the silicone
mat on the cookie sheet. Heat the sugar and water in a
saucepan until the sugar dissolves. Increase the heat and
bring to a boil. Boil, without stirring, until the syrup
turns a golden caramel. Stir in the lemon juice, then
remove from the heat.
7. **Very carefully dip the tops** of the choux puffs in the
hot caramel. Place, dipped side down, on the silicone
mat, to give the puffs a smooth, glossy finish.
8. **Let cool,** then chill. Serve on the same day as they
are made.

Chef's Notes
• Before dipping the choux puffs in the caramel, you
can spread sliced almonds over the silicone baking mat.
As the puffs are dipped, place them, caramel side down,
on the almonds, making sure the nuts stick to the center
of each puff. Let cool, then serve as above.

TARTELETTE CERISES

CHERRY TARTLETS ★

Makes
10

Active time:
10 minutes + making
the shortcrust pastry
and frangipane cream

Chilling time: 1 hour

Cooking time: 20 minutes

INGREDIENTS
Butter for the baking rings
or pans
5 oz. (150 g) sweet
shortcrust pastry dough
(see p. 41)
9 oz. (250 g) fresh
cherries
5 oz. (150 g) frangipane
cream (see p. 62)

Decoration
3½ oz. (100 g) red currant
jelly (see p. 366), warm
(optional)
Shelled pistachios, finely
chopped
Confectioners' sugar,
for dusting

EQUIPMENT
10 × 2½-in. (6-cm) baking
rings or tart pans, ¾ in.
(1.5 cm) deep
Cookie sheet, lined
with parchment paper
if using rings
3½-in. (9-cm) round
cookie cutter

1. **Grease the baking rings or pans** with butter.
Place them on the cookie sheet.
2. **On a lightly floured surface**, roll the pastry dough
to a thickness of about ⅛ in. (3 mm). Take care not
to overwork it.
3. **Cut out 10 circles** using the cookie cutter and line
them into the rings or pans. Chill for 1 hour.
4. **Preheat the oven** to 350°F (180°C/Gas Mark 4).
5. **Wash, halve, and pit** the cherries, setting aside
10 unpitted halves with stalks for decoration.
6. **Fill the tartlet shells** with the frangipane cream.
Arrange the pitted cherry halves in a ring around the
edge, rounded sides up.
7. **Bake for 20 minutes**, until the pastry is golden.
Let the tartlets cool slightly before unmolding.
8. **Place a reserved unpitted cherry half** with stalk
in the center of each tartlet.
9. **Brush the cherries** and pastry edges with warm red
currant jelly, if using. Scatter the pistachios around
the edge of each tartlet. Dust the pistachios with
confectioners' sugar. Serve warm or cold.

TARTELETTE FEUILLETÉE ANANAS

PINEAPPLE

PUFF PASTRY TARTLETS *

Makes
10

Active time: 15 minutes
+ making the puff pastry
and frangipane cream

Chilling time: 1 hour

Cooking time:
35–40 minutes

INGREDIENTS
Puff pastry bases
¾ lb. (350 g) puff pastry
  dough, classic (see p. 28)
  or quick (see p. 29)
1 egg, lightly beaten

Topping
⅓ cup (1 oz./30 g)
  shredded coconut
3½ oz. (100 g) frangipane
  cream (see p. 62)
10½ oz. (300 g) fresh
  pineapple (prepared
  weight)
Apricot glaze, warm
  (optional)

Decoration
Confectioners' sugar,
  for dusting
Finely grated zest
  of 1 lime, preferably
  organic

EQUIPMENT
Large cookie sheet lined
  with parchment paper
8 x 1½-oz. (40-g) "blocks,"
  ¾ in. (2 cm) in height,
  made with dried beans
  or rice wrapped up in
  oven-safe plastic wrap
  (optional)

1. **To prepare the puff pastry bases,** roll the pastry dough on a lightly floured surface into a rectangle measuring 9½ × 14 in. (24 × 35 cm). Prick the dough all over with a fork.
2. **Cut into 2 rectangles** measuring 3¼ × 14 in. (9 × 35 cm) and 4 long strips each measuring ¾ in. × 14 in. (1.5 × 35 cm).
3. **Brush the parchment paper** lightly with water. Place the pastry rectangles on the cookie sheet, leaving space between them. Brush the long pastry edges with water and place the pastry strips on top to form borders. Press down lightly on the inner edge of each strip, then mark indentations along the outer edge at regular intervals using the blunt side of a knife blade.
4. **Brush the pastry** with the lightly beaten egg. If using "blocks," place them at each corner, just inside the border, to prevent the corners from becoming misshapen during baking. Set a wire rack over the "blocks" to keep them in place. Chill the pastry for 1 hour.

5. **Preheat the oven** to 350°F (180°C/Gas Mark 4). Bake the pastry bases for 20 minutes, until lightly golden. Carefully remove the rack and the "blocks," if used, and let the pastry cool on the rack. Leave the oven switched on.
6. **To prepare the topping,** stir the shredded coconut into the frangipane cream. Cut the pineapple into wedges, matchsticks, or other shapes.
7. **Spread the frangipane and coconut cream** over the bases in an even layer. Arrange the pineapple on top. Place in the oven and bake for 15–20 minutes, until the edges of the pineapple caramelize a little. Brush with the warm apricot glaze, if using. Transfer to a wire rack to cool.
8. **When ready to serve,** dust the pastry edges with confectioners' sugar, then sprinkle with lime zest. Cut each rectangle into 5 equal slices using a bread knife.

TARTELETTE FRAISES DES BOIS

STRAWBERRY TARTLETS ★

Makes
10

Active time: 20 minutes
+ making the shortcrust
pastry, frangipane cream,
and strawberry glaze

Chilling time: 1 hour

Cooking time: 20 minutes

INGREDIENTS
Butter for the baking rings
   or pans
5 oz. (150 g) sweet
   shortcrust pastry dough
   (see p. 41)
5 oz. (150 g) frangipane
   cream (see p. 62)
7–9 oz. (200–250 g)
   Fraises des Bois
   (see Chef's Notes)
1 quantity (4½ oz./130 g)
   strawberry glaze
   (see p. 78), warm

EQUIPMENT
10 × 2½-in. (6-cm) baking
   rings or tart pans, ¾ in.
   (1.5 cm) deep
Cookie sheet, lined
   with parchment paper
   if using rings
3½-in. (9-cm) round
   cookie cutter

1. **Grease the baking rings** or pans with butter.
Place them on the cookie sheet.
2. **On a lightly floured surface**, roll the pastry dough
to a thickness of about ⅛ in. (3 mm). Take care not
to overwork it.
3. **Cut out 10 circles** using the cookie cutter and line
them into the baking rings or pans. Chill for 1 hour.
4. **Preheat the oven** to 350°F (180°C/Gas Mark 4).
5. **Fill the tartlet shells** with the frangipane cream.
Bake for 20 minutes, until the pastry is golden and
the frangipane cream is set.
6. **Remove the tartlets** from the oven, let them cool
slightly, then unmold onto a wire rack to cool.
7. **Select the most attractive strawberries,** handling
them as little as possible as they are fragile. Brush the
tartlets with a layer of warm strawberry glaze, then
arrange the strawberries over the glaze. Drizzle over
a little more glaze. Serve on the same day as the tartlets
are made.

Chef's Notes
• If Fraises des Bois are unavailable, use another small,
sweet variety of strawberry.
• To use fewer Fraises des Bois, pipe a dome of Napoleon
cream (pastry cream mixed with Chantilly cream;
see p. 200) on top of each tartlet and arrange the
strawberries attractively over it.

TARTELETTE AUX MIRABELLES

MIRABELLE PLUM TARTLETS ★

Makes
10

Active time: 10 minutes
+ making the shortcrust
pastry and frangipane
cream

Chilling time: 1 hour

Cooking time: 20 minutes

INGREDIENTS
Butter for the baking rings
    or pans
5 oz. (150 g) sweet
    shortcrust pastry dough
    (see p. 41)
10 oz. (300 g) mirabelle
    plums (see Chef's
    Notes)
5¼ oz. (150 g) frangipane
    cream (see p. 62)
3½ oz. (100 g) apricot
    glaze, warm (optional)

EQUIPMENT
10 × 2½-in. (6-cm) baking
    rings or tart pans, ¾ in.
    (1.5 cm) deep
Cookie sheet, lined
    with parchment paper
    if using rings
3½-in. (9-cm) round
    cookie cutter

1. **Grease the baking rings** or pans with butter. Place them on the cookie sheet.
2. **On a lightly floured surface**, roll the pastry dough to a thickness of about ⅛ in. (3 mm). Take care not to overwork it.
3. **Cut out 10 circles** using the cookie cutter and line them into the baking rings or pans. Chill for 1 hour.
4. **Preheat the oven** to 350°F (180°C/Gas Mark 4).
5. **Wash and dry** the plums, then halve and pit them.
6. **Fill the tartlet shells** with the frangipane cream. Arrange the plum halves over the cream, rounded sides up.
7. **Bake for 20 minutes**, until the pastry is golden and the frangipane cream is set.
8. **Remove the tartlets** from the oven, let them cool slightly, then unmold onto a wire rack to cool.
9. **If glazing the tartlets**, brush them with the warm apricot glaze. Serve on the same day as the tartlets are made.

Chef's Notes
• Mirabelle plums are the size of cherries, golden in color, and exceptionally sweet. They are available in cans. However, if fresh plums are preferred and fresh mirabelles are not available, substitute a small, sweet variety such as Sugar Baby or cherry plums.

TARTELETTE AUX FRUITS DE SAISON

SEASONAL FRUIT TARTLETS *

Makes
10

Active time: 20 minutes
+ making the shortcrust
pastry and frangipane
cream

Chilling time: 1 hour

Cooking time:
15–20 minutes

INGREDIENTS
Butter for the baking rings
or pans
5 oz. (150 g) sweet
shortcrust pastry dough
(see p. 41)
5 oz. (150 g) frangipane
cream (see p. 62)
Seasonal fruit
3½ oz. (100 g) apricot
glaze or red fruit jelly
(see Chef's Notes), warm
Confectioners' sugar,
for dusting (optional)

EQUIPMENT
10 × 1½-in. (4-cm) baking
rings or tart pans, ¾ in.
(1.5 cm) deep
Cookie sheet, lined
with parchment paper
if using rings
2¾-in. (7-cm) round
cookie cutter

1. **Grease the baking rings** or pans with butter.
Place them on the cookie sheet.
2. **On a lightly floured surface**, roll the pastry dough
to a thickness of about ⅛ in. (3 mm). Take care not
to overwork it.
3. **Cut out 10 circles** using the cookie cutter and line
them into the baking rings or pans. Chill for 1 hour.
4. **Preheat the oven** to 350°F (180°C/Gas Mark 4).
5. **Fill the tartlet shells** with the frangipane cream.
Bake for 15–20 minutes, until the pastry is golden
and the frangipane cream is set.
6. **Remove the tartlets** from the oven, let them cool
slightly, then unmold onto a wire rack to cool.
7. **Wash and dry the fruit.** Leave it whole or cut it
into smaller pieces, depending on the size.
8. **Brush the tartlets** with a thin layer of warm apricot
glaze or red fruit jelly. Arrange the fruit on top.
One kind of fruit can be used for each tartlet, or an
assortment of different fruits.
9. **Brush another layer of glaze** over the fruit, if desired,
or dust with confectioners' sugar. Serve on the same day
as the tartlets are made.

Chef's Notes
• Smaller fruits can be added to the frangipane cream
before baking. The tartlets can then be topped with
fresh fruit before serving.
• The tartlets can also be brushed with warm strawberry
glaze (see p. 78) or raspberry glaze (see p. 80).

Mini Tartlets (see p. 383):
(clockwise, from top left to center)
peach; red berry; strawberry;
pistachio; lemon meringue;
praline; candied fruit; chocolate-
cacao; Fraise des Bois; red berry

TARTELETTE À LA MANGUE

MANGO TARTLETS ★

Makes	INGREDIENTS	EQUIPMENT
10	Butter for the baking rings or pans	10 × 3-in. (8-cm) baking rings or tart pans, ¾ in. (1.5 cm) deep
Active time: 30 minutes + making the shortcrust pastry and pastry cream	¾ lb. (350 g) sweet shortcrust pastry dough (see p. 41)	Cookie sheet, lined with parchment paper if using rings
	1 egg yolk, lightly beaten	5-in. (12-cm) and 2-in. (5-cm) round cookie cutters
Chilling time: 1 hour	3–4 ripe mangos	
	9 oz. (250 g) pastry cream (see p. 66)	
Cooking time: 20 minutes	4 tsp (20 ml) passion fruit juice	10 × 3-in. (8-cm) parchment paper circles
	Passion fruit glaze (see p. 280) or neutral glaze (see p. 81), warm	Pie weights or dried beans
	Finely grated zest of 1 lime, preferably organic	Pastry bag fitted with a medium plain tip
	Confectioners' sugar, for dusting	

1. **Grease the baking rings** or pans with butter. Place them on the cookie sheet.
2. **On a lightly floured surface**, roll the pastry dough to a thickness of about ⅛ in. (3 mm). Take care not to overwork it.
3. **Cut out 10 circles** using the 5-in. (12-cm) cookie cutter and line them into the baking rings or pans. Chill for 1 hour.
4. **Preheat the oven** to 350°F (180°C/Gas Mark 4).
5. **Line the tartlet shells** with the parchment paper circles, fill with pie weights, and blind-bake for 20 minutes. Remove the parchment paper and pie weights, then brush the pastry with the egg yolk to seal it. Return the tartlet shells to the oven for an additional 3–5 minutes, until golden.
6. **Remove the tartlets** from the oven, let them cool slightly, then unmold onto a wire rack to cool completely.

7. **Peel the mangos.** Cut the flesh lengthwise away from the pits into 10 slices, about ½ in. (1 cm) thick. Cut 10 rounds from the slices using the 2-in (5-cm) cookie cutter and score one side of each in a crisscross pattern using a bread knife. Chill until using.
8. **Whisk together** the pastry cream and passion fruit juice. Spoon into the pastry bag and pipe into the tart shells to fill them completely. If necessary, smooth the top level using a palette knife.
9. **Place a mango round**, scored lines uppermost, on top of each tartlet. Brush with a thin layer of warm glaze. Sprinkle with the lime zest and dust with confectioners' sugar just before serving.

Chef's Notes

• The tartlets can also be filled with coconut and frangipane cream, instead of passion fruit cream. Combine 14 oz. (400 g) frangipane cream (see p. 62) with 1⅓ cups (3½ oz./100 g) shredded coconut. Bake in the tartlet shells, as for the Seasonal Fruit Tartlets recipe (see p. 298) and decorate as above, once the filling has cooled.

TARTELETTE AUX AGRUMES

CITRUS TARTLETS ★

Makes
10

Active time: 20 minutes
+ making the shortcrust
pastry and frangipane
cream

Drying time: 12 minutes

Chilling time: 1 hour

Cooking time: 15 minutes

INGREDIENTS
5¼ oz. (150 g) pink
    grapefruit supremes
5¼ oz. (150 g) orange
    supremes
Butter for the baking rings
    or pans
10½ oz. (300 g) sweet
    shortcrust pastry dough
    (see p. 41)
14 oz. (400 g) frangipane
    cream (see p. 62)
3½ oz. (100 g) apricot
    glaze or apple jelly,
    warm (optional)
10 green pistachios

EQUIPMENT
Silicone baking mat
    on a cookie sheet
10 × 3-in. (8-cm) baking
    rings or tartlet pans,
    ¾ in. (1.5 cm) deep
Cookie sheet, lined with
    parchment paper if
    using rings
5-in. (12-cm) round cookie
    cutter

1. **Preheat the oven** to 425°F (220°C/Gas Mark 7).
2. **Place the pink grapefruit and orange supreme**s
on the silicone baking mat. Dry them out in the oven
for 12 minutes. Let cool on the mat.
3. **Grease the baking rings** or pans with butter.
Place them on the cookie sheet.
4. **On a lightly floured surface**, roll the pastry dough
to a thickness of about ⅛ in. (3 mm). Take care not to
overwork it.
5. **Cut out 10 circles** using the cookie cutter and line
them into the baking rings or pans. Chill for 1 hour.
6. **Preheat the oven** to 350°F (180°C/Gas Mark 4).

7. **Fill the tartlet shells** with the frangipane cream.
Arrange the grapefruit and orange supremes on top.
8. **Bake for 15 minutes**, until the pastry is golden and
the frangipane cream is set.
9. **Remove the tartlets** from the oven, let them cool
slightly, then unmold onto a wire rack to cool.
10. **The tartlets can be brushed** with a thin layer
of warm apricot glaze or apple jelly while still warm,
if desired. Decorate each tartlet with a pistachio.
11. **Serve on the same day** as the tartlets are made.

TARTELETTE AUX MYRTILLES

BLUEBERRY TARTLETS *

Makes	INGREDIENTS	EQUIPMENT
10	Butter for the rings or pans	10 × 3-in. (8-cm) baking
	¾ lb. (350 g) sweet	rings or tart pans, ¾ in.
Active time: 15 minutes	shortcrust pastry dough	(1.5 cm) deep
+ making the shortcrust	(see p. 41)	Cookie sheet, lined
pastry and pastry cream	10½ oz. (300 g) fresh or	with parchment paper
	frozen blueberries	if using rings
	(see Chef's Notes)	5-in. (12-cm) round cookie
Chilling time: 1 hour	2½ tbsp (1 oz./30 g) sugar	cutter
	1 egg yolk, lightly beaten	10 × 4-in. (10-cm)
Cooking time: 20 minutes	¾ lb. (350 g) pastry cream	parchment paper circles
	(see p. 66)	Pie weights or dried beans
	3½ oz. (100 g) red currant	
	jelly (see p. 366), warm	

1. **Grease the baking rings** or pans with butter. Place them on the cookie sheet.

2. **On a lightly floured surface,** roll the pastry dough to a thickness of about ⅛ in. (3 mm). Take care not to overwork it.

3. **Cut out 10 circles** using the cookie cutter and line them into the baking rings or pans. Chill for 1 hour.

4. **Place the blueberries** and sugar in a saucepan over low heat until the sugar dissolves. The berries should soften and begin to release their juices. Remove from the heat and let cool.

5. **Preheat the oven** to 400°F (200°C/Gas Mark 6).

6. **Line the tartlet shells** with the parchment paper circles, fill with pie weights, and blind-bake for 20 minutes. Remove the parchment paper and pie weights, then brush the pastry with the egg yolk to seal it. Return the tartlet shells to the oven for an additional 3–5 minutes, until golden.

7. **Remove the tartlets** from the oven, let them cool slightly, then unmold onto a wire rack to cool completely.

8. **Whisk the pastry cream** until smooth. Divide the cream between the tartlet shells. Top with the blueberries and brush them with a thin layer of warm jelly. Serve immediately.

Chef's Notes
• Fresh raspberries or Fraises des Bois could be used instead of blueberries. There is no need to cook them first: simply arrange them over the pastry cream and brush with the warm jelly.

VAL D'ISÈRE
VAL D'ISÈRE TARTLETS ★★

Makes
12

Active time: 1 hour +
making the shortcrust
pastry, marzipan,
ladyfingers, and chocolate
glaze

Chilling time: At least
1 hour, preferably
overnight

Cooking time: 15 minutes

Storage: Up to 4 days
in the refrigerator

INGREDIENTS
Tartlet shells
(make 1 day ahead)
Butter for the rings or pans
9 oz. (250 g) sweet
    shortcrust pastry dough
    (see p. 41)
1 egg yolk, lightly beaten

Kirsch syrup
½ cup (3½ oz./100 g)
    sugar
¼ cup (60 ml) kirsch

Almond and walnut filling
14 oz. (400 g) homemade
    marzipan (see p. 63),
    chopped
3½ tbsp (50 ml) kirsch
7 tbsp (3½ oz./100 g)
    butter, diced
Scant 1 cup (3½ oz./100 g)
    walnuts, finely ground

To assemble
6 ladyfingers (see p. 24)
14 oz. (400 g) chocolate
    glaze (see p. 76)
36 walnut kernels
    (optional)

EQUIPMENT
12 × 3-in. (8-cm) baking
    rings or tartlet pans,
    ¾ in. (1.5 cm) deep
Cookie sheet, lined
    with parchment paper
    if using rings
5-in. (12-cm) round cookie
    cutter
12 × 3-in. (8-cm)
    parchment paper circles
Pie weights or dried beans
Stand mixer fitted with
    the paddle beater
Instant-read thermometer

1. **Grease the baking rings** or pans with butter.
Place them on the cookie sheet.
2. **On a lightly floured surface,** roll the pastry dough
to a thickness of about ⅛ in. (3 mm). Take care not
to overwork it.
3. **Cut out 12 circles** using the cookie cutter and line
them into the baking rings or pans. Chill for at least
1 hour, or preferably overnight.
4. **Preheat the oven** to 400°F (200°C/Gas Mark 6),
when ready to bake.
5. **Line the tartlet shells** with the parchment paper
circles, fill with pie weights, and blind-bake for
20 minutes. Remove the parchment paper and pie
weights, then brush the pastry with the egg yolk to seal
it. Return the tartlet shells to the oven for an additional
3–5 minutes, until golden.
6. **Remove the tartlets** from the oven, let them
cool slightly, then unmold onto a wire rack to cool
completely.

7. **To prepare the kirsch syrup,** heat the sugar and
kirsch in a saucepan until the sugar dissolves. Increase
the heat and bring to a boil. Remove from the heat and
let cool.
8. **To prepare the almond and walnut filling,** beat the
marzipan and kirsch on low speed in the stand mixer
until smooth. Add the butter and beat for 5 minutes,
until the mixture is light and creamy. Beat in the
ground walnuts.
9. **To assemble the tartlets,** cover the base of each tartlet
shell with a thin layer of the almond and walnut filling.
Cut the ladyfingers in half and dip them in the kirsch
syrup until soaked but still intact. Place one half in each
tartlet shell, then cover with the remaining almond and
walnut filling.
10. **Dip the blade** of a palette knife in water and smooth
the filling into a dome shape. Chill for 15 minutes.
11. **Heat the glaze** in a bowl over a saucepan of barely
simmering water (bain-marie), until the temperature
reaches 104°F (40°C).
12. **Carefully dip the domed tops** of the tartlets in the
glaze, letting the excess drip back into the bowl. Smooth
the edges with a palette knife. Decorate with 3 walnut
kernels per tartlet, if using. Chill until ready to serve.

HOT DESSERTS

BEIGNETS MILLE FRUITS

FRUIT FRITTERS ★

Serves
10

Active time: 10 minutes

Resting time: 2 hours

Soaking time: 1 hour

Cooking time: 8 minutes
per batch

INGREDIENTS
Batter
2 cups (8½ oz./240 g) AP
    flour
Scant ½ cup (100 ml) light
    beer
2 eggs, separated
⅓ oz. (10 g) fresh yeast
    dissolved in 1 tbsp
    (15 ml) whole milk
    (see Chef's Notes)
½ cup (130 ml) whole milk,
    divided
3 tbsp (45 ml) neutral oil
⅓ cup (2½ oz./70 g) sugar

Rum-soaked fruit
Scant ½ cup (100 ml) rum
½ cup (3½ oz./100 g)
    sugar
1¾ lb. (800 g) firm fruit,
    fresh or in syrup and
    well drained
Neutral oil for deep-frying

To serve
Confectioners' sugar,
    for dusting
Red currant jelly
    (see p. 366), optional

EQUIPMENT
Electric hand beater
Deep fryer or large
    saucepan
Instant-read thermometer

1. **To prepare the batter,** sift the flour into a mixing bowl.
2. **Whisk in the beer,** egg yolks, yeast, and 3½ tbsp (50 ml) of the milk until smooth. Whisk in the remaining milk and oil.
3. **Set aside** the egg whites and sugar. Let the batter rest for 2 hours.
4. **To prepare the rum-soaked fruit,** whisk the rum and sugar together in a bowl until the sugar dissolves. If using bananas, peel and cut into ¾-in. (2-cm) slices. To prepare apples, pears, or pineapples, peel and remove the cores. Cut the flesh into ½-in. (1-cm) rings. If using stone fruits, such as apricots, peaches, or plums, wash and dry them, then cut them in half and remove the pits. If using fruit in syrup, drain it well and cut into smaller pieces, if necessary.
5. **Macerate the fruit** in the rum syrup for 1 hour.
6. **When ready to fry** the fritters, finish preparing the batter. Whisk the egg whites until they hold soft peaks, then gradually whisk in the sugar until the peaks are firm. Fold into the batter prepared in steps 1 and 2.
7. **To fry the fritters,** heat the oil in a deep fryer or large saucepan, filling the pan no more than two-thirds full, until the temperature reaches 375°F (190°C). Do not overheat the oil as the batter will burn before the fruit inside is cooked.
8. **Drain the fruit,** reserving any rum syrup left in the bowl (see Chef's Notes).
9. **Dip one piece of fruit at a time** into the batter until it is coated. Lift it out with a fork and lower it into the oil. At first, the fruit will sink to the bottom, but should quickly rise to the surface.

10. **Fry the battered fruit in batches.** Do not place too many in the pan at once, as this will lower the temperature of the oil.
11. **Fry for about 8 minutes,** until the fritters are light gold, turning them over halfway so they brown evenly.
12. **Drain with a slotted spoon** onto a plate lined with paper towel. Repeat until all the battered fruit has been fried.
13. **Dust the fritters** with confectioners' sugar. Serve hot with red currant jelly on the side, if desired.

Chef's Notes

• Store any remaining rum syrup in an airtight container in the refrigerator to use for a fruit salad.
• Any leftover batter can be made into a dessert that is similar to a light clafoutis. Preheat the oven to 350°F (180°C/Gas Mark 4). Grease a baking dish with butter. Roughly chop some fruit and stir it into the leftover batter with 3 tbsp of the rum syrup. Transfer to the baking dish and bake for 15–30 minutes, until set and golden.
• If fresh yeast is unavailable, you can substitute 2¼ tsp (7 g) active dry yeast or 1½ tsp (5 g) instant yeast. Instant yeast must be mixed directly into the flour before any liquid is added, rather than dissolved in the milk, which can be omitted.

CRÊPES SUZETTE *

Makes
30 × 6-in. (15-cm) crêpes

Active time: 1½ hours +
making the pastry cream

Cooking time: 20 minutes
(using 2 pans) +
10 minutes before serving

INGREDIENTS
Crêpe batter
2 cups (9 oz./250 g) AP
   flour
Scant ¼ cup (55 ml)
   neutral oil
Scant ⅓ cup (2 oz./60 g)
   sugar
6 eggs
1 tbsp (15 ml) Grand Marnier
1 tbsp (15 ml) aged rum
Finely grated zest
   of 1 orange, preferably
   organic
5 tbsp (3 oz./80 g) butter,
   melted
3 cups (750 ml) whole
   milk, divided
7 tbsp (3½ oz./100 g)
   butter for the pan, or
   a scant ½ cup (100 ml)
   neutral oil, as needed

Orange pastry cream
2 oranges, preferably
   organic
1 tbsp (15 ml) Grand
   Marnier
1½ quantities (2 lb./900 g)
   pastry cream
   (see p. 66), warm

Grand Marnier syrup
1 stick + 2 tbsp (5¼ oz./
   150 g) butter
¾ cup (5 oz./150 g) sugar
Juice of 2 oranges
⅔ cup (150 ml) Grand
   Marnier (see Chef's
   Notes)

EQUIPMENT
Electric hand beater
   or blender
2 × 6-in. (15-cm) crêpe
   pans or skillets
Skillet large enough
   to hold all the rolled
   crêpes
2 × 16-in. (40-cm) serving
   platters

---

1. **To prepare the crêpe batter,** melt the butter in a saucepan until it begins to color and has a nutty aroma (*beurre noisette*).

2. **Using an electric hand beater or blender,** whisk together or blend the flour, oil, sugar, eggs, Grand Marnier, rum, orange zest, melted butter, and a generous ¾ cup (200 ml) of the milk until smooth.

3. **Add 1½ cups (350 ml) of the milk,** whisking or blending again until smooth. Reserve the remaining milk to thin the batter before cooking, if necessary.

4. **To prepare the orange pastry cream,** finely zest both oranges and juice one of them. Stir the zest, juice, and Grand Marnier into the warm pastry cream. Juice the second zested orange and reserve the juice to make the syrup.

5. **To cook the crêpes,** thin the crêpe batter with more milk, if necessary, until it has the consistency of pouring cream. Set the pans over medium heat and lightly grease with butter or oil. Grease the pans between crêpes as needed.

6. **Add a ladleful of batter** to each pan and swirl so the batter covers the bases in a thin layer. Cook for about 1 minute on each side. As they cook, remove the crêpes from the pans and stack them on a plate. Keep warm in a bain-marie, covered with aluminum foil.

7. **To prepare the Grand Marnier syrup,** heat the butter, sugar, orange juice, and half the Grand Marnier in a skillet large enough to hold all the crêpes when rolled, until the butter melts and the sugar dissolves. Keep the remaining Grand Marnier warm in a small saucepan.

8. **Spoon a little of the Grand Marnier syrup** onto the serving platters. Set the skillet aside.

9. **Fill each crêpe** with a generous 1 tbsp of the orange pastry cream, then roll them up. Keep the crêpes warm on the serving platters.

10. **Place the skillet** with the remaining Grand Marnier syrup over high heat. Lay the rolled crêpes in it. When they are hot, sprinkle over the warm Grand Marnier and carefully flambé. When the flames have died down, transfer the crêpes to the platters. Serve immediately.

Chef's Notes
• A simpler version of this recipe can be made without pastry cream. Fold the crêpes into four and overlap them in a large skillet. Add the syrup and the warm Grand Marnier, then flambé when hot.
The more Grand Marnier you add, the longer the flames will last. Serve when the flames have died down.
• Cognac or aged rum can be added to the Grand Marnier to flambé.

GAUFRES

WAFFLES *

Makes	INGREDIENTS	To serve	EQUIPMENT

Makes
20

Active time: 15 minutes

Cooking time: 4 minutes
per waffle

INGREDIENTS
2½ cups (600 ml) whole
    milk, divided
1 small pinch salt
7 tbsp (3½ oz./100 g)
    butter + more for
    the waffle iron
2 cups (9 oz./250 g) AP
    flour
8 eggs (1¾ cups/400 g),
    beaten
1 cup (250 ml) heavy
    cream

To serve
Confectioners' sugar, jam
    of your choice, Chantilly
    cream (see p. 50), or
    hot chocolate sauce
    (see p. 90)

EQUIPMENT
Stand mixer with the
    paddle beater and whisk
Waffle iron

1. **Heat 1½ cups (350 ml) of the milk** with the salt
in a saucepan. Stir in the butter, then bring to a boil.
2. **Remove from the heat** and immediately stir in the
flour until smooth, using a wooden spatula.
3. **Cook briefly over low heat,** stirring constantly,
until the mixture thickens.
4. **Transfer to the bowl of the stand mixer** fitted with
the paddler beater. Add the eggs a third at a time,
beating on low speed until smooth.
5. **Combine the remaining 1 cup (250 ml) milk** and
cream in a bowl. Fit the stand mixer with the whisk.
Gradually whisk the second mixture into the first on
low speed until combined.
6. **To cook the waffles,** preheat the waffle iron and
lightly grease it with butter. Ladle in a little of the
batter, close the waffle iron, and cook for about
2 minutes on each side, or until golden.
7. **Serve the waffles warm,** dusted with confectioners'
sugar, or topped with jam, Chantilly cream, or hot
chocolate sauce.

OMELETTE SOUFFLÉE À LA BÉNÉDICTINE

SOUFFLÉ OMELET WITH BÉNÉDICTINE LIQUEUR ★★

Serves	INGREDIENTS	EQUIPMENT
6	Butter and sugar, for the serving dish	Oven-safe serving dish
		Electric hand beater
Active time: 15 minutes	6 egg yolks (scant ½ cup/ 120 g)	Large skillet
	1 cup (7 oz./200 g) sugar	
Cooking time: 15 minutes	Generous ¾ cup (200 ml) Bénédictine liqueur, divided	
	8 egg whites (1 cup/240 g)	
	1 pinch salt	
	2 tbsp (30 ml) lemon juice	
	3 tbsp (1¾ oz./50 g) butter	

1. **Preheat the oven** to 400°F (200°C/Gas Mark 6). Grease the serving dish with butter, then sprinkle it with sugar.

2. **Whisk the egg yolks and sugar** with half the Bénédictine liqueur on high speed, until the mixture falls from the whisk in thick ribbons.

3. **Whisk the egg whites** with the salt and lemon juice until they hold firm peaks. Stir a generous tablespoon of the whites into the yolk mixture to loosen it. Gently fold in the remainder using a flexible spatula, taking care not to deflate the mixture.

4. **Melt the 3 tbsp (1¾ oz./50 g) butter** in a large skillet. Cook until it begins to color and has a nutty aroma (*beurre noisette*). Pour in the omelet mixture. Cook for 4–5 minutes, until puffed and lightly golden underneath (lift the edges with a palette knife to check the color).

5. **Slide the omelet** out of the pan into the serving dish, then fold it in half. Bake for about 10 minutes, until puffed and golden.

6. **While the omelet is baking,** heat the remaining Bénédictine liqueur in a saucepan.

7. **Remove the omelet from the oven,** pour the hot liqueur over it, and carefully flambé. Serve the omelet as soon as the flames have died down.

SOUFFLÉ À LA VANILLE

VANILLA SOUFFLÉ ★

Serves	INGREDIENTS	Mixture 2	EQUIPMENT
3	For the soufflé dish	3 egg yolks	6–7-in. (16–18-cm) round
	2 tbsp (25 g) butter	(scant ¼ cup/60 g)	soufflé dish, 2½ in.
Active time: 20 minutes	Sugar	3 egg whites (6½ tbsp/	(6 cm) deep
		90 g)	Electric hand beater
Infusing time: 10 minutes	Mixture 1	1 tbsp + 2 tsp (20 g) sugar	
	1 cup (250 ml) whole milk	Confectioners' sugar,	
Cooling time: 15 minutes	1 vanilla bean, split	for dusting	
	lengthwise		
Cooking time:	⅓ cup (2¼ oz./65 g) sugar		
15–20 minutes	½ cup + 1 tbsp (2½ oz./		
	45 g) AP flour		
	1 tbsp + 1 tsp (20 g) butter		

1. Preheat the oven to 350°F (180°C/Gas Mark 4). Grease the soufflé dish with the butter, then sprinkle with sugar to coat evenly.

2. To prepare mixture 1, pour the milk into a large saucepan, scrape in the seeds of the vanilla bean, and add the bean. Bring to a boil, then remove from the heat. Cover and let infuse for 10 minutes. Remove the vanilla bean.

3. Set aside ¼ cup (60 ml) of the infused milk to cool. Return the saucepan to a low heat to keep the remaining infused milk at a low simmer.

4. Whisk together the sugar, flour, and the ¼ cup (60 ml) of cooled milk. Whisk in a small amount of the hot milk, then return the entire mixture to the saucepan. Let boil for 2 minutes, whisking continuously. Remove from the heat.

5. While the mixture is still warm, stir in the butter until melted. Cover and let cool for 15 minutes.

6. To prepare mixture 2, whisk the egg yolks into mixture 1 to make a smooth custard. Transfer to a mixing bowl.

7. Whisk the egg whites in a separate bowl until they hold soft peaks. Whisk in the sugar until the peaks are medium-firm.

8. Stir one-third of the whites into the custard to lighten it. Gently fold in the remaining whites, using a flexible spatula, until thoroughly incorporated.

9. Pour the batter into the soufflé dish to fill it three-quarters full. Lightly dust the top with confectioners' sugar.

10. Bake for about 20 minutes, until well risen and the tip of a knife pushed into the center comes out clean. Serve immediately.

SOUFFLÉ AU CHOCOLAT

CHOCOLATE SOUFFLÉ ★

Serves	INGREDIENTS	Mixture 2	EQUIPMENT
3	*For the soufflé dish*	3 egg whites (6½ tbsp/	6–7-in. (16–18-cm) round
	2 tbsp (25 g) butter	90 g)	soufflé dish, 2½ in.
Active time: 20 minutes	Sugar	1 tbsp + 2 tsp (20 g) sugar	(6 cm) deep
		2 egg yolks (2½ tbsp/	Instant-read thermometer
		40 g)	Electric hand beater
Cooking time: 20 minutes	*Mixture 1*	Confectioners' sugar,	
	3¼ oz. (90 g) dark	for dusting	
	chocolate, 70% cacao,		
	chopped		
	Scant ⅓ cup (2 oz./60 g)	*To serve*	
	sugar	Chocolate sauce	
	2½ tbsp (40 ml) whole	(see p. 90) or vanilla	
	milk	custard sauce	
		(see p. 86), well chilled	

1. Preheat the oven to 350°F (180°C/Gas Mark 4). Grease the soufflé dish with the butter, then sprinkle with the sugar to coat evenly.

2. To prepare mixture 1, melt the chocolate in a bowl over a saucepan of barely simmering water (bain-marie). Whisk in the sugar and milk until smooth. Remove from the heat and let cool to 140°F (60°C).

3. Meanwhile, prepare mixture 2. Whisk the egg whites until they hold soft peaks. Gradually whisk in the sugar until the peaks are medium-firm.

4. When the chocolate mixture reaches 140°F (60°C), whisk in the egg yolks until smooth. Gently and evenly fold in the egg whites, until thoroughly incorporated.

5. Pour the batter into the soufflé dish. Lightly dust the top with confectioners' sugar.

6. Bake for about 20 minutes, until well risen and the tip of a knife pushed into the center comes out clean.

7. Serve immediately, with well-chilled chocolate sauce or vanilla custard sauce on the side.

SOUFFLÉ AU GRAND-MARNIER

GRAND MARNIER SOUFFLÉ ★

Serves
4

Active time: 25 minutes
+ making the candied
orange

Macerating time:
Overnight

Cooling time: 15 minutes

Cooking time: 20 minutes

INGREDIENTS
*Candied orange
(make 1 day ahead)*
½ orange, preferably
    organic
Scant ½ cup (100 ml)
    water
½ cup minus 1½ tbsp
    (2¾ oz./80 g) sugar

Grand Marnier syrup
Syrup from the candied
    orange (see above)
1 tbsp (15 ml) Grand
    Marnier

Ladyfinger layer
2 ladyfingers (see p. 24)

For the soufflé dish
2 tbsp (25 g) butter
Sugar

Mixture 1
1 cup (250 ml) whole milk,
    divided
Scant ⅓ cup (2 oz./60 g)
    sugar
½ cup + 1 tbsp (2½ oz./
    45 g) AP flour
2 tbsp (1 oz./30 g) butter

Mixture 2
3 egg yolks
    (scant ¼ cup/60 g)
Finely chopped candied
    orange (see left)
2 tbsp (15 ml) Grand
    Marnier
3 egg whites (6½ tbsp/
    90 g)
1 tbsp + 2 tsp (20 g) sugar
Confectioners' sugar,
    for dusting

EQUIPMENT
6–7-in. (16–18-cm) round
    soufflé dish, 2½ in.
    (6 cm) deep
Electric hand beater

1. **A day ahead, prepare the candied orange.** Slice the ½ orange thinly, remove any seeds, and place the slices in a saucepan. Add the water and sugar, then heat until the sugar dissolves. Increase the heat and bring to a boil. Let simmer for 15 minutes.

2. **Remove from the heat,** cover, and let macerate overnight.

3. **The next day,** drain the orange slices over a bowl to reserve the syrup. Chop the slices finely, then set aside.

4. **To prepare the Grand Marnier syrup,** stir the Grand Marnier into the candied orange syrup in a bowl large enough to dip the ladyfingers.

5. **Dip the ladyfingers** in the syrup until soaked but still intact. Cut into small dice, then set aside.

6. **Preheat the oven** to 350°F (180°C/Gas Mark 4). Grease the soufflé dish with the butter, then sprinkle with sugar to coat evenly.

7. **To prepare mixture 1,** bring ¾ cup (190 ml) of the milk to a boil in a large saucepan. Whisk together the sugar, flour, and remaining milk. Whisk in a little of the boiling milk, return the entire mixture to the saucepan, and bring to a boil, whisking continuously. Let boil for 2 minutes, still whisking constantly, then remove from the heat.

8. **While the mixture is still warm,** stir in the butter until melted. Cover and let cool for 15 minutes.

9. **To prepare mixture 2,** whisk the egg yolks into mixture 1 to form a smooth custard. Stir in the chopped candied oranges and the Grand Marnier. Transfer to a mixing bowl.

10. **In a separate bowl,** whisk the egg whites until they hold soft peaks. Gradually whisk in the sugar and keep whisking until the peaks are medium-firm.

11. **Stir one-third of the whites** into the custard to lighten it. Gently fold in the remaining whites using a flexible spatula, until thoroughly incorporated.

12. **Pour half the batter** into the soufflé dish and scatter over the diced ladyfingers. Cover with the remaining batter. Lightly dust the top with confectioners' sugar.

13. **Bake for about 20 minutes,** until well risen and the tip of a knife pushed into the center comes out clean. Serve immediately.

SOUFFLÉ AUX PISTACHES

PISTACHIO SOUFFLÉ ★

Serves
3

Active time: 20 minutes

Cooling time: 15 minutes

Cooking time: 25 minutes

INGREDIENTS

For the soufflé dish
2 tbsp (25 g) butter
Sugar

Mixture 1
⅔ cup (150 ml) whole milk, divided
3 tbsp (1¼ oz./35 g) sugar
1½ tbsp (½ oz./15 g) cornstarch
1 tbsp (20 g) butter

Mixture 2
3 egg yolks (scant ¼ cup/60 g)
Scant ⅓ cup (1 oz./30 g) almond powder
½ cup (2 oz./60 g) shelled pistachios, finely chopped
2 tbsp (30 ml) kirsch
4 egg whites (½ cup/120 g)
1 tbsp + 2 tsp (20 g) sugar
Confectioners' sugar, for dusting

EQUIPMENT
6–7-in. (16–18-cm) round soufflé dish, 2½ in. (6 cm) deep
Electric hand beater

1. **Preheat the oven** to 350°F (180°C/Gas Mark 4). Grease the soufflé dish with the butter, then sprinkle with sugar to coat evenly.
2. **To prepare mixture 1**, bring a scant ½ cup (120 ml) of the milk to a boil in a large saucepan. In a mixing bowl, whisk together the sugar, cornstarch, and remaining milk. Whisk in a small amount of the boiling milk, then return the entire mixture to the saucepan, whisking continuously. Let boil for 2 minutes, still whisking constantly, then remove from the heat.
3. **While the mixture is still warm**, stir in the butter until melted. Cover and let cool for 15 minutes.

4. **To prepare mixture 2**, whisk the egg yolks into mixture 1 to make a smooth custard. Stir in the almond powder, pistachios, and kirsch. Transfer to a mixing bowl.
5. **In a separate bowl,** whisk the egg whites until they hold soft peaks. Gradually add the sugar and keep whisking until the peaks are medium-firm.
6. **Stir one-third of the whites** into the custard to lighten it. Gently fold in the remaining whites using a flexible spatula, until thoroughly incorporated.
7. **Pour the batter** into the soufflé dish to fill it three-quarters full. Lightly dust the top with confectioners' sugar.
8. **Bake for about 20 minutes**, until well risen and the tip of a knife pushed into the center comes out clean. Serve immediately.

SOUFFLÉ AUX POMMES

APPLE SOUFFLÉ ★

Serves
3–4

Active time: 20 minutes

Infusing time: 10 minutes

Cooling time: 15 minutes

Cooking time: 25 minutes

INGREDIENTS

For the soufflé dish
2 tbsp (25 g) butter
Sugar

Mixture 1
1 cup (250 ml) whole milk, divided
¼ vanilla bean, split lengthwise
⅓ cup (2¼ oz./65 g) sugar
⅓ cup (1½ oz./40 g) AP flour
1 tbsp + 1 tsp (20 g) butter
2 tbsp (30 ml) Calvados

Mixture 2
3 egg yolks
   (scant ¼ cup/60 g)
2 firm baking apples (such as Chantecler, Belle de Boskoop, Golden Delicious)
3 egg whites (6½ tbsp/90 g)
1 tbsp + 2 tsp (20 g) sugar
2 tbsp (30 ml) Calvados, for flambéing

EQUIPMENT

6–7-in. (16–18-cm) round soufflé dish, 2½ in. (6 cm) deep, or 4 individual soufflé dishes (see Chef's Notes)
Electric hand beater

---

1. **Preheat the oven** to 350°F (180°C/Gas Mark 4). Grease the soufflé dish with the butter, then sprinkle with sugar to coat evenly.

2. **To prepare mixture 1**, pour the milk into a large saucepan, scrape in the seeds of the vanilla bean, and add the bean. Bring to a boil, then remove from the heat. Cover and let infuse for 10 minutes. Remove the vanilla bean.

3. **Set aside** ¼ cup (60 ml) of the infused milk to cool. Return the saucepan to a low heat to keep the remaining infused milk at a low simmer.

4. **Whisk together** the sugar, flour, and the ¼ cup (60 ml) cooled milk. Whisk in a small amount of the boiling milk, then return the entire mixture to the saucepan, whisking continuously. Let boil for 2 minutes, still whisking constantly, then remove from the heat.

5. **While the mixture is still warm**, stir in the butter and Calvados, until the butter has melted. Cover and let cool for 15 minutes.

6. **To prepare mixture 2**, whisk the egg yolks into mixture 1 to make a smooth custard. Transfer to a mixing bowl.

7. **Peel and core the apples.** Cut them into very thin slices.

8. **Whisk the egg whites** in a separate bowl until they hold soft peaks. Add the sugar and keep whisking until the peaks are medium-firm.

9. **Stir one-third of the whites** into the custard to lighten it. Gently fold in the remainder using a flexible spatula, until thoroughly incorporated.

10. **Pour one-third of the batter** into the soufflé dish. Set aside 4 apple slices for decoration and cover the batter with half the remaining apple slices. Pour in another third of the batter and cover with the rest of the apple slices. Pour over the remaining batter, then decorate the top with the 4 reserved apple slices. Lightly dust the top with confectioners' sugar.

11. **Bake for about 25 minutes**, until well risen and the tip of a knife pushed into the center comes out clean.

12. **When the soufflé** is almost ready, heat the Calvados in a small saucepan. Remove the soufflé from the oven, pour the hot Calvados over it, and carefully flambé. Serve as soon as the flames have died down.

Chef's Notes
• If making individual soufflés, reduce the cooking time by about 5 minutes.

SOUFFLÉ PRALINÉ

PRALINE SOUFFLÉ *

Serves	INGREDIENTS	*Mixture 2*	EQUIPMENT
4	*For the soufflé dish*	3 egg yolks	6–7-in. (16–18-cm) round
	2 tbsp (25 g) butter	(scant ¼ cup/60 g)	soufflé dish, 2½ in.
Active time: 20 minutes	Sugar	3½ oz. (100 g) almond	(6 cm) deep
		praline powder	Electric hand beater
Cooling time: 15 minutes	*Mixture 1*	(see Chef's Notes)	
	1 cup (250 ml) whole milk,	1 tbsp (15 ml) aged rum	
Cooking time: 25 minutes	divided	4 egg whites (½ cup/120 g)	
	3½ tbsp (1½ oz./40 g) sugar	1 tbsp + 2 tsp (20 g) sugar	
	⅓ cup (1½ oz./40 g) AP	2¾ oz. (80 g) pralines	
	flour	Confectioners' sugar,	
	1 tbsp + 1 tsp (20 g) butter	for dusting	

1. **Preheat the oven** to 350°F (180°C/Gas Mark 4). Grease the soufflé dish with the butter, then sprinkle with sugar to coat evenly.
2. **To prepare mixture 1,** bring ¾ cup (190 ml) of the milk to a boil in a saucepan. In a mixing bowl, whisk together the sugar, flour, and remaining milk. Whisk in a small amount of the boiling milk, then return the entire mixture to the saucepan, whisking continuously. Let boil for 2 minutes, still whisking constantly, then remove from the heat.
3. **While the mixture is still warm,** stir in the butter until melted. Cover and let cool for 15 minutes.
4. **To prepare mixture 2,** whisk the egg yolks into mixture 1 to make a smooth custard. Stir in the almond praline powder and rum.
5. **In a separate bowl,** whisk the egg whites until they hold soft peaks. Add the sugar and keep whisking until the peaks are medium-firm.

6. **Stir one-third of the whites** into the custard to lighten it. Gently fold in the remainder using a flexible spatula, until thoroughly incorporated.
7. **Roughly crush** the pralines with a rolling pin.
8. **Pour half the batter** into the soufflé dish and scatter the crushed pralines over it. Cover with the remaining batter. Lightly dust the top with confectioners' sugar.
9. **Bake for about 20 minutes,** until well risen and the tip of a knife pushed into the center comes out clean. Serve immediately.

Chef's Notes

• Hazelnut praline powder can be used instead of almond, if preferred. If powder is unavailable, substitute almond or hazelnut praline spread.

SOUFFLÉ AU CITRON ÉTOILE

LEMON SOUFFLÉ ★

Serves	INGREDIENTS	Mixture 1	EQUIPMENT
4	*Candied lemon*	1 cup (250 ml) whole milk,	6–7-in. (16–18-cm) round
	1 lemon, preferably	divided	soufflé dish, 2½ in.
Active time: 30 minutes	organic	Scant ⅓ cup (2 oz./60 g)	(6 cm) deep
	Scant ½ cup (100 ml)	sugar	Electric hand beater
Cooling time: 15 minutes	water	½ cup + 1 tbsp (2½ oz./	
	⅓ cup (2¾ oz./75 g) sugar	45 g) AP flour	
Cooking time: 35 minutes		1 tbsp + 1 tsp (20 g) butter	
	For the soufflé dish		
	2 tbsp (25 g) butter	*Mixture 2*	
	Sugar	4 egg yolks (scant ⅓ cup/	
		80 g)	
		4 egg whites (½ cup/	
		120 g)	
		1 tbsp + 2 tsp (20 g) sugar	
		Confectioners' sugar,	
		for dusting	

1. To prepare the candied lemon, remove 6 strips of zest from the lemon using a vegetable peeler. Cut the lemon in half crosswise. Thinly slice one half and juice the other half, reserving the juice for the soufflé batter.

2. Heat the water and sugar in a saucepan with the lemon zest and slices until the sugar dissolves. Increase the heat, bring to a boil, then let simmer for 15 minutes. Remove from the heat and let cool completely. Remove the zest and set aside for decoration. Drain the lemon slices, then chop them finely.

3. Preheat the oven to 350°F (180°C/Gas Mark 4). Grease the soufflé dish with the butter, then sprinkle with sugar to coat evenly.

4. To prepare mixture 1, bring ¾ cup (190 ml) of the milk to a boil in a saucepan. In a mixing bowl, whisk together the sugar, flour, and remaining milk. Whisk in a small amount of the boiling milk, then return the entire mixture to the saucepan, whisking continuously. Let boil for 2 minutes, still whisking constantly, then remove from the heat.

5. While the mixture is still warm, stir in the butter until melted. Cover and let cool for 15 minutes.

6. To prepare mixture 2, whisk the egg yolks into mixture 1 to make a smooth custard. Stir in the chopped candied lemon and lemon juice.

7. In a separate bowl, whisk the egg whites until they hold soft peaks. Gradually add the sugar and keep whisking until the peaks are medium-firm.

8. Stir one-third of the whites into the custard to lighten it. Gently fold in the remainder, using a flexible spatula, until thoroughly incorporated.

9. Pour the batter into the soufflé dish to fill it three-quarters full. Arrange the strips of candied lemon zest over the batter in a star pattern. Lightly dust with confectioners' sugar.

10. Bake for about 20 minutes, until well risen and the tip of a knife pushed into the center comes out clean. Serve immediately.

COLD DESSERTS

ABRICOTS AU SIROP

APRICOTS

IN WHITE WINE SYRUP *

Active time: 10 minutes

Soaking time: 2 hours,
if using dried apricots

Cooking time: 15 minutes

Storage: Up to 5 days
in the refrigerator

INGREDIENTS
2 lb. (1 kg) ripe but firm
   fresh apricots, or
   1 lb. 2 oz. (500 g) dried
   apricots

White wine syrup
75-cl bottle dry white wine
2 cups (14 oz./400 g)
   sugar
1 lemon, sliced

EQUIPMENT
Jars with airtight lids

1. **If using dried apricots**, soak them in warm water
for 2 hours to make them swell.
2. **If using fresh apricots**, wash and dry them.
Cut them in half and remove the pits.
3. **To prepare the white wine syrup**, combine the white
wine, sugar, and lemon slices in a saucepan. Heat gently
until the sugar dissolves, then bring to a simmer.
4. **Add the apricots**—there should be enough liquid to
just cover the fruit—and poach them for 15 minutes,
until they are tender but still hold their shape.
5. **Transfer the apricots** and lemon slices to the jars.
Pour the syrup over them.
6. **Let cool**, then seal tightly with the lids. Store in the
refrigerator.

ABRICOTS FRAIS AVEC LEURS NOYAUX

WHOLE POACHED APRICOTS ★

Active time: 10 minutes

Cooking time: 15–20 minutes

Macerating time: At least 3 hours

Storage: Up to 5 days in the refrigerator

INGREDIENTS
3½ lb. (1.5 kg) firm fresh apricots

Syrup
4 cups (1 L) water
1½ cups (10½ oz./300 g) sugar
Scant 1 cup (10½ oz./ 300 g) acacia honey
A few small pieces candied ginger

EQUIPMENT
Jars with airtight lids

1. **Wash and dry** the apricots, leaving them whole.
2. **To prepare the syrup**, combine the water, sugar, honey, and ginger in a saucepan. Heat gently until the sugar dissolves, then bring to a simmer.
3. **Add the apricots** to the syrup and poach for 20 minutes, until the fruit is tender when pierced with the tip of a knife.
4. **Remove from the heat.** Let macerate for at least 3 hours.
5. **Drain the apricots** from the syrup. Place in the jars and seal tightly with the lids. Store in the refrigerator.

BREAD AND BUTTER PUDDING ★

Serves	INGREDIENTS	To serve (optional)	EQUIPMENT
6	1 cup (250 ml) water	Vanilla custard sauce	Toaster oven or broiler
	Scant ¼ cup (1 oz./30 g)	(see p. 86) or raspberry	12½-in. (32-cm) baking
Active time: 20 minutes	raisins	coulis (see p. 51)	dish
	2 tbsp (30 ml) dark rum		Large roasting pan
Soaking time: 15 minutes	2 cups (500 ml) whole		for the bain-marie
	milk		
Cooking time: 30 minutes	1 vanilla bean, split		
	lengthwise		
	7 oz. (200 g) white		
	sandwich bread (*pain de mie*), thinly sliced and crusts removed		
	5 tbsp (2½ oz./70 g) butter		
	3 eggs (⅔ cup/150 g)		
	2 egg yolks (2½ tbsp/40 g)		
	½ cup (3½ oz./100 g) sugar		

1. **Bring the water to a boil.** Put the raisins in a heatproof bowl, pour over the boiling water, and let soak for 15 minutes to plump them up.
2. **Drain the raisins**, return them to the bowl, and add the rum. Let soak until ready to use.
3. **Preheat the oven** to 430°F (220°C/Gas Mark 7).
4. **Heat the milk** and vanilla bean in a saucepan, ensuring the milk does not come to a boil. Keep warm.
5. **Spread the slices of bread** thinly with butter. Cut each slice in half to make 2 triangles. Toast or broil briefly until the buttered sides are golden.
6. **Arrange the triangles**, buttered side up, over the base of the baking dish with the corners pointing upward. Pack them tightly together in overlapping rows so that the base of the dish is covered.
7. **Whisk together** the eggs, egg yolks, and sugar. Remove the vanilla bean from the warm milk. Pour the milk onto the eggs and sugar, whisking continuously.

8. **Pour the mixture** slowly and carefully over the bread triangles. Use a palette knife to prevent the triangles from floating and to ensure they remain in neat rows in the dish.
9. **Place the baking dish** in the roasting pan. Pour in enough hot water to come halfway up the sides of the dish.
10. **Carefully transfer** to the oven and bake for 30 minutes. At the start of the cooking time, press down on the triangles a few times with a palette knife, as they tend to float to the surface while the custard is still runny.
11. **Let cool**, then chill in the dish until ready to serve.
12. **Just before serving**, drain the raisins and scatter them over. The pudding can also be served warm, with vanilla custard sauce or raspberry coulis.

COMMENT ÉVIDER UNE BRIOCHE

HOW TO HOLLOW OUT A BRIOCHE

A brioche can be hollowed out and the crumb replaced
with a variety of fillings, such as Bavarian cream
(see p. 44), chocolate mousse (see pp. 82–83), chopped
fresh fruit, or pastry cream (see p. 66).

A Parisian brioche is a little easier to hollow out than
a brioche mousseline.

1. **Cut off** the top or "head" of the brioche using
a bread knife.
2. **Carefully cut** an opening by pushing the knife
vertically through the top, ½ in. (1 cm) from the crust,
to within ¾ in. (2 cm) of the base. Take care not to cut
all the way through the base.
3. **Cut around the inside** of the brioche, leaving
a ½-in. (1-cm) border.
4. **To release the crumb**, cut a small opening,
¾ in. (2 cm) above the base, by inserting the knife
horizontally into the side. Through this opening, move
the knife from side to side in an arc until the crumb
comes away in a cylinder that detaches from the crust.
5. **Carefully remove the crumb** without damaging
the crust, which will be fragile. The crumb can be used
in other desserts such as Brioche Bread Pudding
(see p. 230) or Almond Brioche Toast (see p. 96).

BRIOCHE ESTELLE À LA PASSION

PASSION FRUIT BRIOCHE ★★

Serves
8

Active time: 30 minutes + making the brioche

Chilling time: 5 hours

INGREDIENTS

Passion fruit mousse
⅔ cup (160 ml) heavy cream, well chilled
3 sheets gelatin, 180–200 Bloom
2 egg whites (¼ cup/60 g)
½ cup (3½ oz./100 g) sugar
2 tbsp (30 ml) water
6 oz. (175 g) passion fruit puree

Brioche
1 Parisian brioche (see p. 104), made a day ahead
Generous ¾ cup (200 ml) simple syrup (see p. 91)

EQUIPMENT
Stand mixer fitted with the whisk
Instant-read thermometer

1. **To prepare the passion fruit mousse**, whip the cream until it holds its shape. Chill until using. Soak the gelatin in a bowl of cold water until softened.
2. **To make an Italian meringue** for the mousse, place the egg whites in the stand mixer bowl. Dissolve the sugar in the water in a saucepan over low heat, then increase the heat and bring to a boil.
3. **As soon as the syrup** begins to boil, whisk the egg whites on high speed until firm peaks form (about 5 minutes in total).
4. **Check the temperature** of the sugar syrup. When it reaches 250°F (121°C), reduce the mixer speed to low and very carefully drizzle the syrup into the whisked whites. Do not let the hot syrup touch the whisk, as it could spray up and burn you.
5. **Continue whisking** on low speed for about 5 minutes, until the meringue is firm and glossy, and it has cooled to room temperature.
6. **Whisk the passion fruit puree** into the meringue. Squeeze the gelatin to remove excess water, then microwave in a bowl on high for 5 seconds or until melted. Whisk the gelatin into the meringue. Gently fold in the whipped cream using a flexible spatula.
7. **Hollow out the brioche** following the instructions on p. 334. Reserve the crumb. Brush the syrup over the inside of the base and over the crumb side of the "head."
8. **Fill the brioche** with the passion fruit mousse. If the filling does not reach the top, cut some of the reserved crumb into small dice and add them into the mousse to fill the brioche.
9. **Chill for at least 5 hours.** Remove the brioche from the refrigerator 30 minutes before serving and place the "head" on top.

Chef's Notes
• The brioche can also be filled with a passion fruit-flavored Bavarian cream instead of passion fruit mousse. Make up ½ quantity (12¼ oz./350 g) Bavarian cream (see p. 44) and, while it is still warm, stir in 6 oz. (175 g) passion fruit puree. Immediately spoon into the brioche before the cream has time to set. Chill as indicated above.

CHARLOTTE AUX FRAISES OU AUX FRAMBOISES

STRAWBERRY OR RASPBERRY CHARLOTTE ★★

Serves
7–8

Active time: 20 minutes +
making the ladyfingers
and coulis

Chilling time: 2 hours

Storage: Up to 6 hours
in the refrigerator
(before unmolding)

INGREDIENTS
Vanilla Bavarian cream
2 sheets gelatin,
    180–200 Bloom
1 quantity (12¼ oz./350 g)
    vanilla custard sauce
    (see p. 86), hot
Generous ¾ cup
    (200 ml) heavy cream,
    well chilled

To assemble
Butter and sugar
    for the pan
About 20 ladyfingers
    (see p. 24 and
    Chef's Notes)
7 oz. (200 g) fresh
    strawberries or
    raspberries + more
    for decoration
¼ cup (1¾ oz./50 g) sugar
½ quantity (5¾ oz./165 g)
    strawberry or raspberry
    coulis (see p. 51),
    well chilled

EQUIPMENT
Instant-read thermometer
9-in. (23-cm) fluted
    charlotte pan

1. **To prepare the Bavarian cream**, soak the gelatin in a bowl of cold water until softened. Squeeze the sheets to remove excess water. Whisk into the hot custard until melted.
2. **Place the custard** over a bowl filled halfway with ice water. Cool until the temperature reaches 64°F–68°F (18°C–20°C). Whip the cream until it holds its shape.
3. **As soon as the custard** reaches the required temperature, fold in the whipped cream.
4. **To assemble the charlotte**, lightly grease the sides of the pan with butter. Line the sides with ladyfingers, making sure they are placed tightly together. Trim the tops flush with the top of the pan and reserve the trimmings. Sprinkle a little sugar over the base of the pan, as this will make unmolding the charlotte easier.
5. **Wash and dry** the fruit. If using strawberries, trim the tops and, if large, cut them into smaller pieces. Gently toss the fruit in the sugar.

6. **Fill the charlotte** with alternate layers of Bavarian cream and fruit, beginning with the cream. If the layers do not reach the top, cut the ladyfinger trimmings into small dice and add them to fill the pan. Chill for 2 hours.
7. **Immediately before serving,** dip the base of the pan briefly in hot water to release the charlotte. Invert it onto a serving plate. Decorate with berries and spoon some of the coulis over them. Serve well chilled with the remaining coulis on the side.

Chef's Notes
• Instead of lining the mold with individual ladyfingers and then adding the filling, the charlotte pan can be filled with the cream and fruit first, and chilled for 2 hours. After unmolding, carefully wrap a band of ladyfingers around the charlotte and press gently to fix them to the cream. To make a band of ladyfingers, pipe them close together on the sheet so that they join together during baking.

CHARLOTTE AUX MARRONS

CHESTNUT CHARLOTTE ★★

Serves
7–8

Active time: 20 minutes +
making the ladyfingers

Chilling time: 3 hours

Storage: Up to 24 hours
in the refrigerator
(before unmolding and
decorating)

INGREDIENTS

Chestnut mousse
2 sheets gelatin,
  180–200 Bloom
1 lb. 2 oz. (500 g) *crème
  de marrons* (chestnut
  spread)
3½ tbsp (50 ml) whisky
1¼ cups (300 ml) heavy
  cream, well chilled,
  divided

To assemble
Butter for the pan
About 20 ladyfingers
  (see p. 24)
1¾ oz. (50 g) candied
  chestnuts, finely
  chopped

Glaze (make 1 day ahead)
7 oz. (200 g) chocolate
  glaze (see p. 76)

Decoration
Confectioners' sugar,
  for dusting
½ oz. (15 g) *crème de
  marrons* (chestnut
  spread)
1 candied chestnut

EQUIPMENT
Electric hand beater
9-in (23-cm) fluted
  charlotte pan
Instant-read thermometer
Pastry bag fitted
  with a small plain tip

---

1. **To prepare the chestnut mousse,** soak the gelatin in a bowl of cold water until softened. Place the *crème de marrons* in a mixing bowl. Whisk until smooth, then mix in the whisky.

2. **Heat 2 tbsp (30 ml) of the cream** in a heatproof bowl over a saucepan of barely simmering water (bain-marie). Squeeze the gelatin to remove excess water, then microwave in a bowl on high for 5 seconds or until melted. Whisk the gelatin into the cream and keep the bowl over the bain-marie to prevent the gelatin from setting again too quickly.

3. **Whisk one-third** of the chestnut mixture into the gelatin cream to loosen it, then pour back into the mixing bowl.

4. **Whip the rest of the cream** until it holds its shape. Fold half of it into the chestnut mixture, then repeat with the other half.

5. **To assemble the charlotte,** lightly grease the sides of the pan with butter. Line the base with a circle of parchment paper to make unmolding easier. Line the sides of the pan with the ladyfingers, making sure they are placed tightly together. Trim the tops flush with the top of the pan.

6. **Fill the charlotte** with alternate layers of chestnut mousse and finely chopped candied chestnuts, beginning with the mousse. Chill for at least 3 hours.

7. **To glaze the charlotte,** heat the chocolate glaze to 104°F (40°C) in a bowl over a saucepan of barely simmering water (bain-marie). Make sure not to create air bubbles when stirring.

8. **Remove the charlotte** from the refrigerator. Dip the base of the pan briefly in hot water to release the charlotte and carefully invert it onto a serving plate. Remove the parchment paper. Dust the ladyfingers with confectioners' sugar. Pour the glaze into the center to cover the top. Spoon a little *crème de marrons* into the pastry bag and pipe small pearls between each ladyfinger. Place the candied chestnut on top. Chill briefly for the glaze to set before serving.

Chef's Notes
• The charlotte can also be assembled in a 7- × 2¾- × 2¾-in. (18- × 7- × 7-cm) Yule log mold. Lightly grease the mold with butter and line with parchment paper. Cut the ladyfingers in half and line the sides of the pan with them, cut side up, making sure they are placed tightly together. Proceed with step 6, filling the mold to within ½ in. (1 cm) of the top. Cut the remaining ladyfingers to the width of the mold and cover the top with them. Chill for at least 3 hours, then proceed with steps 7 and 8.

CHARLOTTE CÉCILE

CHOCOLATE AND VANILLA
CHARLOTTE ★★

Serves
7–8

Active time: 45 minutes + making the ladyfingers and chocolate mousse

Chilling time: 1½ hours

Storage: Up to 2 days in the refrigerator (before unmolding)

INGREDIENTS
To assemble
Butter for the pan
About 20 ladyfingers (see p. 24)
1 quantity (12¼ oz./350 g) chocolate mousse (see p. 82)

Vanilla Bavarian cream
2 sheets gelatin, 180–200 Bloom
1 quantity (12¼ oz./350 g) vanilla custard sauce (see p. 86), hot
½ cup (125 ml) heavy cream, well chilled

Decoration
1¾ oz. (50 g) dark chocolate
Confectioners' sugar, for dusting

EQUIPMENT
9-in. (23-cm) fluted charlotte pan
Instant-read thermometer

1. **To assemble the charlotte,** lightly grease the sides of the pan with butter. Line the sides with the ladyfingers, making sure they are placed tightly together. Trim the tops flush with the top of the pan.
2. **Add the chocolate mousse** to fill the pan halfway. Chill for 30 minutes.
3. **To prepare the vanilla Bavarian cream,** soak the gelatin in a bowl of cold water until softened. Squeeze the sheets to remove excess water, then whisk them into the hot custard until melted.
4. **Set the custard** over a bowl filled halfway with ice water. Let cool until the temperature reaches 64°F–68°F (18°C–20°C). Meanwhile, whip the cream until it holds its shape. As soon as the custard reaches the required temperature, fold in the whipped cream.

5. **Pour the Bavarian cream** over the chocolate mousse to fill the pan completely. Chill for at least 1 hour.
6. **Shave the chocolate** into curls using a vegetable peeler.
7. **Immediately before serving,** dip the base of the pan briefly in hot water to release the charlotte. Invert it onto a serving plate. Dust the ladyfingers with confectioners' sugar. Pile the chocolate curls on top, then dust them lightly with confectioners' sugar.

CHARLOTTE AUX POMMES À L'ANCIENNE

OLD-FASHIONED
APPLE CHARLOTTE ★

Serves
6

Active time: 45 minutes +
baking the apples

Cooking time: 1 hour

Chilling time: Overnight

Cooling time: 30 minutes

INGREDIENTS
Baked apples
(make 1 day ahead,
see Chef's Notes)
2 lb. (900 g) firm
  baking apples (such
  as Chantecler, Belle
  de Boskoop, Golden
  Delicious)
4 tbsp (2 oz./60 g) butter,
  melted
Scant ⅓ cup (2 oz./60 g)
  vanilla sugar

Toasted bread
7 tbsp (3½ oz./100 g)
  butter
½ cup (3½ oz./100 g)
  brown sugar
White sandwich loaf
  (*pain de mie*), sliced

For the pan
Butter
Sugar

To serve
Apricot coulis (see p. 51)
  or vanilla custard sauce
  (see p. 86)

EQUIPMENT
Baking dish
Rimmed baking sheet
6-in. (16-cm) charlotte
  pan, 4 in. (10 cm) deep
3-in. (8-cm), 4½-in.
  (11-cm), and 5½-in.
  (14-cm) round cookie
  cutters

---

1. **A day ahead**, prepare the baked apples. Preheat the oven to 340°F (170°C/Gas Mark 3). Peel, halve, and core the apples. Place them in a single layer in the baking dish, rounded sides up. Pour the melted butter over them, then sprinkle with the vanilla sugar.
2. **Bake for 30 minutes**, until the apples are tender when pierced with the tip of a knife. Let cool. Cover and refrigerate overnight.
3. **The following day, prepare the toasted bread.** Preheat the broiler. Beat the butter until softened, then beat in the brown sugar. Trim the crusts off the bread and spread 13 slices with a thin layer of the butter and sugar. Set on the baking sheet, buttered side up, and broil until golden.
4. **Preheat the oven** to 340°F (170°C/Gas Mark 3). Lightly grease the charlotte pan with butter, then sprinkle with sugar to coat.
5. **Cut 10 of the toasted bread slices** lengthwise into 3 equal pieces. Line the sides of the pan with them, buttered sides against the pan, overlapping them slightly.

6. **Use the cookie cutters** to cut 3 circles (one of each size) from the remaining toasted bread slices.
7. **Place the smallest (3-in./8-cm) bread circle** at the bottom of the charlotte pan, buttered side down. Cover with half the apples, pressing them down into an even layer. Place the 4½-in. (11-cm) circle on top, followed by the remaining apples. Finish with the 5½-in. (14-cm) circle, buttered side uppermost.
8. **Place the charlotte** on the baking sheet and bake for 30 minutes. Cool in the pan for 30 minutes, then turn out onto a serving plate. Serve warm or cold, with apricot coulis or vanilla custard sauce on the side.

Chef's Notes
• Instead of baked apples, you can fill the charlotte with 1 quantity (about 2 lb./900 g) Apple Compote (see p. 348).

CHOUCHOU VANILLE FRAMBOISE

RASPBERRY AND VANILLA CHOUCHOU ★★★

Serves
6

Active time: 1½ hours

Cooking time: 25 minutes

Freezing time: At least
2 hours

INGREDIENTS
Choux puffs
7 oz. (200 g) choux pastry
  dough (see p. 38)
Scant ¼ cup (1 oz./30 g)
  blanched almonds,
  coarsely ground

Crispy praline layer
Generous 2 tbsp (20 g)
  shelled sunflower seeds
1½ oz. (40 g) hazelnut
  praline paste
½ oz. (15 g) plain crêpe
  dentelle cookies or crisp
  lace wafers, crushed
⅓ oz. (10 g) milk
  chocolate, chopped
2 tsp (10 g) butter, diced

Vanilla crémeux
1 sheet gelatin, 180–200
  Bloom
Scant ½ cup (100 ml)
  heavy cream
¼ Bourbon Madagascar
  vanilla bean, split
  lengthwise
2 egg yolks (2½ tbsp/40 g)
1 tbsp (15 g) sugar
1 tbsp (20 g) butter, diced

Vanilla mousse
½ sheet gelatin,
  180–200 Bloom
1 quantity (12¼ oz./350 g)
  vanilla custard sauce
  (see p. 86)
⅓ cup (85 ml) heavy
  cream, well chilled

To assemble
Generous ¼ cup (3½ oz./
  100 g) raspberry jam,
  divided
Confectioners' sugar, for
  dusting
2½ oz. (70 g) raspberry
  glaze (see p. 80)

Glaze
9 oz. (250 g) neutral glaze
  (see p. 81)

To serve
Fresh raspberries
Raspberry coulis
  (see p. 51), well chilled

EQUIPMENT
Pastry bags fitted with
  a ½-in. (1-cm) plain tip,
  3 × ⅛-in. (3-mm) plain
  tips, and 2 × large plain
  tips
7-cm (17-cm) ring mold,
  1½ in. (4 cm) deep
Cookie sheet lined with
  parchment paper
Instant-read thermometer
Immersion blender

---

1. **Preheat the oven** to 350°F (180°C/Gas Mark 4).
2. **To prepare the choux puffs,** spoon most of the choux pastry dough into the pastry bag with a ½-in. (1-cm) plain tip. Pipe out 18 puffs measuring ¾ in. (2 cm) in diameter on the cookie sheet. Sprinkle with the almonds. Pipe the remaining dough into mini choux puffs using a pastry bag with an ⅛-in. (3-mm) tip. Bake for 20–25 minutes, until golden and crisp. Let cool on a wire rack.
3. **To prepare the crispy praline layer,** toast the sunflower seeds, then let cool. In a mixing bowl, stir together the praline paste, mini choux puffs, crêpe dentelle cookies, and toasted sunflower seeds. Melt the chocolate and butter in the microwave in separate bowls. Stir into the praline mixture. Transfer to a pastry bag with a large plain tip.

4. **Using a pencil,** draw around the outside edge and the hole in the center of the mold to trace a ring on the parchment. Place on the cookie sheet with the pencil lines underneath. Pipe the praline mixture into the drawn ring, so it is slightly smaller than the mold. Freeze until using.
5. **To prepare the vanilla crémeux,** soak the gelatin in cold water until softened. Use the cream, vanilla bean, egg yolks, and sugar to make a custard, following the instructions on p. 86. Squeeze excess water from the gelatin, then whisk it into the hot custard until melted. Set the pan over a bowl filled halfway with ice water to stop the custard cooking. Let it cool until the temperature reaches 104°F (40°C), stirring often. Gradually beat in the butter using the immersion blender. Transfer the custard to a plate, then press plastic wrap over the surface and chill.

6. **To prepare the vanilla mousse,** soak the gelatin in cold water until softened. Squeeze the gelatin to remove excess water. Microwave in a bowl on high for 5 seconds, or until melted. Stir into the custard sauce. Let cool until the temperatures reaches 59°F (15°C). Whip the cream until it holds its shape, then fold in.

7. **To assemble the ring,** spoon the vanilla mousse into the mold. Remove the praline layer from the freezer and, using a pastry bag with a large plain tip, pipe 3 tbsp (2½ oz./70 g) of raspberry jam over it. Place the praline layer on top of the mousse, jam side down. Press it down gently so it is flush with the top of the mold. Smooth over any excess mousse with a palette knife. Freeze for 2 hours.

8. **To fill the 18 choux puffs,** spoon the remaining raspberry jam and vanilla crémeux into separate pastry bags both fitted with plain ⅛-in. (3-mm) tips. Pierce a hole in the side of each puff and fill half of them with equal quantities of jam and crémeux and the remaining puffs with just crémeux. Dust the tops of the crémeux-filled puffs with confectioners' sugar. Coat the tops of those filled with jam and crémeux with a thin layer of raspberry glaze. Chill the puffs, tops uppermost, until needed.

9. **Shortly before serving,** melt the neutral glaze in a bowl over a saucepan of barely simmering water (bain-marie) until the temperature reaches 104°F (40°C). Remove the ring from the freezer. Briefly dip the base of the mold in hot water to release the ring. Invert it onto a rack and pour the glaze over it until evenly coated. Transfer the ring to a serving plate large enough to add the choux puffs around it later. Chill until serving.

10. **Immediately before serving,** arrange the choux puffs around the ring, alternating the colors. Fill the center of the ring with fresh raspberries (fill them with raspberry coulis, if desired). Serve with chilled raspberry coulis on the side.

COMPOTE DE POMMES

APPLE COMPOTE ⋆

Serves
4 (makes about 2 lb./
900 g)

Active time: 15 minutes

Cooking time: 20 minutes

Storage: Up to 4 days in
the refrigerator, covered

INGREDIENTS
1½ lb. (750 g) tart apples
    (such as Chantecler,
    Belle de Boskoop,
    Braeburn, or Honeycrisp)
Lemon juice, as needed
¼ cup (1¾ oz./50 g) sugar
Scant ½ cup (100 ml)
    water
½ vanilla bean, split
    lengthwise

EQUIPMENT
Rimmed baking sheet
    lined with parchment
    paper

1. **Preheat the oven** to 340°F (170°C/Gas Mark 3).
2. **Wash, peel, and core the apples.** Cut one-third into
quarters, then coat with lemon juice to prevent them
from browning.
3. **Chop the remaining apples** into small dice and
spread them over the baking sheet. Bake for about
15 minutes, until the apples are tender. Let cool.
4. **Place the apple quarters,** sugar, water, and vanilla
bean in a saucepan. Cook over low heat for about
20 minutes, until the apples are tender. Remove the
vanilla bean. Let cool, then stir in the roasted diced
apples.
5. **Transfer to a covered container** and store in the
refrigerator until serving.

COMPOTE DE RHUBARBE

RHUBARB COMPOTE ★

Serves
4–5 (makes about
2½ lb./1.2 kg)

Active time: 15 minutes

Cooking time: 30 minutes

Storage: Up to 5 days in
the refrigerator, covered

INGREDIENTS
2 lb. (1 kg) rhubarb
1 cup (7 oz./200 g) sugar
1 vanilla bean, split
   lengthwise
3½ tbsp (50 ml) water

1. **Wash, trim, and peel** the rhubarb. Cut the stalks into small pieces.
2. **Place in a saucepan**, alternating layers of rhubarb with layers of sugar.
3. **Add the vanilla bean** and water. Bring to a simmer over low heat. Simmer very gently for 30 minutes, stirring occasionally.
4. **Remove from the heat** and let cool.
5. **Chill in a covered container** until serving.

Chef's Notes
• For a sweeter compote, blanch the rhubarb first, before simmering it with the sugar.

COMPOTE DE RHUBARBE FRAISE

STRAWBERRY AND RHUBARB COMPOTE ★

Serves
6 (makes 3¼ lb./1.5 kg)

Active time: 20 minutes

Cooking time: 30 minutes

Storage: Up to 5 days in
the refrigerator, covered

INGREDIENTS
2 lb. (1 kg) rhubarb
1 cup (7 oz./200 g) sugar
3½ tbsp (50 ml) water
10½ oz. (300 g)
  strawberries

1. **Wash, trim, and peel** the rhubarb. Cut the stalks into small pieces.
2. **Place in a saucepan**, alternating layers of rhubarb with layers of sugar. Add the water.
3. **Bring to a simmer** over low heat. Let simmer very gently for 25 minutes, stirring often, until the rhubarb is tender.
4. **Wash and hull** the strawberries. Halve or quarter them, depending on their size.
5. **Add the strawberries** to the rhubarb. Cook for 5 minutes, stirring continuously. Remove from the heat and let cool.
6. **Chill in a covered container** until serving.

Chef's Notes
• For a sweeter compote, blanch the rhubarb first, before simmering it with the sugar.

CRÈME À LA VANILLE D'ANNIE

ANNIE'S VANILLA CARAMEL CUSTARD ★

Serves
8

Active time: 15 minutes

Cooking time: 40 minutes

Storage: Up to 3 days
in the refrigerator

INGREDIENTS
Caramel
1 cup (7 oz./200 g) sugar
2 tbsp (30 ml) water
A few drops lemon juice

Custard
4 cups (1 L) whole milk
1 Bourbon Madagascar
  vanilla bean, split
  lengthwise
4 eggs (¾ cup + 2 tbsp/
  200 g)
8 egg yolks
  (scant ⅔ cup/160 g)
¾ cup (5 oz./150 g) sugar

To serve (optional)
1 quantity (12¼ oz./350 g)
  vanilla custard sauce
  (see p. 86), well chilled
Raspberry coulis (see
  p. 51), well chilled

EQUIPMENT
2-qt. (2-L) soufflé dish
  or 8 individual oven-safe
  bowls or ramekins
Electric hand beater
Fine-mesh sieve
Baking pan with high sides
  for the bain-marie

---

1. **To prepare the caramel**, combine the sugar, water, and lemon juice in a small saucepan. Heat until the sugar dissolves, then bring to a boil. Boil for 8–10 minutes, until the syrup turns into an amber-colored caramel. Immediately pour into the soufflé dish or ramekins and swirl to coat the base and sides.
2. **Preheat the oven** to 340°F (170°C/Gas Mark 3).
3. **To prepare the custard**, pour the milk into a large saucepan. Scrape in the vanilla seeds and add the bean. Bring to a boil.
4. **Whisk together** the eggs, egg yolks, and sugar in a mixing bowl. Place the fine-mesh sieve over the bowl and pour in the hot milk, whisking continuously until the two mixtures are combined. Pour into the soufflé dish or ramekins.
5. **Place in the baking pan** and pour in enough hot water to come halfway up the sides of the dish or ramekins. Carefully transfer to the oven and bake for 40 minutes if making a large custard or about 15 minutes if making individual ones (depending on the size of the ramekin), until the tip of a knife inserted into the center comes out clean. If necessary, return the custard to the oven to continue baking.
6. **Let the custard cool** in the dish(es). Chill until serving.
7. **To serve**, either invert the custard onto a serving plate (run a knife around the inside of the dish first to release the custard) or serve it from the dish. Serve individual custards in their bowls or ramekins. Serve well chilled, with vanilla custard sauce or raspberry coulis on the side, if desired.

Chef's Notes
• Instead of pouring the hot caramel into the dish(es), it can be stirred into the boiling milk to infuse it with a caramel flavor. Grease the dish(es) with butter, then dust with sugar before pouring in the custard. The caramel can also be poured over the top of the custard. Bake as above.

FIGUES AU VIN / POIRES AU VIN

FIGS OR PEARS

IN SPICED RED WINE ★

Serves
6–8

Active time: 15 minutes

Cooking time: 10 minutes
(for figs and pears in
syrup), 45 minutes (for
fresh pears)

Storage: Up to 3 days in
the refrigerator, covered

INGREDIENTS

2 lb. (1 kg) fresh figs, fresh
   pears, or pears in syrup
   (see p. 372)
½ cup (130 ml) water
3 cups (750 ml) red wine
½ cup minus 1½ tbsp
   (2¾ oz./80 g) sugar
1 whole clove
1 stick cinnamon
1 vanilla bean, split
   lengthwise
3 star anise

1. **Wash fresh figs or pears.** If using figs, slice off the
hard tips of the stems at an angle. If using fresh pears,
peel and core from the base, leaving the stalks attached:
this will help the pears absorb the poaching syrup.
2. **Pour the water and wine** into a large saucepan.
Add the sugar and spices. Heat and stir until the sugar
dissolves. Bring to a very gentle simmer. Add the fruit
and, if using figs or poached pears, cook for 10 minutes.
Remove the saucepan from the heat and let the fruit
cool in the syrup.
3. **If using fresh pears,** simmer them very gently for
30–45 minutes, until tender. The length of time will
depend on the ripeness of the pears. Remove from the
heat and let cool in the syrup.
4. **Chill the fruit and syrup** in a covered container until
serving.

Chef's Notes
• The fruit is delicious served on its own. If desired,
the syrup can be reduced to a glaze, then poured over
the fruit before serving.

FRAISES AU PÉCHARMANT

STRAWBERRIES
IN PÉCHARMANT WINE ⋆

Serves
6

Active time: 15 minutes

Cooking time: 15 minutes

Storage: Up to 3 days in
the refrigerator, covered

INGREDIENTS
2 cups (500 ml)
   Pécharmant red wine
   or light red Bordeaux
Scant 1 cup (5½ oz./160 g)
   sugar
1 tea bag
6 green peppercorns
2 lb. (1 kg) strawberries

To serve (optional)
A few fresh mint leaves,
   thinly sliced, or vanilla
   ice cream

EQUIPMENT
Fine-mesh sieve

1. **Heat the wine gently** in a large saucepan. Stir in the sugar until dissolved. Add the tea bag and peppercorns and bring to a simmer. Let simmer over low heat until it turns into a light syrup.
2. **While the syrup is simmering**, wash and hull the strawberries.
3. **Strain the syrup** through a fine-mesh sieve. Return it to the saucepan and add the strawberries, immersing them in the syrup. Simmer gently for 3 minutes.
4. **Remove from the heat.** Let cool, then chill in a covered container until serving.
5. **Serve well chilled or warm.** If serving chilled, sprinkle the strawberries with fresh mint. If serving warm, accompany with a scoop of vanilla ice cream (see Chef's Notes).

Chef's Notes
• At Easter in south-west France, these strawberries are often served warm, accompanied by a slice of *Coque de Moissac*: a round brioche topped with candied fruits. A slice of Bordeaux Brioche (p. 98) would make an equally good accompaniment.

FRAISES AU SIROP

STRAWBERRIES IN SYRUP ★

Serves	INGREDIENTS
6	2 lb. (1 kg) large, firm strawberries
Active time: 15 minutes	Juice of 1–2 lemons
	1–2 cups (7–14 oz./ 200–400 g) sugar
Macerating time: 30 minutes	2 cups (500 ml) water or 1 cup (250 ml) water + 1 cup (250 ml) sweet white wine
Cooking time: 5 minutes	
Storage: Up to 12 hours in the refrigerator, covered	1 vanilla bean, split lengthwise

1. **Wash, dry, and hull** the strawberries. Place them in a bowl and drizzle with lemon juice until coated. Sprinkle with a little of the sugar (depending on how sweet the strawberries are).

2. **Let macerate** for 30 minutes.

3. **Pour the water,** or the mix of water and white wine, into a saucepan. Add the vanilla bean and sugar, reducing the amount of sugar if you are using a sweet wine. Heat gently until the sugar dissolves. Increase the heat and bring to a boil, stirring often.

4. **Reduce the heat** to low. Add the strawberries and simmer gently for 5 minutes.

5. **Let cool.** Chill in a covered container for up to 12 hours before serving.

FRUITS AU SIROP

FRUIT IN SYRUP ★

Serves
6–8

Active time: 20 minutes

Cooking time: 20 minutes

Macerating time:
2–3 hours or overnight

Storage: Up to 4 days
in the refrigerator,
depending on the fruit,
covered

INGREDIENTS
2 lb. (1 kg) fresh fruit
    of your choice
    (see Chef's Notes)
4 cups (1 L) water
3–4 cups (600–800 g)
    sugar, to taste
1 vanilla bean, split
    lengthwise

1. **Wash and dry** the fruit. Prepare as necessary by peeling and/or removing pits.
2. **To prepare the syrup**, combine the water, sugar, and vanilla bean in a saucepan. Heat gently until the sugar dissolves. Increase the heat and bring to a boil, stirring often.
3. **Reduce the heat** to low and add the fruit. There should be enough syrup to just cover the fruit when it begins to poach.
4. **Poach the fruit** gently over very low heat for 15–20 minutes, without letting the syrup boil. The cooking time will depend on the size and ripeness of the fruit. The fruit is ready when it can be pierced easily with the tip of a knife.
5. **Remove from the heat**, cover, and let the fruit cool in the syrup. Macerate at room temperature for 2–3 hours, or preferably overnight.
6. **Keep chilled** in a covered container until serving.

Chef's Notes
• Use this recipe as a base for the recipes that follow, in which spice blends have been added to the poaching syrups of popular fruits. Some of the combinations might be surprising but, hopefully, will allow you to create your own ideas for adding variety to fruit desserts.

BANANES AU SIROP

BANANAS IN SYRUP ★

Serves
6–8

Active time: 10 minutes

Cooking time: 15 minutes

Storage: Up to 3 days in
the refrigerator, covered

INGREDIENTS
2 cups (500 ml) water
2 cups (500 ml) aged rum
1½ cups (10½ oz./300 g)
    granulated sugar
Scant 2 tsp (7.5 g) vanilla
    sugar
1¾ lb. (800 g) bananas
    (unpeeled weight)

---

1. **Combine the water**, rum, granulated sugar, and vanilla sugar in a saucepan. Heat gently until the sugars dissolve. Increase the heat and bring to a boil, stirring often.
2. **While the syrup is heating**, peel and slice the bananas.
3. **Reduce the heat** to low and add the bananas. Simmer very gently for 15 minutes, without letting the syrup boil.
4. **Transfer to a bowl**, cover, and let macerate in the syrup until cool.

Chef's Notes
• The bananas can be kept chilled in a covered container for up to 3 days.

PRUNEAUX AU SAUTERNES

PRUNES IN SAUTERNES ★

Serves
8

Active time: 10 minutes

Cooking time: 10 minutes

Macerating time: 3 days

Storage: Up to 5 days in
the refrigerator, covered

INGREDIENTS
75-cl bottle Sauternes
  wine
½ cup + 1 tbsp
  (4 oz./110 g) sugar
1 small stick cinnamon,
  broken into short
  lengths
1¾ lb. (800 g) prunes,
  pitted

To serve (optional)
Brioche slices
  (see pp. 100–106)
Financiers (see p. 118)

1. **Pour the Sauternes** into a saucepan and add the sugar
and cinnamon stick.
2. **Heat gently** until the sugar dissolves.
Increase the heat and bring to a boil, stirring often.
3. **Add the prunes**, then remove from the heat.
4. **Let cool.** Transfer to a covered container.
5. **Let macerate** in the syrup for 3 days,
in the refrigerator, before serving.
6. **Serve with slices of brioche** or with financiers,
if desired.

FRUITS PANACHÉS AU SIROP

FRUIT AND NUTS
IN RED WINE SYRUP ★

Serves
8

Active time: 20 minutes

Macerating time:
Overnight

Cooking time: 20 minutes

Storage: Up to 5 days in
the refrigerator, covered

INGREDIENTS
3½ lb. (1.5 kg) fresh pears,
    preferably a small,
    firm variety
1 lb. 2 oz. (500 g) prunes,
    pitted
5 oz. (150 g) walnut halves
3 × 75-cl bottles full-
    bodied red wine
    (such as Madiran)
3 cups (1¼ lb./600 g)
    sugar
1 stick cinnamon
4 bay leaves

1. **Peel and core the pears** from the base, leaving
the stalks attached.
2. **Place the pears in a saucepan** with the prunes
and walnuts. Pour in enough red wine to cover them.
Add the sugar, cinnamon stick, and bay leaves.
3. **Heat to a gentle simmer** until the sugar dissolves.
4. **Cook over very low heat**, without letting the syrup
boil, until the pears are tender when pierced with the
tip of a knife.
5. **Transfer to a bowl.** Cover and let macerate at room
temperature overnight.
6. **Serve at room temperature** or chilled.

LITCHIS AU SIROP

LYCHEES IN SYRUP ★

Serves
4–5

Active time: 5–10 minutes

Macerating time: 24 hours

Cooking time:
5–15 minutes

Storage: Up to 5 days in
the refrigerator, covered

INGREDIENTS

If using fresh lychees
1 cup (250 ml) water
¾ cup (5¼ oz./150 g)
    sugar
Juice and finely grated
    zest of 2 small limes,
    preferably organic
9 oz. (250 g) peeled fresh
    lychees

If using canned lychees
Syrup from the lychee
    cans
⅓ cup (2¼ oz./65 g) sugar
Juice and finely grated
    zest of 2 small limes,
    preferably organic
9 oz. (250 g) lychees
    canned in syrup
    (drained weight)

Fresh lychees

1. **Combine the water**, sugar, lime juice, and zest in
a saucepan. Heat gently until the sugar dissolves.
Increase the heat and bring to a boil, stirring often.
2. **Reduce the heat to low** and add the lychees.
Cook at a gentle simmer for 15 minutes.
3. **Transfer to a bowl**, cover, and let macerate at room
temperature for 24 hours.
4. **Serve at room temperature** or chilled.

Canned lychees

1. **Pour the syrup** from the cans into a saucepan.
Add the sugar, lime juice, and zest. Heat gently until
the sugar dissolves. Increase the heat and bring to a boil,
stirring often.
2. **Add the lychees**, remove from the heat, and transfer
to a bowl. Cover and let macerate at room temperature
for 24 hours.
3. **Serve at room temperature** or chilled.

Chef's Notes

• The lychees are a perfect accompaniment to the
Pineapple and Mango Singapour (see p. 218).

GÂTEAU DE SEMOULE AUX RAISINS

SEMOLINA PUDDING

WITH RAISINS ⋆

Serves
8

Active time: 15 minutes

Soaking time: 2 hours

Cooking time: 20 minutes

Chilling time: 2 hours

Storage: Up to 2 days in the refrigerator, covered

INGREDIENTS
⅔ cup (3½ oz./100 g)
    raisins
Scant ½ cup (100 ml)
    aged rum
3 cups (750 ml) whole milk
½ cup (3½ oz./100 g)
    sugar
Finely grated zest of
    ½ lemon, preferably
    organic
1 pinch salt
¾ cup (4½ oz./125 g)
    fine semolina
5 tbsp (2½ oz./75 g)
    butter, diced
2 eggs (scant ½ cup/100 g)

To serve (optional)
Fresh fruit coulis
    (see p. 51)
Fresh fruit

1. **Soak the raisins** in the rum for 2 hours.
2. **Place the milk**, sugar, lemon zest, and salt
in a saucepan and heat until the sugar dissolves.
Bring to a boil, then add the semolina in a thin, steady
stream, stirring constantly to avoid lumps forming.
3. **Reduce the heat to low.** Cover and cook for about
20 minutes, until the semolina has completely absorbed
the milk. Stir occasionally to prevent the semolina
from sticking to the base of the pan.
4. **Remove from the heat.** Stir in the butter, then
the eggs one by one. Stir in the rum-soaked raisins.
5. **Divide the mixture** between 8 bowls. Cool, then chill
for 2 hours.
6. **Serve the semolina chilled,** either on its own or with
a fruit coulis and fresh fruit, if desired.

GÊLÉE DE GROSEILLES

RED CURRANT JELLY ★

Makes
2 lb. (1 kg)

Active time: 15 minutes

Cooking time: 15 minutes

Storage: Up to 1 month
in the refrigerator

INGREDIENTS
½ cup (125 ml) water
Sugar equal in weight to
    that of the red currant
    juice (see Chef's Notes)
Juice of 1 lb. 2 oz. (500 g)
    red currants

EQUIPMENT
Instant-read thermometer
Stand mixer fitted with
    the paddle beater
4 × 1-cup (250-ml) canning
    jars, sterilized

1. **Heat the water and sugar** in a saucepan until the sugar dissolves. Increase the heat and bring to a boil. Boil until the temperature of the syrup reaches 265°F (130°C)—this is known as the soft-crack stage (see Chef's Notes).
2. **Pour the red currant juice** into the syrup. Heat to 203°F (95°C) and cook for 5 minutes, stirring constantly. Remove from the heat.
3. **Pour into the stand mixer bowl** and beat on low speed for 15 minutes to cool.
4. **Pour the jelly** into the sterilized jars. Let cool completely, then seal tightly with the lids.

Chef's Notes
• There should be equal quantities in weight of fruit juice and sugar. Weigh the juice, then weigh out the same amount of sugar.
• It is best to check the temperature of the syrup using a thermometer. However, it can also be tested by dropping a teaspoon of the syrup into a bowl of cold water: it should form firm but pliable threads.

ŒUFS À LA NEIGE

FLOATING ISLANDS ★★

Serves	INGREDIENTS	To serve	EQUIPMENT
8	*Meringues*	1 quantity (12¼ oz./350 g)	Silicone molds with 2½-in.
	Neutral oil for the molds	vanilla custard sauce	(6-cm) half-sphere
Active time: 30 minutes	10 egg whites (1⅓ cups/	(see p. 86)	cavities
	300 g)		Stand mixer fitted
Cooking time: 10 minutes	3–4 drops lemon juice	*Caramel*	with the whisk
	⅔ cup (4½ oz./125 g)	(see Chef's Notes)	Pastry bag fitted
	superfine sugar	1 cup (7 oz./200 g) sugar	with a large plain tip

1. **To prepare the meringues,** very lightly grease the cavities of the silicone molds with a neutral oil. If using a steam oven, preheat it to 185°F (85°C). If not, the meringues can be microwaved.

2. **Whisk the egg whites** until frothy. Add the lemon juice, then gradually whisk in the sugar until the egg whites form firm peaks. When all the sugar has been added, continue whisking on low speed for about 30 seconds, until stiff and shiny.

3. **Spoon the meringue** into the pastry bag and pipe into the molds to fill the cavities three-quarters full. Cook in batches, if necessary (24 meringues in total are needed, 3 per serving).

4. **Cook the meringue** in a steam oven at 185°F (85°C) for 3 minutes, or microwave for 30–40 seconds on high. The meringues should be firm to the touch. Turn them out of the molds into a shallow dish and let cool.

5. **When ready to serve,** divide the vanilla custard sauce between 8 bowls. Place 3 meringues in each bowl.

6. **To prepare the caramel,** set a saucepan over low heat. Add 2½ tbsp (1 oz./30 g) of the sugar and make a dry caramel (see p. 46). Let the sugar dissolve into a clear syrup, without stirring, then gradually add the remaining sugar in the same way. When the syrup begins to color, carefully swirl the saucepan to encourage even browning.

7. **When the desired color** has been reached, drizzle the caramel over the meringues. Serve immediately.

Chef's Notes
• The floating islands can be drizzled with liquid caramel (see p. 47), if preferred.
• Caramel decorations can also be prepared in advance. Line a cookie sheet with parchment paper or use a marble slab. Make a dry caramel and, when it reaches the desired color, let it cool slightly. Transfer to a piping cone made with 2–3 layers of parchment paper (to protect your hand, as the caramel will be hot) and pipe decorative shapes over the cookie sheet or slab, or drizzle it over the sheet or slab using a spoon. Let cool, then lift off the shapes. Place them on the meringues immediately before serving.
• Stenciled caramel shapes are another alternative. When the caramel has reached the desired color, pour it over a cookie sheet lined with parchment paper. Let cool completely. Grind the caramel to a fine powder in a small food processor. Line the cookie sheet with fresh parchment paper and place a silicone stencil mat on it. Sift the ground caramel through a fine-mesh sieve over the stencil. Place in an oven preheated to 350°F (180°C/ Gas Mark 4) for a few minutes, until the caramel has melted. Let cool. Place the caramel shapes on the meringues immediately before serving.

PÊCHES AU SIROP

PEACHES

IN RED WINE SYRUP ★

Serves
7–8

Active time: 15 minutes

Cooking time: 15 minutes

Macerating time: At least
2 hours

Storage: Up to 5 days in
the refrigerator, covered

INGREDIENTS
2 lb. (1 kg) fresh peaches
75-cl bottle full-bodied
    red wine (such as
    Madiran)
Scant ½ cup (100 ml) dry
    Madeira
1 cup (7 oz./200 g) sugar
1 tsp black peppercorns

1. **Wash the peaches.** To peel, plunge them in boiling water for a few seconds, if necessary, to loosen their skins, then cut a small cross in the base of each one and peel away the skin.
2. **Combine the wine**, Madeira, and sugar in a saucepan. Add the peppercorns. Heat until the sugar dissolves, then bring to a simmer.
3. **Add the peaches** to the syrup. They need to be covered with syrup, so add more wine and sugar as necessary. Poach gently for 15 minutes, until the peaches are tender when pierced with the tip of a knife.
4. **Remove from the heat.** Cover and let macerate for at least 2 hours.
5. **Chill in a covered container** until ready to serve.

POIRES AU SIROP

PEARS IN SYRUP ★

Serves
7–8

Active time: 15 minutes

Cooking time:
10–15 minutes

Macerating time:
Overnight

Storage: Up to 5 days in
the refrigerator, covered

INGREDIENTS
2 lb. (1 kg) fresh pears
    (such as Bartlett,
    Comice, Beurré Hardy,
    Passe-Crassane, or
    small wild pears)
Juice of 1 lemon
4 cups (1 L) water
1 cup (7 oz./200 g) sugar
Generous ½ cup
    (7 oz./200 g) honey
1 vanilla bean, split
    lengthwise
3 bay leaves
2 whole cloves
1 tsp black peppercorns

1. **Wash and peel the pears.** Core them from the base, leaving the stalks attached. Coat with lemon juice to prevent them from turning brown.

2. **Combine the water**, sugar, and honey in a saucepan. Add the vanilla bean, bay leaves, cloves, and peppercorns. Heat until the sugar dissolves, then bring to a simmer.

3. **Add the pears** to the syrup and simmer gently for 10–15 minutes, just until they are tender when pierced with the tip of a knife. Be careful not to overcook the pears.

4. **Remove from the heat.** Cover and let macerate overnight at room temperature.

5. **Chill in a covered container** until ready to serve.

RIZ IMPÉRATRICE

EMPRESS RICE PUDDING ⋆

Serves
10

Active time: 1 hour

Cooking time: 35 minutes

Chilling time: 3 hours

Storage: Up to 3 days in
the refrigerator (before
unmolding)

INGREDIENTS
2½ oz. (70 g) candied
 fruit, finely chopped
Rum for soaking
 the candied fruit
3 cups (750 ml) water
1 cup (7 oz./200 g) round
 or short-grain rice
3⅓ cups (800 ml) whole
 milk
3 tbsp (1½ oz./40 g)
 butter
Finely grated zest of
 1 orange, preferably
 organic
1 Bourbon Madagascar
 vanilla bean, split
 lengthwise

½ cup (3½ oz./100 g)
 sugar + 1 tbsp (15 g)
 for the heavy cream
¼ tsp (1 g) fine salt
3 sheets gelatin,
 180–200 Bloom
1 quantity (12¼ oz./350 g)
 vanilla custard sauce
 (see p. 86), divided
1 tsp (5 ml) kirsch
⅔ cup (150 ml) heavy
 cream, well chilled

To serve
1 quantity (4½ oz./130 g)
 raspberry coulis
 (see p. 51)
Candied fruit slices

EQUIPMENT
11-in. (28-cm) round
 fluted mold

1. **Place the candied fruit** in a bowl and pour in enough rum to cover it. Let soak until using.
2. **Bring the water** to a boil in a saucepan. Add the rice and let boil for 2 minutes. Drain the rice, then rinse in the strainer under running cold water to remove excess starch.
3. **Pour the milk** into the saucepan. Add the butter, orange zest, and vanilla bean, then bring to a boil. Add the rice, ½ cup (3½ oz./100 g) sugar, and salt. Cook over low heat, stirring from time to time, for 25 minutes, or until all the milk has been absorbed by the rice.
4. **Remove from the heat.** Let cool, then remove the vanilla bean and scrape in any remaining seeds.
5. **Soak the gelatin** in a bowl of cold water until softened. Weigh out 5¼ oz. (150 g) of the vanilla custard sauce and transfer to a sauce boat. Chill until ready to serve.

6. **Reheat the remaining custard** (7 oz./200 g). Squeeze the gelatin to remove excess water, then whisk it into the custard until melted. Whisk in the kirsch. Stir the custard with a spatula as it cools to prevent a skin from forming, or set it over a bowl filled halfway with ice water to speed up the cooling process.
7. **Whip the heavy cream** with the 1 tbsp (15 g) sugar until it holds its shape. Fold into the custard.
8. **Stir the rum-soaked candied fruit** into the rice and, using a flexible spatula, very gently fold in the custard and cream mixture. Pour into the mold. Chill for at least 3 hours to set.
9. **Immediately before serving,** briefly dip the base of the mold in hot water to release the pudding, then invert it onto a serving plate. Pour a little raspberry coulis on top and decorate the serving plate with slices of candied fruit.
10. **Serve well chilled** with the remaining raspberry coulis and vanilla custard sauce on the side.

TIRAMISU ★★

Serves
6

Active time: 30 minutes +
making the ladyfingers

Cooking time: 20 minutes

Storage: Up to 2 days
in the refrigerator

INGREDIENTS
Ladyfinger layer
12 ladyfingers (see p. 24)
⅓ quantity (½ cup/120 ml)
   coffee syrup, Opéra
   cake recipe (see p. 208),
   warm

Mascarpone mousse
1 sheet gelatin,
   180–200 Bloom
Scant ½ cup (3¼ oz./90 g)
   sugar
1½ tbsp (25 ml) water
3 egg yolks
   (scant ¼ cup/60 g)
Scant ¾ cup (6 oz./170 g)
   mascarpone
Scant ¾ cup (170 ml)
   heavy cream,
   well chilled
Unsweetened cocoa
   powder

EQUIPMENT
Instant-read thermometer
Electric hand beater
Pastry bag fitted with a
   ¾-in. (1.5-cm) plain tip

1. **To prepare the ladyfinger layer**, briefly dip the ladyfingers in the warm coffee syrup until soaked but still intact. Set aside.
2. **To prepare the mascarpone mousse**, soak the gelatin in a bowl of cold water until softened.
3. **Heat the sugar and water** in a saucepan until the sugar dissolves. Increase the heat and bring to a boil. Boil until the temperature reaches 250°F (120°C).
4. **While the syrup is boiling**, whisk the egg yolks until creamy. Once the syrup reaches the required temperature, very carefully drizzle it into the yolks, whisking constantly. Take care not to let the hot syrup touch the whisk, as it could spray up and burn you. Continue whisking until cool.
5. **Whisk the mascarpone** in a separate bowl until smooth. Whisk in the egg yolk and syrup mixture until combined.
6. **Squeeze the gelatin** to remove excess water. Microwave in a bowl on high for 5 seconds, or until melted. Whisk a little of the mascarpone mixture into the melted gelatin until blended. Mix back into the rest of the mixture in the bowl, then whisk until smooth.
7. **Whip the cream** until it holds its shape. Fold into the mascarpone mixture using a flexible spatula. Transfer to the pastry bag.
8. **To assemble the tiramisu**, place 6 ladyfingers side by side on a serving plate. Pipe logs of mousse over them. Place a second layer of ladyfingers on top, followed by another layer of mousse piped in logs. Chill until ready to serve.
9. **Dust with cocoa powder** just before serving.

Chef's Notes
• There are many ways to serve this tiramisu. It can be served on 6 serving plates as individual portions, or assembled in individual glasses, ramekins, or even chocolate cups, with the ladyfingers trimmed to the required size.

PETITS FOURS

Mini Chocolate and
  Coffee Éclairs ** 382
Mini Fruit Tartlets * 383
Concerto Petits Fours *** 386
Opéra Petits Fours *** 386
Fruits in Jelly ** 388
Lady Rose Choux Puffs ** 390

CAROLINE CAFÉ ET CHOCOLAT

MINI CHOCOLATE AND COFFEE ÉCLAIRS **

Makes
40–50

Active time: 20 minutes +
making the choux pastry,
pastry cream, and glaze

Cooking time: 20 minutes

INGREDIENTS
Mini éclairs
10½ oz. (300 g) choux
    pastry dough (see p. 38)

Filling
1 lb. 2 oz. (500 g)
    chocolate pastry cream
    (see p. 68) or coffee
    pastry cream (see p. 67),
    or half and half
    (see Chef's Notes)

Glaze
1 quantity (about 1 lb./
    500 g) chocolate glaze
    (see p. 76) or mocha
    glaze (see p. 75), or half
    and half (see Chef's
    Notes)

EQUIPMENT
2 pastry bags fitted with
    ½-in. (1-cm) and ⅛-in.
    (3-mm) plain tips
2 cookie sheets lined
    with parchment paper

1. **Preheat the oven** to 425°F (220°C/Gas Mark 7).
2. **Transfer the choux pastry dough** to the pastry bag
with a ½-in. (1-cm) tip.
3. **Pipe 20–25 logs** measuring 2–2½ in. (5–6 cm)
in length on each cookie sheet (40–50 in total).
4. **Place in the oven** and prop the door ajar with the
handle of a wooden spoon. Bake for 20 minutes, until
the éclairs are golden brown and crisp on the outside
but still soft on the inside. Transfer to a wire rack and
let cool completely.
5. **To fill the éclairs,** beat the pastry cream so that it
is smooth. Spoon it into the pastry bag with an ⅛-in.
(3-mm) tip.
6. **Cut a slit or pierce a small hole** in the base of each
éclair using the tip of a knife or pastry tip. Pipe in the
pastry cream to fill the éclairs.
7. **Glaze the éclairs** with the glaze that matches the
filling. Place the glaze in a bowl large enough to dip the
éclairs and melt over a saucepan of barely simmering
water (bain-marie), until the temperature reaches 104°F
(40°C).
8. **Dip the tops of the éclairs** in the glaze. Hold them
briefly over the bowl to allow excess to drip off.
9. **Place upright** to let the glaze set, then chill. Serve on
the same day as they are made.

Chef's Notes
• All chocolate or all coffee éclairs can be made,
or a mixture of both, as desired.

MINI TARTELETTES AUX FRUITS

MINI FRUIT TARTLETS *

Makes
20

Active time: 20 minutes
+ making the shortcrust
pastry and frangipane
cream

Chilling time: 1 hour

Cooking time:
10–15 minutes

INGREDIENTS
Butter for the pans
8½ oz. (240 g) sweet
   shortcrust pastry dough
   (see p. 41)
Fresh fruit or canned fruit
   in syrup
7 oz. (200 g) frangipane
   cream (see p. 62)
3½ oz. (100 g) apricot
   glaze or neutral glaze
   (see p. 81), warm

EQUIPMENT
20 × 2–2¾-in. (5–7-cm)
   mini tartlet pans
Cookie sheet lined with
   parchment paper
Cookie cutter slightly
   larger than the tartlet
   pans

1. **Grease the tartlet pans** with butter. Place them on the cookie sheet.
2. **On a lightly floured surface**, roll the pastry dough to a thickness of about ⅛ in. (3 mm). Take care not to overwork it. Prick the dough all over with a fork.
3. **Cut out 20 circles** using the cookie cutter and line them into the tartlet pans. Chill for 1 hour.

If using fresh fruit
Fruits such as strawberries, raspberries, mangos, red currants, and lychees are best used fresh. They should be added after baking.

1. **Preheat the oven** to 350°F (180°C/Gas Mark 4).
2. **Fill the tartlet shells** with the frangipane cream.
3. **Bake for 15 minutes**, until the pastry is golden and the frangipane cream is set.
4. **While the shells are baking**, wash and dry the fruit. Cut into smaller pieces, if necessary.
5. **Remove the tartlets** from the oven, let them cool slightly, then unmold onto a wire rack to cool.
6. **While still warm**, brush the tartlets with a thin layer of warm apricot glaze or neutral glaze. Arrange the fruit over the top.

If using canned fruit
Canned fruit, such as pears, apricots, peaches, and plums, should be baked in the tartlet shells.

1. **Preheat the oven** to 340°F (170°C/Gas Mark 3).
2. **Drain the fruit** and cut into small pieces or slice thinly.
3. **Fill the tartlet shells** with the frangipane cream. Place the pieces of fruit in the cream.
4. **Bake for 10–15 minutes**, until the pastry is golden and the frangipane cream is set.
5. **Remove the tartlets** from the oven, let them cool slightly, then unmold onto a wire rack to cool.
6. **While still warm**, brush the tartlets with a thin layer of **warm** apricot glaze or neutral glaze. Let cool before serving.

Chef's Notes
• Many different fruit combinations can be used: experiment with colors, flavors, and shapes. Here are a few suggestions: fig and strawberry; raspberry and red currant; lychee, raspberry, and coconut; pineapple and mango; or lemon topped with tiny pieces of meringue. If using coconut, pineapple, or mango, glaze the tartlets with passion fruit glaze (see p. 280) for a tropical fruit flavor.

See photo p. 299

CONCERTO PETIT FOUR

CONCERTO PETITS FOURS ★★★

Makes
60

Active time: 15 minutes +
making the Concerto

INGREDIENTS
1 Concerto (see p. 174),
   chilled

EQUIPMENT
Kitchen torch (optional)
Bread knife

1. **If not using a kitchen torch** to warm the knife blade, bring a saucepan of water to a boil.
2. **Dampen a warm dishcloth** to wipe the knife blade clean when cutting.
3. **When ready to cut the Concerto**, remove the cake from the refrigerator.
4. **Heat the knife blade** using the kitchen torch, or dip it in the hot water, then wipe dry.

5. **With the hot, dry knife**, cut the Concerto into 1-in. (2.5-cm) squares. Wipe the blade clean with the damp cloth and reheat it between each cut.
6. **Arrange the petits fours** on a serving platter. Chill until ready to serve.

OPÉRA PETIT FOUR

OPÉRA PETITS FOURS ★★★

Makes
70–84

Active time: 15 minutes +
making the Opéra

INGREDIENTS
1 Opéra (see p. 208),
   chilled

EQUIPMENT
Kitchen torch (optional)
Bread knife

1. **Remove the Opéra** from the refrigerator 15 minutes before cutting.
2. **If not using a kitchen torch** to warm the knife blade, bring a saucepan of water to a boil.
3. **Dampen a warm dishcloth** to wipe the knife blade clean when cutting.
4. **Heat the knife blade** using the kitchen torch, or dip it in the hot water, then wipe dry.

5. **With the hot, dry knife,** cut the Opéra into 70 × 1⅓-in. (3.5-cm) squares, or into 84 rectangles measuring 2⅓ × ¾ in. (78 rectangles measuring 6 × 2 cm). Wipe the blade clean with the damp cloth and reheat it between each cut.
6. **Arrange the petits fours** on a serving platter. Chill until ready to serve.

FRUITS EN GELÉE

FRUITS IN JELLY ★★

Makes
20

Active time: 30 minutes
+ making the shortcrust
pastry

Cooking time: 15 minutes

Chilling time: At least
1 hour

INGREDIENTS
Fruit jellies
2 sheets gelatin,
   180–200 Bloom
20 raspberries or small,
   sweet strawberries,
   preferably Fraises
   des Bois
Generous ⅓ cup (90 ml)
   simple syrup
   (see p. 91), warm
Scant ¾ cup (170 ml)
   water
1 tbsp (15 ml)
   strawberry liqueur
   (see Chef's Notes)

Pastry bases
7 oz. (200 g) sweet
   shortcrust pastry dough
   (see p. 41)

Decoration (optional)
Large red currants, halved

EQUIPMENT
Instant-read thermometer
Silicone mold with
   20 × 1½-in. (4-cm)
   half-sphere cavities
2-in. (5-cm) round cookie
   cutter
Cookie sheet lined
   with parchment paper
Hair dryer or hot-air gun

1. **To prepare the fruit jellies,** soak the gelatin in a bowl of cold water until softened.
2. **Wash and dry the berries.** Hull and trim the tops so that they will fit inside the cavities of the mold.
3. **Heat the syrup** to a simmer, then take off the heat. Squeeze the gelatin to remove excess water, then whisk it into the warm syrup until melted. Whisk in the water and strawberry liqueur. Let cool until the temperature reaches 68°F–72°F (20°C–22°C). The pan can be set over a bowl filled halfway with ice water to speed up the cooling process.
4. **Pour a little jelly** into the cavities of the mold. Place in the refrigerator for 10 minutes, to set a little. Place a berry upright on the jelly in each cavity, then cover completely with the remaining jelly. Chill for at least 1 hour, or until set.
5. **Preheat the oven** to 350°F (180°C/Gas Mark 4).

6. **To prepare the pastry bases,** roll the pastry dough on a lightly floured surface to a thickness of about ¼ in. (5 mm). Take care not to overwork it. Prick the dough all over with a fork.
7. **Cut out 20 circles** using the cookie cutter. Place them on the baking sheet.
8. **Bake for 15 minutes,** until golden. Let cool on a wire rack.
9. **To assemble,** warm the base of the silicone mold with a hair dryer or hot-air gun to release the jellies. Place them flat side down on the pastry bases.
10. **Chill until ready to serve.** Serve on the same day as they are made, topped with halved red currants, if desired.

Chef's Notes
• Strawberry syrup can be used instead of liqueur, but the quantity of simple syrup must be reduced to a scant ⅓ cup (70 ml).

CHOUX LADY ROSE

LADY ROSE CHOUX PUFFS ★★

Makes
50

Active time: 20 minutes
+ making the choux pastry

Cooking time: 20 minutes

Infusing time: 10 minutes

INGREDIENTS
Choux puffs
10½ oz. (300 g) choux
    pastry dough
    (see p. 38)

Strawberry crémeux
3 sheets gelatin,
    180–200 Bloom
Scant ½ cup (100 ml)
    heavy cream
1 tsp (5 g) dried hibiscus
    flowers
8 oz. (220 g) strawberry
    puree
3½ oz. (100 g) Fraises des
    Bois, or wild strawberry
    puree
6 egg yolks
    (scant ½ cup/120 g)
¼ cup (1¾ oz./50 g) sugar

Decoration
10½ oz. (300 g) white
    poured fondant
    (see Chef's Notes)
Blue poppy seeds

EQUIPMENT
2 pastry bags fitted with
    ½-in. (1-cm) and ⅛-in.
    (3-mm) plain tips
Cookie sheet lined with
    parchment paper
Fine-mesh sieve
Immersion blender
Electric hand beater
Instant-read thermometer

1. **Preheat the oven** to 425°F (220°C/Gas Mark 7).
2. **Transfer the choux pastry dough** to the pastry bag fitted with a ½-in. (1-cm) tip.
3. **Pipe 50 ovals** measuring 1¼ in. (3 cm) in length onto the cookie sheet, pulling the pastry tip up slightly at the end of each oval to form a teardrop shape.
4. **Place in the oven** and prop the door ajar with the handle of a wooden spoon. Bake for 20 minutes, until the puffs are golden brown and crisp on the outside but still soft on the inside. Transfer to a wire rack to cool.
5. **To prepare the strawberry crémeux**, soak the gelatin in a bowl of cold water until softened. Bring the cream to a simmer in a large saucepan, then remove from the heat and add the hibiscus flowers. Cover and let infuse for 10 minutes. Strain through the fine-mesh sieve into a mixing bowl.
6. **Stir in the strawberry puree** and the whole Fraises des Bois or wild strawberry puree. If using whole strawberries, puree with the immersion blender until smooth. Transfer to a saucepan and bring to a simmer.
7. **While the strawberry mixture is heating,** whisk together the egg yolks and sugar until pale and thick. Slowly pour the yolk mixture into the hot puree, whisking continuously. Cook until the temperature reaches 185°F (85°C), then remove from the heat.

8. **Squeeze the gelatin** to remove excess water, add it to the hot crémeux mixture, and process with the immersion blender until smooth. Pour into a shallow dish, then press plastic wrap over the surface. Let cool.
9. **To fill the puffs,** transfer the strawberry crémeux to the pastry bag with an ⅛-in. (3-mm) tip. Cut a slit or pierce a small hole in the base of each puff using the tip of a knife or a pastry tip. Pipe in the crémeux.
10. **To ice the puffs,** heat the fondant in a saucepan over low heat until the temperature reaches 86°F (30°C), or microwave in a bowl wide enough to dip the puffs. Spread out the poppy seeds on a plate.
11. **Dip the tops** of the puffs in the warm fondant, holding them briefly over the pan or bowl, with the teardrop end pointing downward, to let excess fondant drip off. When the fondant is no longer runny but still soft, dip the rounded ends of the puffs into the poppy seeds.
12. **Place the puffs upright** and let the icing set. Chill until ready to serve. Serve on the same day as they are made.

Chef's Notes
• Unlike rolled fondant, which is rolled out thinly and used to cover cakes, poured (or liquid) fondant is softer and has a pourable consistency. It can be purchased ready to use from cake decorating stores or online.

SMALL CAKES AND COOKIES

ALLUMETTES GLACÉES

LEMON-ICED ALLUMETTES ★★

Makes
36

Active time: 15 minutes +
making the puff pastry

Cooking time: 10 minutes

Storage: Up to 10 days
in an airtight container
in a dry place

INGREDIENTS
Royal icing
½ egg white
Generous 1 cup
  (5¼ oz./150 g)
  confectioners' sugar
3 drops lemon juice

Pastry layer
7 oz. (200 g) puff pastry
  dough, classic
  (see p. 28) or quick
  (see p. 29)

Decoration
Sliced almonds, toasted

EQUIPMENT
Ruler
Cookie sheet lined
  with parchment paper
  and brushed lightly
  with water
Pastry bag fitted with
  a very small round tip
  or paper piping cone

1. **Preheat the oven** to 350°F (180°C/Gas Mark 4).
2. **To prepare the royal icing,** lightly whisk the egg white with a fork to loosen it. Using a flexible spatula, work in the confectioners' sugar. Mix for about 2 minutes until the icing is smooth and light. Stir in the lemon juice.
3. **To prepare the pastry layer,** roll the dough on a lightly floured surface into a rectangle measuring approximately 8 × 16 in. (20 × 40 cm).
4. **Cut into 3 equal strips,** measuring 16 in. (40 cm) in length, using a ruler as a guide. Fold 2 of the strips in half and chill until using.
5. **Lay the third strip** on the cookie sheet. Using an angled palette knife, spread the royal icing over the pastry in a thin layer (approximately ½₀ in./1 mm thick), as evenly as possible.
6. **Dampen the blade** of a bread knife. Cut the strip vertically into 12 equally sized matchsticks. There is no need to separate them at this stage.
7. **Repeat with the remaining** 2 pastry strips to make 36. Place them on the cookie sheet and let the royal icing dry completely. Set aside the remaining icing.

8. **Place a small oven-safe mold,** ¾ in. (2 cm) in height, in each corner of the sheet and position a wire rack on top. This will help the allumettes rise evenly.
9. **Place in the oven** and prop the door ajar with the handle of a wooden spoon. Bake for 15 minutes, until the allumettes are puffed and pale gold on top. If their tops are coloring too quickly, reduce the oven temperature to 340°F (170°C/Gas Mark 3). The allumettes should shrink and separate as they bake. If the royal icing sticks and prevents this, cut them apart toward the end of the cooking time using a bread knife.
10. **Slide the allumettes,** still on the parchment paper, onto a wire rack. Let cool.
11. **Transfer the remaining royal icing** to the pastry bag or paper piping cone. Snip off the tip if using a cone. Pipe a small dot of icing on each allumette and lightly press a sliced almond on top. Handle the allumettes carefully, as the royal icing will mark easily. Store in an airtight container.

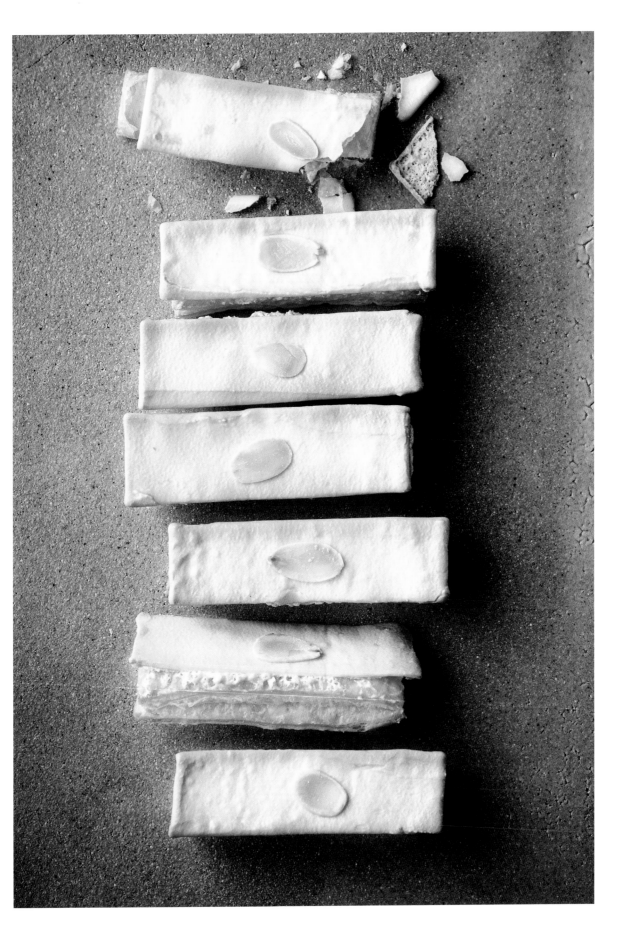

ARLETTES FEUILLETÉES

PUFF PASTRY ARLETTES ★

Makes
about 50

Active time: 30 minutes +
making the puff pastry

Chilling time: At least
3 hours

Cooking time: 20 minutes

Storage: Up to 10 days
in an airtight container
in a dry place

INGREDIENTS
10½ oz. (300 g) puff
     pastry dough, classic
     (see p. 28) or quick
     (see p. 29)
Generous 1 cup
     (5¼ oz./150 g)
     confectioners' sugar,
     sifted + more for
     dusting
Seeds of ½ vanilla bean

To serve (optional)
Chantilly cream,
     for dipping

EQUIPMENT
Cookie sheet lined
     with parchment paper

1. **Roll the pastry dough** on a lightly floured surface into a rectangle measuring approximately 8 × 24 in. (20 × 60 cm).
2. **Dampen one long side** of the pastry by brushing it with water. Roll up tightly from the opposite side, pressing the dampened pastry edge against the roll to seal it. Cover with plastic wrap and chill for 1 hour or until firm.
3. **Cut the roll** into ¼-in. (5-mm) slices using a bread knife. Place the slices flat on a board or tray. Chill for at least 2 hours.
4. **Preheat the oven** to 350°F (180°C/Gas Mark 4).
5. **Stir the confectioners' sugar** and vanilla seeds together. Generously dust the work surface with more sugar. Lay 3 pastry slices on it, then turn them over so both sides are coated with sugar. This will prevent the slices from sticking when rolled out.

6. **Roll each slice** into a very thin, long oval. Place on the cookie sheet. Repeat with the remaining slices, dusting the work surface with more sugar as necessary.
7. **Bake for about 15 minutes**, until golden. While the arlettes are baking, preheat the broiler.
8. **Remove from the oven** and place briefly under the broiler to caramelize the sugar on one side. Let cool on a wire rack.
9. **Serve with Chantilly cream** on the side, for dipping, if desired.

DIAMANTS VANILLE

VANILLA DIAMOND COOKIES *

Makes	INGREDIENTS	"Diamond" coating	EQUIPMENT
60	*Cookie dough*	1 egg yolk	Stand mixer fitted
	1¾ sticks (6½ oz./190 g)	½ cup (3½ oz./100 g)	with the paddle beater
Active time: 30 minutes	cultured butter,	brown sugar	Cookie sheet lined
	82% fat, diced		with parchment paper
	½ cup (3½ oz./100 g)		
Chilling time: 45 minutes	sugar		
	1 tsp (4 g) vanilla powder		
Cooking time: 45 minutes	2 cups (9 oz./250 g) AP		
	flour (see Chef's Notes)		
Storage: Up to 10 days	1 pinch salt		
in an airtight container			

1. **To prepare the cookie dough,** cream together the butter, sugar, and vanilla powder in the stand mixer on low speed.

2. **Add all the flour and salt** and beat until smooth. This should take no longer than 2 minutes: take care not to overmix the dough or it will harden and the cookies will lose their crumbly texture. Cover with plastic wrap and chill for about 30 minutes to firm up.

3. **Divide the dough** into 3 equal amounts. Using plastic wrap, shape each piece into a cylinder measuring 1¼ in. (3 cm) in diameter. Chill for another 15 minutes.

4. **Preheat the oven** to 340°F (170°C/Gas Mark 3).

5. **To prepare the "diamond" coating,** lightly beat the egg yolk. Spread the brown sugar over a sheet of parchment paper. Lightly brush each cylinder of dough all over with the egg yolk, then roll in the sugar until evenly coated.

6. **Cut into ¾-in. (1.5-cm) thick slices** and lay them flat on the cookie sheet.

7. **Bake for about 15 minutes,** until lightly golden. To check the cookies are done, remove one, let it cool briefly, then bite into it. The texture should be soft, crumbly, and melt-in-the-mouth.

8. **Slide the cookies,** still on the parchment paper, onto a wire rack to cool.

Chef's Notes
• This recipe can be varied by using different flour combinations, such as replacing one-quarter of AP flour with cornstarch.

DIAMANTS CHOCOLAT

CHOCOLATE DIAMOND COOKIES *

Makes
60

Active time: 30 minutes

Chilling time: 45 minutes

Cooking time: 45 minutes

Storage: Up to 10 days
in an airtight container

INGREDIENTS

Cookie dough
3 oz. (80 g) milk
    chocolate, chopped
1¾ cups (8¼ oz./235 g)
    AP flour
Scant ¼ cup (1¼ oz./35 g)
    cornstarch
2 tbsp (15 g) unsweetened
    cocoa powder
2 sticks (7¾ oz./220 g)
    cultured butter,
    82% fat, diced
¾ cup (3½ oz./100 g)
    confectioners' sugar
1 pinch salt
½ egg yolk (1¾ tsp/10 g)

"Diamond" coating
1 egg yolk (1½ tbsp/20 g)
½ cup (3½ oz./100 g)
    brown sugar

EQUIPMENT
Instant-read thermometer
Fine-mesh sieve
Stand mixer fitted
    with the paddle beater
Cookie sheet lined
    with parchment paper

1. **To prepare the cookie dough,** melt the chocolate in a bowl over a saucepan of barely simmering water (bain-marie) until the temperature reaches 104°F (40°C), or in the microwave. Sift the flour, cornstarch, and cocoa powder into a bowl.

2. **Beat together** the butter, confectioners' sugar, and salt in the stand mixer on low speed. Beat in the dry ingredients, then the melted chocolate and ½ egg yolk. Mix until smooth. This should take no longer than 2 minutes: take care not to overmix the dough or it will harden and the cookies will lose their crumbly texture. Cover with plastic wrap and chill for about 30 minutes to firm up.

3. **Divide the dough** into 3 equal amounts. Using plastic wrap, shape each piece into a cylinder measuring 1¼ in. (3 cm) in diameter. Chill for another 15 minutes.

4. **Preheat the oven** to 340°F (170°C/Gas Mark 3).

5. **To prepare the "diamond" coating,** lightly beat the egg yolk. Spread the brown sugar over a sheet of parchment paper. Lightly brush each cylinder of dough all over with the egg yolk, then roll in the sugar until evenly coated.

6. **Cut into ¾-in. (1.5-cm) thick slices** and lay them flat on the cookie sheet.

7. **Bake for about 15 minutes,** until lightly golden. To check the cookies are done, remove one, let it cool briefly, then bite into it. The texture should be soft, crumbly, and melt-in-the-mouth.

8. **Slide the cookies,** still on the parchment paper, onto a wire rack to cool.

FINANCIERS FRAMBOISE

RASPBERRY FINANCIERS *

Makes
10

Active time: 15 minutes

Cooking time:
8–10 minutes

Storage: Up to 5 days
in an airtight container

INGREDIENTS

Butter for the pan,
  if needed
½ cup minus 1 tbsp
  (1¾ oz./50 g) AP flour
1 cup (4½ oz./ 130 g)
  confectioners' sugar
¼ tsp (1 g) baking powder
½ cup (1¾ oz./50 g)
  almond powder
5 tbsp (2½ oz./70 g)
  butter
4 egg whites (½ cup/130 g)
2 tsp (10 g) honey
1 tsp (5 ml) raspberry
  brandy
10 fresh raspberries

EQUIPMENT

Stainless steel or silicone
  financier pan with
  1½- × 3-in. (4- × 8-cm)
  cavities
Cookie sheet, if using
  a silicone mold
Instant-read thermometer
Fine-mesh sieve
Pastry bag fitted with
  a ½-in. (1-cm) plain tip

1. **Preheat the oven** to 425°F (220°C/Gas Mark 7).
If using a stainless steel pan, grease it with butter.
If using a silicone pan, place it on the cookie sheet
without greasing.
2. **Sift the flour, confectioners' sugar, and baking
powder** into a mixing bowl. Stir in the almond powder.
3. **Melt the butter** in a saucepan over medium heat,
whisking until it is golden brown and has a nutty
aroma (*beurre noisette*). The temperature should reach
300°F–311°F (150°C–155°C). Remove the butter
from the heat and strain it into a bowl to remove any
impurities. Stir into the dry ingredients using a wooden
spoon.

4. **Gradually mix in the egg whites** until smooth.
Finally, stir in the honey and raspberry brandy.
5. **Transfer the batter** to the pastry bag. Pipe it into
the mold and fill the cavities almost to the top, leaving
a little space for the financiers to rise.
6. Place a raspberry in the center of each one, without
pressing it down into the batter, as the raspberries will
sink during baking.
7. **Bake for 5 minutes.** Reduce the oven temperature
to 400°F (200°C/Gas Mark 6) and bake for an
additional 5 minutes, or until the financiers are golden.
8. **Remove from the oven** and immediately turn the
financiers out onto a wire rack. Let cool.

MACARONS FRAMBOISE

RASPBERRY MACARONS **

Makes
25–30

Active time: 45 minutes

Cooking time:
10–12 minutes per batch

Resting time: Overnight–
3 days (see Chef's Notes)

Storage: Up to 2 weeks
in the freezer
(see Chef's Notes)

INGREDIENTS
Macaron shells
1½ cups (7 oz./200 g)
 confectioners' sugar
1⅓ cups (4½ oz./125 g)
 almond powder
Scant 1½ tbsp (10 g)
 freeze-dried raspberry
 powder
4 egg whites (½ cup/120 g)
2 tbsp (25 g) superfine
 sugar

Filling
¾ cup (9 oz./250 g)
 raspberry jam

EQUIPMENT
Food processor
Fine-mesh sieve
Electric hand beater
Pastry bag fitted with
 ⅓-in. (8-mm) plain tip
2 cookie sheets lined
 with parchment paper

1. **Preheat the oven** to 340°F (170°C/Gas Mark 3).
2. **To prepare the macaron shells,** finely grind the confectioners' sugar and almond powder in the food processor. Sift with the raspberry powder through a fine-mesh sieve into a mixing bowl.
3. **Whisk the egg whites** in a separate bowl until they hold soft peaks. Add the superfine sugar and continue whisking until the peaks are firm.
4. **Vigorously stir** one-third of the egg whites into the dry ingredients. Gently fold in the remainder using a spatula. The mixture should fall from the spatula in thick ribbons and not be too runny.
5. **Spoon the batter** into the pastry bag . Pipe 1¼-in. (3-cm) mounds in staggered rows on the cookie sheets. Let rest for 3 minutes.
6. **Bake for 10–12 minutes,** one sheet at a time, until the macaron shells are shiny but not colored.
7. **Remove from the oven** and place the sheet next to the kitchen sink. Drizzle a little cold water between the cookie sheet and the parchment paper to create steam, as this will help release the macarons from the parchment. Let the shells cool on a wire rack.
8. **To fill the macarons,** spoon a little raspberry jam into the center of the flat side of half the shells. Press the remaining shells lightly on top, so that the jam spreads to the edges. Cover with plastic wrap. Let the macarons "ripen" overnight (or preferably for up to 2–3 days) in the refrigerator before serving.

Chef's Notes
• The macarons will improve if they are "ripened" for 2–3 days in the refrigerator, covered with plastic wrap. This gives them time to develop their characteristic soft and chewy texture.
• If freezing, place the macarons on a cookie sheet, then freeze until solid. Remove from the sheet and stack them on top of one another in an airtight container. Let come to room temperature before serving.

MACARONS AU CHOCOLAT

CHOCOLATE MACARONS ★★

Makes
25–30

Active time: 45 minutes

Cooking time:
10–12 minutes per batch

Resting time: Overnight–
3 days (see Chef's Notes)

Storage: Up to 2 weeks
in the freezer
(see Chef's Notes)

INGREDIENTS
Chocolate ganache
4½ oz. (125 g) chocolate,
    50% cacao, chopped
Scant ½ cup (100 ml)
    heavy cream
2 tbsp (25 g) butter, diced

Macaron shells
1½ cups (7 oz./200 g)
    confectioners' sugar
1⅓ cups (4½ oz./125 g)
    almond powder
1 tbsp + 2 tsp (12 g)
    unsweetened cocoa
    powder
3 egg whites (scant ½ cup/
    100 g)
2 tbsp (25 g) superfine
    sugar

EQUIPMENT
Instant-read thermometer
Electric hand beater
Food processor
Fine-mesh sieve
2 pastry bags fitted with
    ⅓-in. (8-mm) and ⅛-in.
    (4-mm) plain tips
2 cookie sheets lined
    with parchment paper

1. **To prepare the chocolate ganache,** melt the chocolate in a bowl over a saucepan of barely simmering water (bain-marie) until the temperature reaches 104°F (40°C).

2. **In a saucepan,** heat the cream until the temperature reaches 140°F (60°C).

3. **Remove the bowl of melted chocolate** from the saucepan and place on the work surface. Whisk in the butter and cream until smooth. Cool, then chill until using.

4. **Preheat the oven** to 340°F (170°C/Gas Mark 3).

5. **To prepare the macaron shells,** finely grind the confectioners' sugar and almond powder in the food processor. Sift with the cocoa powder through a fine-mesh sieve into a mixing bowl.

6. **Whisk the egg whites** in a separate bowl until they hold soft peaks. Add the superfine sugar and continue whisking until the peaks are firm.

7. **Vigorously stir** one-third of the egg whites into the dry ingredients. Gently fold in the remainder using a spatula. The mixture should fall from the spatula in thick ribbons and not be too runny.

8. **Spoon the batter** into the pastry bag with the ⅓-in. (8-mm) tip. Pipe 1¼-in. (3-cm) mounds in staggered rows on the cookie sheets. Let rest for 3 minutes.

9. **Bake for 10–12 minutes,** one sheet at a time, until the macaron shells are shiny but not colored.

10. **Remove from the oven** and place the sheet next to the kitchen sink. Drizzle a little cold water between the cookie sheet and the parchment paper to create steam, as this will help release the macarons from the parchment. Let the shells cool on a wire rack.

11. **To fill the macarons,** transfer the chocolate ganache to the pastry bag with an ⅛-in. (4-mm) tip and pipe it over the flat side of half the shells. Press the remaining shells lightly on top, so that the ganache spreads to the edges. Cover with plastic wrap. Let the macarons "ripen" overnight (or preferably for up to 2–3 days) in the refrigerator before serving.

Chef's Notes
• The macarons will improve if they are "ripened" for 2–3 days in the refrigerator, covered with plastic wrap. This gives them time to develop their characteristic soft and chewy texture.
• If freezing, place the macarons on a cookie sheet, then freeze until solid. Remove from the sheet and stack them on top of one another in an airtight container. Let come to room temperature before serving.

MACARONS VANILLE

VANILLA MACARONS ★★

Makes
25–30

Active time: 45 minutes

Cooking time:
10–12 minutes per batch

Resting time: Overnight–
3 days (see Chef's Notes)

Storage: Up to 2 weeks
in the freezer
(see Chef's Notes)

INGREDIENTS
Macaron shells
1½ cups (7 oz./200 g)
   confectioners' sugar
1⅓ cups (4½ oz./125 g)
   almond powder
⅓ oz. (10 g) vanilla powder
3 egg whites (scant ½ cup/
   100 g)
2 tbsp (25 g) superfine
   sugar

*Strawberry mousseline
cream filling*
2½ oz. (70 g) vanilla pastry
   cream (see p. 66)
6 oz. (175 g) plain
   buttercream
   (see p. 54), at room
   temperature
1½ tsp (7.5 ml) raspberry
   brandy
1 tsp (5 g) butter,
   melted and cooled

EQUIPMENT
Food processor
Fine-mesh sieve
Electric hand beater
Pastry bag fitted with
   a ⅓-in. (8-mm) plain tip
2 cookie sheets lined
   with parchment paper

---

1. **Preheat the oven** to 340°F (170°C/Gas Mark 3).
2. **To prepare the macaron shells,** finely grind the confectioners' sugar, almond powder, and vanilla powder in the food processor. Sift through a fine-mesh sieve into a mixing bowl.
3. **Whisk the egg whites** in a separate bowl until they hold soft peaks. Add the superfine sugar and continue whisking until the peaks are firm.
4. **Vigorously stir** one-third of the egg whites into the dry ingredients. Gently fold in the remainder using a spatula. The mixture should fall from the spatula in thick ribbons and not be too runny.
5. **Spoon the batter** into the pastry bag . Pipe 1¼-in. (3-cm) mounds in staggered rows on the cookie sheets. Let rest for 3 minutes.
6. **Bake for 10–12 minutes,** one sheet at a time, until the macaron shells are shiny but not colored.
7. **Remove from the oven** and place the sheet next to the kitchen sink. Drizzle a little cold water between the cookie sheet and the parchment paper to create steam, as this will help release the macarons from the parchment. Let the shells cool on a wire rack.

8. **To prepare the filling,** whisk the pastry cream and buttercream in separate bowls until smooth. Whisk the raspberry brandy into the pastry cream, then whisk in the buttercream and melted butter.
9. **To fill the macarons,** spoon a little mousseline cream into the center of the flat side of half the shells. Press the remaining shells lightly on top, so that the cream spreads to the edges. Cover with plastic wrap. Let the macarons "ripen" overnight (or preferably for up to 2–3 days) in the refrigerator before serving.

Chef's Notes
• The macarons will improve if they are "ripened" for 2–3 days in the refrigerator, covered with plastic wrap. This gives them time to develop their characteristic soft and chewy texture.
• If freezing, place the macarons on a cookie sheet, then freeze until solid. Remove from the sheet and stack them on top of one another in an airtight container. Let come to room temperature before serving.

PALETS AUX RAISINS

RAISIN PALETS ★

Makes
about 50

Active time: 5 minutes +
making the marzipan

Soaking time: 1–2 hours

Cooking time: 15 minutes
per batch

Storage: Up to 4 days
in an airtight container
in the refrigerator

INGREDIENTS
½ cup (2½ oz./70 g)
    raisins
Scant ½ cup (100 ml) rum,
    lukewarm
Butter for the pan if needed
9 oz. (250 g) homemade
    marzipan, 50% almonds,
    (see p. 63), chopped
2½ eggs (½ cup/125 g),
    lightly beaten
4 tbsp (2½ oz./65 g)
    butter

EQUIPMENT
Stainless steel or silicone
    mold with 1½-in. (4-cm)
    cylindrical cavities, ¾ in.
    (2 cm) deep
Cookie sheet if using
    a silicone mold
Stand mixer fitted
    with the paddle beater
Instant-read thermometer
Disposable pastry bag

1. **Soak the raisins** in the rum for 1–2 hours.
2. **Preheat the oven** to 350°F (180°C/Gas Mark 4). If using a stainless steel mold, lightly grease the cavities with butter. If using a silicone mold, place it on the cookie sheet without greasing.
3. **Beat the marzipan** in the stand mixer until softened. Gradually beat in the eggs until the mixture is smooth.
4. **Heat the butter** in a saucepan until melted and the temperature reaches about 140°F (60°C). Beat the butter into the almond paste mixture.
5. **Drain the raisins**, reserving any rum that has not been absorbed. Fold the raisins into the batter using a flexible spatula.

6. **Spoon the batter** into the pastry bag and snip off the tip. Pipe into the cavities in the mold to fill them three-quarters full (about ⅓ oz./10 g in each one).
7. **Bake each batch** until risen and lightly golden. If using a stainless steel mold, the baking time will be about 12 minutes. If using a silicone mold, allow 15 minutes.
8. **Let cool**, then unmold onto a wire rack. Any rum left from soaking the raisins can be drizzled over the top of the palets, if desired.

PALMIERS ★★

Makes
60

Active time: 15 minutes +
making the puff pastry

Freezing time: 10 minutes

Cooking time: 10 minutes
per batch

Storage: Up to 1 week
in an airtight container
in a dry place

INGREDIENTS
⅔ cup (2¾ oz./80 g)
    vanilla confectioners'
    sugar (see Chef's
    Notes)
7 oz. (200 g) classic puff
    pastry dough, made
    with 4 single turns
    (see p. 28), 1 day ahead

EQUIPMENT
2 cookie sheets lined
    with parchment paper

1. **Preheat the oven** to 400°F (200°C/Gas Mark 6).
2. **Sprinkle the work surface** generously with the vanilla sugar. Place the pastry on the sugar to prevent it from sticking. Roll out and give the pastry two additional single turns (see p. 28). Freeze for 5 minutes.
3. **Cut the pastry in half.** Sprinkle the work surface with more sugar and roll each half into a rectangle measuring approximately 6 × 12 in. (15 × 30 cm).
4. **Fold over** the shorter ends so that they meet in the middle, then fold the pastry in half to make 4 layers. Place the two pieces of folded pastry on a flat plate. Freeze for 5 minutes to firm them up a little.
5. **Remove one piece of pastry** from the freezer and cut it into ¼-in (5-mm) thick slices (about 30 slices). Lay them flat on one of the cookie sheets, leaving plenty of space between them as they will expand during baking.
6. **Bake for about 10 minutes**, until golden. Halfway through the baking time, prepare the remaining slices and lay them flat on the second cookie sheet, ready to go in the oven.
7. **Slide the baked palmiers**, still on the parchment paper, onto a wire rack to cool (see Chef's Notes). Stack or store them when they have cooled completely, or they will stick together.

Chef's Notes
• The palmiers can be caramelized on one side, if desired. When golden, remove from the oven and place briefly under a preheated broiler to caramelize. Slide onto a wire rack to cool.

ROCHERS CONGOLAIS

COCONUT PYRAMIDS ★

Makes	INGREDIENTS	EQUIPMENT
30	4 egg whites	Electric hand beater
	(scant ⅓ cup/130 g)	Instant-read thermometer
Active time: 15 minutes	1½ cups (10½ oz./300 g)	Cookie sheet lined
	sugar	with baking parchment
Cooking time: 20 minutes	1 tbsp apple compote	
	(see p. 348) or pear	
Storage: Up to 10 days	compote	
in the refrigerator	4 cups (10½ oz./300 g)	
in an airtight container	unsweetened shredded	
	coconut	

1. **Preheat the oven** to 400°F (200°C/Gas Mark 6).
2. **In a bowl** over a saucepan of barely simmering water (bain-marie), whisk together the egg whites and sugar until hot to the touch (113°F/45°C).
3. **Remove from the bain-marie.** Add the apple or pear compote and the shredded coconut. Whisk for 3 minutes until smooth.
4. **Scoop out rounded tablespoonfuls** of the mixture, about the size of a small egg, and place on the cookie sheet. With damp hands, shape into pyramids.
5. **Bake for 20 minutes,** until lightly golden on the outside but still soft on the inside. Let cool on a wire rack.

SABLÉS ARLÉSIENS

ARLESIAN SHORTBREAD COOKIES ★

Makes
88–96

Active time: 15 minutes

Chilling time: At least
1 hour, or preferably
overnight (see Chef's
Notes)

Cooking time: 10 minutes
per batch

Storage: Up to 10 days
in an airtight container
in a dry place

INGREDIENTS
⅔ cup (2 oz./60 g)
    almond powder
⅔ cup (3 oz./85 g)
    confectioners' sugar,
    divided
1 stick + 2 tbsp
    (5¼ oz./150 g) butter,
    diced
1 extra-large egg yolk
    (1¾ tbsp/30 g)
1 pinch salt
Finely grated zest of
    1 lemon, preferably
    organic
1⅓ cups (5¾ oz./165 g)
    AP flour

EQUIPMENT
Stand mixer fitted
    with the paddle beater
2 cookie sheets
Ruler
Fluted pastry wheel

1. **Make the cookie dough** a day ahead, if possible.
In a mixing bowl, stir together the almond powder and
a scant ½ cup (2 oz./60 g) of the confectioners' sugar.
2. **In the stand mixer,** beat together the butter, egg yolk,
remaining 3 tbsp (1 oz./25 g) confectioners' sugar, salt,
and lemon zest until smooth.
3. **Beat in** the mixture of almond powder and
confectioners' sugar, then the flour, until just combined.
Take care not to overwork the dough.
4. **Gather the dough** into a ball, flatten it into a disk,
and cover with plastic wrap. Chill for at least 1 hour,
or preferably overnight.
5. **Roll the dough** between two sheets of parchment
paper into a rectangle measuring 13¾ × 10 in.
or 36 × 24 cm, with a thickness of ¼ in. (5 mm).
Slide it carefully onto a cookie sheet. Chill for about
30 minutes to firm the dough up a little.
6. **Preheat the oven** to 350°F (180°C/Gas Mark 4).
Remove the top sheet of parchment paper.

7. **Using the pastry wheel** and a ruler, cut the dough
into 1¼-in. (3-cm) squares, making 88 × 1¼-in. squares
or 96 × 3-cm squares in total. Line the second cookie
sheet with parchment paper and carefully transfer half
the squares to the second sheet using a palette knife.
Do this carefully as the dough will break easily.
Chill the remaining squares while the first batch bakes.
8. **Bake each batch** for 10 minutes, until the cookies
are golden around the edges. Let cool for a few minutes
on the cookie sheet. Slide them, still on the parchment
paper, onto a wire rack and let cool. These cookies are
fragile so handle them with care.

Chef's Notes
• Chilling the dough overnight makes it much easier
to work with.
• Cookies larger than 1¼ in. (3 cm) can be made,
but a longer resting time is needed to ensure that the
dough holds together.

SABLÉS AUX NOISETTES

HAZELNUT SHORTBREAD COOKIES *

Makes
about 60

Active time: 15 minutes

Cooking time:
8–10 minutes

Storage: Up to 10 days
in an airtight container
in a dry place

INGREDIENTS
Scant ½ cup (2½ oz./75 g)
   hazelnuts
¾ cup + 2 tbsp (3½ oz./
   100 g) AP flour
Scant ½ cup (1½ oz./40 g)
   hazelnut powder
7 tbsp (3½ oz./100 g)
   butter, diced
½ cup (3½ oz./100 g)
   sugar
3 eggs (⅔ cup/150 g)
Scant 2 tsp (7.5 g) vanilla
   sugar

EQUIPMENT
Mortar and pestle
Electric hand beater
Pastry bag fitted with
   a ½-in. (1-cm) plain tip
Cookie sheet lined
   with parchment paper

1. **Preheat the oven** to 400°F (200°C/Gas Mark 6).
2. **Roughly crush the hazelnuts** using the mortar
and pestle, leaving some pieces the size of small peas.
Combine the flour and hazelnut powder.
3. **Cream the butter and sugar** together in a bowl over
a saucepan of barely simmering water (bain-marie).
Whisk in the eggs one by one, then whisk in the vanilla
sugar. The heat from the bain-marie will help prevent
the mixture from separating.
4. **Remove from the heat.** Fold in the flour and hazelnut
powder until combined. Take care not to overmix.
Transfer to the pastry bag.
5. **Pipe out** walnut-size mounds or "S" shapes onto
the cookie sheet. Sprinkle with the crushed hazelnuts.
6. **Bake for 8–10 minutes,** until golden around the
edges. Rotate the cookie sheet from front to back
halfway through the cooking time.
7. **Slide the cookies,** still on the parchment paper,
onto a wire rack and let cool.

SACRISTAINS *

Makes
80

Active time: 15 minutes +
making the puff pastry

Cooking time: 30 minutes
per batch

Storage: Up to 6 days
in an airtight container
in a dry place

INGREDIENTS
Generous 1 cup
(5½ oz./160 g) almonds,
finely chopped
1 cup minus 3 tbsp
(5½ oz./160 g) pearl
sugar, if possible,
or granulated sugar
1 lb. (450 g) puff pastry
dough, classic
(see p. 28) or quick
(see p. 29), well chilled
(see Chef's Notes)
1 egg, lightly beaten

EQUIPMENT
2 cookie sheets lined
with parchment paper

1. **Preheat the oven** to 400°F (200°C/Gas Mark 6).
2. **Stir the almonds and sugar together.** Divide equally
between four bowls.
3. **Roll the pastry** on a lightly floured surface into
a rectangle measuring approximately 5½ × 16 in.
(14 × 40 cm), with a thickness of about ¹⁄₁₆ in.
(2 mm). Cut lengthwise into 2 equal strips.
Fold one strip in half and chill until using.
4. **Brush the other strip** with lightly beaten egg.
Scatter almonds and sugar from one bowl over it.
5. **Run a rolling pin** lightly over the top so that the
almonds and sugar stick to the pastry. Turn the strip
over, brush with egg, and cover with almonds and sugar
from the second bowl. Cut into smaller strips measuring
¾ × 2¾ in. (2 × 7 cm).
6. **Pick up each strip** and twist it twice like a candy
wrapper. Place the twists quite close together on the
cookie sheet. There should be room for about 40,
as the sacristains will shrink lengthwise as they bake.
7. **Bake for 10 minutes.** Reduce the oven temperature to
325°F (160°C/Gas Mark 3) and bake for an additional
20 minutes, until golden. While the first batch is baking,
prepare the second batch in the same way, using the
reserved strip of pastry and two remaining bowls of
almonds and sugar. Place on the second cookie sheet
and bake as per the previous batch.
8. **Slide the sacristains,** still on the parchment paper,
onto a wire rack and let cool.

Chef's Notes
• It is important to ensure that the puff pastry is very
cold and to work quickly. If the pastry is too soft, it will
be difficult to twist the strips without them collapsing.

TUILES AUX AMANDES

ALMOND TUILES ⋆

Makes
about 50

Active time:
15 minutes

Chilling time: At least
1½ hours, or preferably
3 days (see Chef's Notes)

Cooking time: 8 minutes
per batch

Storage: Up to 6 days
in an airtight container
in a dry place

INGREDIENTS
2⅓ cups (7 oz./200 g)
   sliced almonds
Scant 1 cup (6½ oz./185 g)
   sugar
3 tbsp (1 oz./30 g) AP flour
3 extra-large egg whites
   (½ cup/110 g;
   see Chef's Notes)
3 tbsp (1½ oz./40 g)
   butter, melted and
   cooled
Milk

EQUIPMENT
3 cookie sheets lined
   with parchment paper
Rolling pin or baba mold
   (optional; see Chef's
   Notes)

1. **Combine the almonds,** sugar, and flour in a mixing bowl. Using a flexible spatula, stir in the egg whites and butter. Cover with plastic wrap and chill for at least 1½ hours, or preferably 3 days.
2. **Preheat the oven** to 350°F (180°C/Gas Mark 4).
3. **Spoon 16–18 mounds** of batter onto each cookie sheet using a tablespoon, leaving space between them. Dip the tines of a fork in milk and use to flatten the mounds. If they are not sufficiently flat, the centers of the tuiles will not bake evenly.
4. **Bake for 8–10 minutes,** one sheet at a time, until golden.
5. **Slide the tuiles,** still on the parchment paper, onto a wire rack and let them cool flat (see Chef's Notes).

Chef's Notes
• The tuiles will be even tastier if the batter is made 3 days ahead, as the almonds will develop their flavor. Keep the mixture in a covered bowl in the refrigerator and stir once a day.
• It is very important to add the right amount of egg white. If too much is added, the batter will be too runny; if too little is used, the mixture will be dry.
• To give the tuiles their traditional curved French roof tile shape, bake them in smaller batches. Remove from the cookie sheet using a palette knife as soon as they come out of the oven and drape them over a rolling pin or press them into a baba mold. Let cool completely before removing.

INDEX

ACKNOWLEDGMENTS

The Publisher wishes to thank Sylvie Gille-Naves Lenôtre and Alain Lenôtre for their dedication and hard work in creating this beautiful book.

Flammarion also extends its thanks to the following people for their collaboration and participation: Mme. Nathalie Bellon-Szabo, President of the Société Lenôtre S.A.; Olivier Voarick, Chief Executive Officer; Guy Krenzer, Executive Chef and Creative Director; Christophe Gaumer, Patisserie Creative Chef; Stéphane Durand, International Creative Chef; and all the teams at Maison Lenôtre.

The English editor wishes to express her sincere thanks to Guy, Christophe, and Stéphane at Maison Lenôtre, as well as Christelle Pradat, Head of the Baking and Pastry Department at the Culinary Institute Lenôtre, and her team, for their invaluable assistance.

A personal dedication from Christian Lacour, a chef at Lenôtre since 1968: "I owe my deepest gratitude to Gaston Lenôtre, who imbued me with his philosophy and legendary love of good food."

Caroline Faccioli would like to thank chef Guy Krenzer and all the team at Maison Lenôtre—whose superlative talent and unparalleled expertise have left a lasting impression on her—for once again believing in this delectable book. Thanks also to Marion Chatelain, for her brilliant ideas and boundless energy; Margaux Besnier for her tireless commitment and constant good humor; and Ryma Bouzid for her trust and support on this magnificent project.

Marion Chatelain wishes to thank Guy for his renewed faith in this book and for sharing his gastronomic passion; Christophe, Julie, and the whole Lenôtre team for their generosity; Caroline for embarking on this new adventure; and Ryma for believing in this ambitious project.

She would also like to thank the following creative artists:

Laurette Broll for her inspirational ceramics.
www.laurettebroll.com
Studio: 47 Avenue Gambetta, 75020 Paris
Photographs pp. 16, 79, 105, 109, 113, 115, 123, 125, 130–31, 148–49, 153, 155, 195, 211, 241, 243, 274–75, 293, 299, 301, 307, 311, 314–15, 319, 333, 341, 347, 367, 375, 377, 378–79, 413.

Annie M for her natural yet elegant ceramics and Raku ware.
www.anniem.net
Studio: 8 Rue Buzenval, 75020 Paris
Photographs pp. 4, 7, 10–11, 25, 52–53, 56–57, 61, 70–71, 95, 103, 139, 157, 159, 177, 181, 183, 203, 205, 207, 211, 217, 219, 221, 231, 240, 245, 251, 269, 289, 295, 355, 385, 397, 399, 411, 415, 418–19.

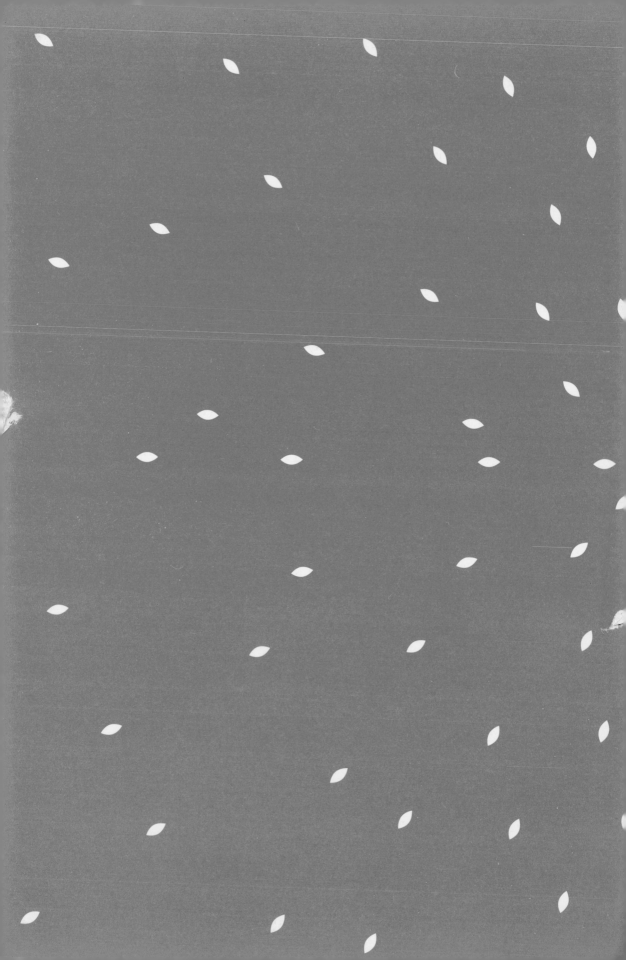